AMERICAN NOMAD

ALSO BY STEVE ERICKSON

Days Between Stations

Rubicon Beach

Tours of the Black Clock

Leap Year

Arc d'X

Amnesiascope

AMERICAN NOMAD

STEVE ERICKSON

Henry Holt and Company • New York

Henry Holt and Company, Inc.
Publishers since 1866
115 West 18th Street
New York, New York 10011

Henry Holt® is a registered trademark
of Henry Holt and Company, Inc.

Published in Canada by Fitzhenry & Whiteside Ltd.,
195 Allstate Parkway, Markham, Ontario L3R 4T8.

Library of Congress Cataloging-in-Publication Data

Erickson, Steve.
American nomad / Steve Erickson.—1st ed.
p.   cm.
1. Presidents—United States—Election—1996.   2. United States—
Politics and government—1993–   3. Erickson, Steve.   I. Title.
E888.E75   1997   97-1532
324.973'0929—dc21   CIP

ISBN 0-8050-5155-4

Henry Holt books are available for special promotions
and premiums. *For details contact:* Director, Special Markets.

Printed in the United States of America
All first editions are printed on acid-free paper. ∞

1   3   5   7   9   10   8   6   4   2

The mystic chords of memory . . . will yet swell the chorus of the Union, when again touched, as surely they will be, by the better angels of our nature.

—ABRAHAM LINCOLN

I'm an American artist; I have no guilt.

—PATTI SMITH

AMERICAN NOMAD

1

They told you it was a war for the soul of America, but you didn't believe them. They kept saying you were the Enemy, but you wouldn't accept that, because you didn't feel like an enemy. Now you know they meant every word, and more. Now, as the Twentieth Century slips America's hold on it, you have become the Enemy they always said you were.

2

When the spring came, we ran for the hills.

Actually, it was the last day of winter. I moved out of the old Hotel Hamblin where I had lived five years, down off the Sunset Strip near Hollywood. Viv and I took a house in one of the canyons that perforate Los Angeles: Laurel, Beachwood, Coldwater, Benedict, Santa Monica, Temescal, Topanga, Malibu. . . . I can't tell you which one. Viv has it in her head that right-wing Christians, among others, will come after me. Suffice it to say that in the city of Los Angeles I now live in a place that looks nothing like Los Angeles, in hills that remind me of Hawaii some days, Scotland others—with tree-canopied lanes and a white fog that flows like milk up the pass at night beneath our windows, curdling among the ravines. Precariously the house juts out high over the canyon. From the road in the canyon below, Viv insists the house looks crooked, like it's about to topple over; I promise her the house is straight, it's the canyon that's crooked. "But this is a dream," a friend insisted when he first saw the house, "you guys are living the dream that everyone comes to Los Angeles for," and that dream feels as precarious as the house, verging on the moment of falling into space. As though it presented itself to our lives far too soon to have any hope of being real beyond morning. Viv and I were, at the outset, confronted by three omens. The first was a small earthquake, the night we moved in.

3

The second was the peacock. Below our house is a small ranch, with several cows, a couple of horses, either sheep or goats—I can't be sure by their bleat—geese, and a peacock. We hear the screech of the peacock all day, a terrible scream that fills the canyon and alarms ignorant visitors; at its sound delivery boys fall to the ground, expecting to be strafed by enemy aircraft. Our first actual sighting was the morning when, having left the front door open, we looked up to see the bird in our doorway. It did not open its fan for us, which for some reason filled me with a primal relief. The peacock was there only a moment and then gone, sauntering down the street, taking flight for stretches of the road. Now and then, watching from the huge windows of our house that explode out into the canyon, I see the peacock below, among the cows. Though it would not fan for us, it fans for the cows, dark blue and foliage green, so that at first, from a distance, I mistake it for a bush. The cows are the bird's sullen audience.

The third omen was nothing more or less than our address. It is right there, in black numbers, on the white mailbox at the end of our driveway. 1996.

4

I was fleeing my life and Los Angeles. The destruction that racked the city over the first half of the Nineties had become a cliché even before the litany was over: riot, fire, flood, quake. Viv and I, together four years, had been through most of it. We had been together the night of the Quake, when the old red bricks of the Hotel Hamblin that had been so reassuring during the riot a couple of years before suddenly seemed so treacherous. Along with the other tenants we stumbled downstairs out onto the sidewalk in the pitch black, and then I had it in my head, against all Viv's protests, to go back into the building and up the stairs to the roof where I had watched the fires of the riots, surrounding me in a red ring. I wanted to see L.A. as its true self, the Anti-City. I don't think it's a coincidence that anti-city and anarchy sound like the same word.

Reaching the top of the roof, I turned where I stood and took it all in, from the ocean in the west to Century City circling south, Baldwin Hills and the Miracle Mile, Downtown to the east and Silverlake above it, Hollywood and the Hollywood Hills to the north, looming in the dark. I turned where I stood to see all of it—except there was nothing to be seen. My mouth fell. For the first and only time in the city's history all the electricity was out, from one horizon to the other, and there was nothing but blackness. It was far more frightening than any ring of fire.

5

Now, another two years later, L.A. having subsided from actual violence into a psychosis of violence that permeates everything, the view from our house in the canyon was the blackness of peace. The lights of other little houses flickered in the hills, the night sky above dashed with stars. When the moon was full, it lit up the canyon so one could see the leaves of the trees on the other side.

What for several years had been anarchic exhilaration, in an anti-city of no laws or borders, had slowly metamorphosed in Viv and me to benumbed dread. Moving to the canyon wasn't going to change that completely, of course: one day at lunch coming out of a local eatery I stopped to the sound of helicopters above and the whiff of smoke around me, and everyone else around me stopped as well, scanning the horizon and sniffing the air for the glint and smell of fire exactly the way animals in the woods freeze in their tracks at the same scent. In those few minutes I inhaled a new understanding of doom. Even so, it was different from nights of Viv waking in her Venice studio to the sound of gunfire. So we had traded our courage for a modicum of common sense, and our past, as Viv put it, vanished behind us like a vapor trail.

At the same time my life seemed as precarious as the house and the dream it represented. I had just lost the biggest job of my life, and the promise of a financially secure year was not merely reneged but replaced with a taunt of disaster. For weeks and then months I waited for a sign of what to do next, but all I had were visions in the delirium of the L.A. twilight, looking out the huge windows of our house and waiting for the earth's greatest seizure yet, which would bring the Pacific Ocean rolling through all the L.A. canyons, rendering the high green hills small green islands. And out of the corner of my eye I could see the flickers of my past that had not yet vaporized, on the television against the far wall. "So what's going on with the campaign?" people asked at dinner.

"I'm not covering the campaign anymore," I mumbled in return. "I don't care," and turned the TV off.

Wave goodbye to your country, I once wrote to whomever was listening, with the hand that isn't busy throwing it away. That was another election, and though it was only eight years ago, it was a different America, then only threatening to vanish in the dust of inertia; now, eight years later, something more malevolent and violent fractured the landscape, something more malevolent and violent fractured me. If it was a different America now, I was a different American, the distance between the America in my head and the America beneath my feet much farther than the length of my body; and I

4

thought I had made my bitter peace with this. There was no reason to assume America had to be the name of my spiritual crisis. Let America be the name of its own fucking crisis. I could be, along with the rest of us, a Post-American as easily as I was ever an American—well, easier, since being an American was never easy, or at least never supposed to be. For a brief moment in the mid-Nineties I had the strange, disorienting sensation of not thinking about America at all. I liked it.

6

I unpacked. I emptied boxes, I filled shelves. I moved furniture. I put up blinds and painted, I set up my office. Viv arranged her studio, with her sculptures. I organized dishes, books, videos, compact discs; it became a *very* organized house. I went to the grocery store in town and stocked up for that day a cataclysm would be lapping at our back door. Every morning I made my rounds to scoop up from the floor the corpses of bugs; there were bugs like I had never seen. Ones that crawled and ones that flew and ones that crawled and flew. Viv was working on a series of pieces in which she constructed, in the patterns of stained-glass windows, intricate, fantastic mosaics of butterfly wings, chopped into fragments of color and iridescence; these stained-glass butterfly windows were enshrouded by huge steel mandalas and pyramids. Now, when the butterflies and moths hurled themselves at our house in the night, the porch and outer halls strewn with their bodies at dawn, it was not clear if they were sacrificing themselves to Viv's art or mounting a protest against it, like Buddhist monks setting themselves on fire. I changed lightbulbs, hung prints, strapped bookshelves to the walls as one does in earthquake country. The straps, get this, are made of *velcro*. We're going to have an earthquake the magnitude of Hiroshima and the house will be held together by velcro? All that will be left, after the concrete pylons have crumpled and the wood girders have snapped and the metal studs have disintegrated, will be velcroed walls floating in space.

7

But then everything in America seemed to be hanging in space. People discounted the true math of the Millennium, supposedly measured from the birth of Jesus and giving the Year of Our Lord 2000 its particular transcendent and ominous implications—except that, of course, Jesus was not really born in the Year One, or for that matter the Year Zero. Jesus, by most historical reckoning, was actually born closer to 4 B.C., which means that the new Millennium began not in the year 2000, but the year 1996. In the year 1996, at the junction of winter and spring, in a year when nature seemed to especially love the recriminations of the first and resent the healing of the second, we were having a Millennium and didn't even know it: a Secret Millennium, or at least an unconscious one.

Here was what was happening in America. Jesus was on the cover of the country's three major newsmagazines, all in the same week. Two rich young men in Los Angeles, who had breezily admitted to murdering their mother and father, even going back for another shot at the mother as she twitched untowardly following the initial shotgun blast, were convicted in their second trial, the first having sputtered to misconclusion when in the confusion of all the mayhem the jury apparently couldn't decide if the boys were actually guilty or not. In an America where the growing discussion of morality and values grew ever more severe, and where a lack of moral proportion grew ever more unyielding, a Navy admiral fatally shot himself through the heart for wearing the wrong medal. The country seriously considered the question of whether seven-year-old children should be allowed to fly airplanes—a deliberation one would not have thought mentally or morally taxing—after the airplane that one small girl was flying crashed upon takeoff, killing her, her father, and her flight instructor. A cabinet secretary was killed in another airplane crash on the other side of the world amidst a crusade to bring Big Macs to the Balkans, whose ongoing dementia seemed the one thing that characterized all four corners of the Twentieth Century.

The government of the United States decided on a national budget seven months after the budget was to have gone into effect, and after the government had ground to a halt twice. A compound of American fascists in Montana was surrounded by federal authorities and implored with reasonableness, apparently in the hope that Montana might be the birthplace of an altogether new political species, reasonable fascists. The country celebrated, if that is the word, the first anniversary of an explosion in the Midwest that executed a hundred and sixty-nine people for the crime of working for the government, while the two men accused of detonating the explosion were about to go on trial. A reclusive American Cain who, by evil and ingenious means, had allegedly been blowing up airline and university offices for seventeen years with impunity, was turned in to the FBI by his American Abel, slightly less reclusive and only slightly less a genius. Also in the Midwest, where such weirdness was so rampant at this junction of winter and spring, a little girl with two heads, two minds and two souls, which by a more insightful definition must be called, in fact, two little girls, started kindergarten and seemed to be negotiating life with a sanguinity and joy that could only lead one to wonder what if the Kaczynski Brothers had been so physically conjoined, or the Menendez Brothers. Would the good David Kaczynski have somehow preempted the evil Ted, disarming the bombs with the right hand as fast as his brother was making them with the left? Would the Menendezes have done twice the evil twice as fast or twice as soon, or would—as in algebra—two negatives have canceled each other out? And perhaps it was only the whacked-out deluge of my visions, as I waited for my life to return to me high above the clouds, that led me to wonder about two other wounded American siamese twins of the American heartland, born within a few hundred miles of each other, each to troubled circumstances and difficult childhoods, separated at birth only by the mere generation between them, conjoined at some more mysterious junction than the Kaczynski psyche or the Menendez soul, or little Abigail and Brittany Hensel's body. That junction was the consuming desire to be President of the United States.

8

In an obscure Sixties novel called *Dr. Bloodmoney*, which takes place in a post-apocalyptic California, a young girl has constant conversations with an "imaginary friend," to the annoyance of her mother, who finally takes the little girl to see a doctor. Upon investigation the doctor discovers that living in the girl's side is a twin brother, roughly the size of a baby rabbit. He shares her brain and body, perhaps even her soul; he has shared everything with her except her birth. The author of *Dr. Bloodmoney*, Philip K. Dick, was himself haunted by a twin sister who died at the age of one month. Now, as nature split itself between the Cain of winter and the Abel of spring, the first so clearly dominating the second, I began turning the TV back on, watching from time to time the presidential campaign of 1996, albeit with dazed detachment, my interest only truly piqued by the question of whether Bill Clinton was the lost twin brother living in Bob Dole's side, or whether it was Bob Dole living in Bill Clinton's.

9

Since mid-February, hurtling frenzied down through the days of March, had been a series of Republican Party primaries of which, as a correspondent covering the presidential campaign for *Rolling Stone* magazine not so long before, I was a small part. I had had my own itinerary, according to which New Hampshire would lead me to Arizona and South Carolina, and from those places to Georgia and Florida and Texas, finally back to California. Now my only connection to the presidential race was the length of cable running from my hilltop television to, I supposed, a satellite dish somewhere, not so far away; without a moment's decompression I suddenly found myself outside the collective event, and my non-interest was not unlike most Americans'. But truth be told, unlike for most Americans, it was a sore point. Or, perhaps it was a sore point for most Americans as well, but for different reasons. "You have a great job, man," James Carville had told me in Washington almost six months to the day before I fled to the canyon, and at the time I had no reason to suppose he was wrong.

10

If anything, I only wondered how it was that *I* had happened to land such a great job—and I wasn't the only one wondering. On my first day I had gone to the congressional press gallery in Washington, D.C., to get my credentials, a business I took seriously enough to wear a coat and tie for, for all the good it did me. Fully credentialed, fully coated and tied, among twenty or thirty other reporters covering the United States Senate in session, I hadn't been in the gallery three minutes before a sergeant-at-arms approached and said, "Can I help you?" by which he clearly meant, "Who are you; what are you doing here; you don't suppose that press badge actually fools anyone do you; please leave; we hate you." I did not leave but took his point anyway. I could be credentialed from the Capitol all the way back to L.A. and it would never change the fact that, in the eyes of the Senate, I didn't belong here.

The night I arrived in Washington in September 1995, the Capitol had gleamed in my hotel window through a bitter rain, while the trees were swept by a black winter wind that either didn't know or didn't care it was still too early for winter. This was a wind that had blown up from out of the American heart, where winter now lived the year-round. By the time Indian summer returned a few days later the corridors of Congress were still cold from the political gust that had whipped through the previous week: Republicans and Democrats had nearly come to blows over Medicare "hearings" that weren't really hearings, and the air was so thick with bitterness and blood that the fumes seemed to have induced mass derangement. On the Senate floor below me Dale Bumpers, a Democrat from Arkansas, was railing against financing what he called a "condo to Mars," by which I believed he meant a space station, and over the course of the next thirty minutes other senators entered one door of the chamber and exited another like the revolving figures of an old Swiss cuckoo clock, long enough to vote yes or no on the condo to Mars with a leering Robert Dole, leader of the Republicans and candidate for President, making the climactic entrance to register a literal thumb's down. (It was one of those strangely worded pieces of legislation where a no vote meant you were for it and a yes vote meant you were against.) From the vantage point of the gallery I was stunned by how ancient they all looked. Their walk was the aging, constipated waddle of power so desperately entwined with such a slim sense of identity that the two have become impossible to separate. But there was also something else.

Now they were also clearly in the grip of the Terror. It had finally sunk in that the country was on the eve of some looming electoral rampage: American Thermidor, with the guillotine erected in the Capitol rotunda. First the Old Guard would go at the hands of the New, Daniel Patrick Moynihan's head lopped off by some young snot like Pennsylvania Republican Rick Santorum; but as happens with Terrors, sooner or later the Santorums would not only get theirs, but get it worst of all. The original ideological logic of revolutions is the first thing washed away in the bloodbath. Though in the atmosphere of fall 1995 the Republicans were having their way with the nation, saving America from a lot of sick old parasites whining for their Medicaid, in order to build condominiums on Mars, by now even the victors had begun to suspect the pyrrhic implications of passing a budget that was very impressive in its boldness, if you could just leave aside for the moment its immorality. Watching the Senate floor below me I was interested to note who was persona non grata. Barbara Boxer of California—fresh from her role in bringing down another senator for good-naturedly raping his female employees from time to time—rushed around trying to glad-hand everyone who recoiled from her, while Alfonse D'Amato strutted down the aisles as though just returning from a particularly profitable hand of poker, *Mean Streets'* Johnny Boy having gone on to become the most powerful man in New York. Calling out to this colleague or that,

D'Amato was either oblivious or indifferent to the palpable disgust he engendered, throwing back his head and laughing when the others pointedly turned away.

"I assume," Carville said a few hours later, "they plan to do exactly what they say, which is tear it all down." I had come to Carville's townhouse to talk about the presidential election of 1996, but things had changed so much so fast in this country that the man who only three years before authored the undisputed masterpiece of modern presidential campaigns had about him the air of someone time had already passed by; during the most momentous week of the most momentous session of Congress since 1965, if not 1933, James Carville was lying on a couch with his arms folded watching—as had been everyone in the Senate Press Gallery—not C-SPAN hearings on the budget or farm subsidies or even condos to Mars, but the closing arguments of a murder trial three thousand miles away. Within arm's reach his three-month-old daughter rocked in her cradle. Gangly puppies bounded across the floor, various assistants rushed to and fro. Upon my arrival I was disarmed to be greeted not by Carville but his wife Mary Matalin, a former George Bush spokeswoman I spent much of 1992 shaking my fist at whenever she came on television. Upstairs in his office, while Carville read a travel brochure, I babbled with all the authoritative confidence of someone who, even in coat and tie with press credential in full view, had almost gotten kicked out of the Senate half an hour earlier, for no other reason than that I so manifestly appeared not to belong there. "You mean," I said, "the federal government."

"Tear it all down and replace it with four hundred and thirty-five fiefdoms," he snapped, finally tossing the brochure aside and putting his feet on the desk. "Everything good that's happened in this country in the last thirty years has come from the federal government. Medicare. Civil rights."

"So are we talking about returning to a pre–Civil War America?" I asked. "Where people say, 'The United States *are* . . .' instead of 'The United States *is* . . .'?" The southerner wasn't sure how to answer that. "You could put it that way," he finally allowed, his eyes settling on the wall of his office where his blunt legendary maxim, "The Economy, Stupid," had been replaced with "We're Right, They're Wrong." Everywhere I went, I told Carville, I was struck by a sense of the coming election as cataclysm. It didn't matter that there was no cataclysmic issue—slavery, depression, war, scandal—or that the sense of calamity was contradicted by numbers: crime statistics down, not up; illegitimate births down, not up; the deficit half what it was three years before; the combined inflation and unemployment rate the lowest in twenty-five years. Somehow the public understood that the meaning of the election was bigger than numbers, amorphous, "something in the psyche," Carville admitted. The President of the United States himself had tried to get at this when, in his own artless way, he had recently referred to a national "funk," only to backpedal furiously from the characterization when the media went nuts over it.

But if there was anyone who felt more uncomfortable with such metaphysics than the American political media, it was an American political strategist like James Carville, because if there was one thing a meat-and-potatoes strategist didn't want to have to run against, it was a country's psyche. So just as soon as he said it, he backed away as fast as the President had: "Wage stagnation and the decline of the two-parent family" was the line he was trying out that day, and the same one they were using at the White House, for all I knew. Still not having quite honed the requisite reportorial rudeness the job required, I may have been a little too delicate asking if Carville's role in Clinton's reelection was really defined yet, particularly vis-à-vis new Clinton gurus who once were more inclined to manage campaigns for Jesse Helms. If indeed time had passed him by, then Carville was now the wandering nomad of campaign managers; and when he said, "If they want me to go over and run it like I did in '92, I'll do that," he *almost* succeeded in not sounding wistful, he *almost* succeeded in not sounding envious when he told me, "You have a great job this year," and I thought, Yeah, as the wandering nomad of political writers. Slapping me on the back, he became a lot friendlier when I was leaving, though that may have been because I was leaving. "This," he explained matter-of factly, "is only going to be the most interesting election of our political consciousness."

11

More than fourteen months away from it, one couldn't be blamed for having thought so, even as the public remained unengaged, in part because it considered the presidential election with so much dread it couldn't bear to face it. If the election of Bill Clinton in 1992 was attended with hope, if the repudiation of Bill Clinton in the congressional election of 1994 was attended with rage, now between hope and rage no feeling quite measured up to the most interesting election of our political consciousness, particularly one that was a referendum on nothing more or less specific than the American soul. Millennial America was a state of entropy, where not only the political and moral gravity had imploded but a gravity of the spirit, and where the America originally conceived as a floating crap game of benign Jeffersonian anarchy perilously approached a twisted, malignant version of that—Thomas Jefferson's anti-country having given way to Timothy McVeigh's. In the last presidential election of the Millennium, on the bicentennial of the first contested election in the country's history (between Jefferson and John Adams, whose philosophical dispute about the power of the federal government was unnervingly similar to the same one the country was still having two hundred years later), having won everything America meant to win, having established its supremacy over the whims of history and, long after having put a chicken in every pot and two cars in every garage, having put a VCR in every home, which another thousand years from now may be the only thing about the Twentieth Century that anyone really remembers, America had, along with James Carville and myself, become a country of nomads, who wandered the hallways of the American soul not sure if they were in a funhouse or a cancer ward.

Even to many who didn't support him, or who became disillusioned quickly, Bill Clinton was the Last-Chance President. Three years after his election, a year following his humiliation by the smashing election of a Republican Congress, it was already understood perfectly by most people that Clinton's presidency was over and that he was doomed to defeat, assuming he decided to stand for reelection at all, and assuming the Democratic Party didn't cast him aside for Bill Bradley or Robert Kerrey or Richard Gephardt. At the outset of 1995 Clinton was obviously the politically deadest man of all time, running consistently behind in the polls for the better part of the year, often by as much as fifteen percent against the clear next President of the United States, Bob Dole. But now, in the last months leading up to 1996, the Republican Congress's standing with the public was plummeting faster than Clinton's, and if this went on much longer, one institution after another falling into disrepute, something really scary might happen: we might almost have to conclude that the fault of things lay with ourselves. It might be that the secret of the next presidential election, the secret of why it was so important and why we so dreaded it, was that a Moment of Truth was upon us in a way it hadn't been since 1860, the last time the landscape of presidential politics fractured into an array of minority parties without a majority anywhere to be seen, electing in the process a President who provoked such hostility that half the country, you may remember, went to war with the other half.

In the aftermath of the 1995 bombing of a federal building in Oklahoma City, with the country north of us teetering on the edge of its own breakup, the notion of Utah and Arizona and Michigan going to war with the rest of the United States seemed only slightly less preposterous than it had before. It might even be argued that the nation was already at war with itself, what with talk at the 1992 Republican National Convention about Real Americans and Other Americans. So in the fall of 1995 the Moment of Truth took many forms, and these included the high-mindedly metaphorical, which contemplated whether the only person who could save America was an ex-general on a national book tour who a hundred and fifty years ago would have been a slave, and tabloid verities, which couldn't fully explain why I was running around the country writing a story about an election no one wanted to hear about, while the only story that *everyone* wanted to hear about was unfolding in my own hometown, in my absence.

On the night of the Verdict, the moon was half white and half black. Perhaps only in a city as surreal as Los Angeles, where in the fall of 1995 three-fourths of the county's mental institutions were on the verge of closing for lack of funds, thus releasing into the streets a veritable India of lunatics, could tabloid verity converge so glibly with high-minded metaphor. Immediately afterward, the Verdict confused the only thing about the election of 1996 that had thus far captured America's imagination, because Colin Powell was nothing politically if not a redemptive figure, the man by whom white America could redeem itself. For white America, Powell's race was part of his attraction insofar as it allowed whites to persuade themselves that his race in particular, and therefore race itself, was not an issue in America anymore; his possible election as President offered white America the chance to forgive itself for a past that African-Americans were not ready to forgive. Thus black America viewed the redemption that Powell offered as specious, a reflex of moral narcissism by which white people could just "feel good about themselves," in the process absolving themselves of more sins and responsibilities for the past than could be counted, let alone absolved. At any rate the upshot was that by mid-autumn, just as Powell's possible candidacy was beginning to focus people's minds on the 1996 election and provide the hope many Americans had despaired of ever having again, Powell's doppelganger, another black man who had lived the life of a white hero, was acquitted of murder in a social orgy of denial, which included white people in denial of racism and police corruption, and black people in denial of DNA and common sense. Thereupon O. J. Simpson threw a party with balloons. Thereupon white America said, Fuck redemption.

As Simpson was the dark side, Powell was the light side of Joe Christmas. Joe Christmas is the central figure of William Faulkner's 1932 novel *Light in August*, a man who literally does not know if he is white or black, a fact that drives him first to madness and then to a terrible mayhem by which he first kills the woman who loves him and then applies his wrathful blade literally to the gonads of authority. Given a little discipline early in life, perhaps the firm love of parents followed by the loving firmness of the military, Joe Christmas might

15

have killed for America instead, which is all the difference between pathology and patriotism. But in the fall of 1995 he still would have ended up where Colin Powell was, a million books sold but a man without a race, which, in this country, might as well mean a man without a country. It might be argued that in a nation of nomads this made Powell the perfect President, and never more perfect than at the moment he announced he would not run. Spurning the yearning of his country, Powell was the embodiment of history rejecting America as America once supposed it could reject history, cutting itself loose of history's moorings; and in all the contradictions of his refusal, he was a perfect metaphor for a country torn between its heart and soul, wanting a savior who would deliver America from its problems as opposed to a leader who could tell America the bad news and call upon it to deliver itself. Declaring himself a Republican, Powell not only declined to endorse any of the Republicans running, but even refused to commit himself to endorsing the eventual nominee. Praising the party's "energy" and vowing to help move the Party of Lincoln "closer to the spirit of Lincoln," he also admitted in so many words that, darn it, some of those Republicans were a mean, nasty bunch of people when you got right down to it. Which is to say that whatever his newly professed allegiance, Powell knew he was not only a man without a race but a man without a party as well: "Eight million Republicans out there," James Carville told me upon contemplating a Powell campaign, "and the best they can come up with is a Democrat."

12

Then, at the same time that the racial zeitgeist was going haywire in America—white Americans both seeking redemption and saying the hell with it, black Americans actually booing Powell's name at a mass march in Washington—the hard facts of life culminated in an extraordinary press conference by a mob of conservative intellectual gangsters who threatened Powell with political obliteration even before he made his decision. Such preemptive intimidation was entirely the point, of course. Whether Powell, had he run, would have transcended people like these, not to mention the limitations of his country at large, was one thing; there was only so much he could have done about that. Whether he would have transcended his own limitations was something else. At the same moment that we lamented the lost opportunity to elect a sane, dignified man to the White House, not as savior but as a figure of momentous metaphoric import, we had to confront how profoundly wrongheaded Powell's deliberations were in the first place. Not only should it have been obvious from the beginning that running as a Republican would be a disastrous miscalculation, since it was clear the Party of Lincoln had moved much too far from the spirit of Lincoln ever to nominate a man who truly represented Lincoln's legacy, the very consideration of it was a failure of imagination so monumental on Powell's part as to almost disqualify him from the job. To anyone with a glimmer of vision it was always an independent candidacy, its inherent problems of money and organization and ballot registration notwithstanding, that was in keeping with the nature of both the man and the moment. Joe Christmas, even on his calm days, was never a Republican.

Now we were a country of Joe Christmases, not knowing if we're white or black, racially nomadic in the color of our minds if not our faces—and maybe it was the Joe Christmas in me that was drawn to the Lincoln Memorial every time I was in Washington. Inside the memorial, engraved in one wall on Lincoln's right, is the Gettysburg Address, and on his left the Second Inaugural; and it is the last half of that particular speech I always found myself reading again and again. In it Lincoln contemplates the approaching end of the Civil War. He contemplates the national resurrection to follow. And then he suggests that slavery is America's original sin, and that the Civil War is the price the country must pay for having defiled God's gracious gift of America by "wringing [its] bread from the sweat of other men's faces," and that God may well have it that the nation must go right on fighting the war into eternity, forever locked in a death's grip with itself. And at the same time that the country may be damned to this hell of its own making, like an American Jesus (to be assassinated on

17

Good Friday) Lincoln absolves the enemy and assumes the sins of the country's history: "With malice toward none, with charity for all, with firmness in the right as God gives us to see the right, let us strive on to finish the work we are in, to bind up the nation's wounds, to care for him who shall have borne the battle, and for his widow, and his orphan. . . ."

It's an astonishing speech, Lincoln's greatest and the last great speech of his life. Never forgetting that the enemy of the war was other Americans, reaching out to those Americans the hand of forgiveness and friendship (even as he rather shrewdly states for the record of history their responsibility for the war), the Second Inaugural has the sort of incalculable, almost blinding moral generosity for which the godfathers of American morality in 1995 had no capacity. It is a speech as visionary as it is openhearted, because it could save the country again, five generations later, if enough people believed it. But to believe it again would require not only a great collective leap of faith but a man with the courage and genius to say it, and one shouldn't doubt for a second that if any President today got up and started talking about how America must redeem its original sin of slavery, he'd be impeached in two minutes. When, on the day of Louis Farrakhan's Million Man March in Washington, Bill Clinton gave a measured, fairly innocuous speech in Austin about race, Bob Dole vented his outrage that the President of the United States could possibly suggest America had ever been a racist country. These depressing ruminations were on my mind the night that, prowling the French Quarter of New Orleans, I was almost certain I sighted a big familiar Irishman sloshing a Hurricane in one hand and shaking the other in a fist while ranting about white European culture, as he disappeared into a strip joint called the Bourbon Saloon. I ran up to the door where one of the establishment's entertainers sat outside, a lovely young woman in an elegant long black dress with long black gloves who identified herself as "Summer." "Say," I asked Summer, "wasn't that Pat Buchanan?"

"Who's Pat Buchanan?" she said.

"He's running for President."

"Yes," Summer nodded sagely, "I'm sure that was him, then." I wasn't going in to find out. Ever since getting to New Orleans I'd been trying to track that rascal down, all over the French Quarter among the jazz clubs and blues bars and gumbo joints and voodoo shops and Hurricane stands, because we had an interview scheduled; but if I cornered him now in a strip joint on Bourbon Street he would only deny it later, and probably wouldn't talk to me at all when I finally caught up with him the next day in a hotel lobby out by the airport, where he had just finished a press conference. The conservative commentator and former speech writer for Richard Nixon, Spiro Agnew, and Ronald Reagan, now a candidate for the Republican presidential nomination, had come to Louisiana to interject himself in the state's ongoing controversy regarding legalized gambling, not to mention the state's odd gubernatorial politics. Odd presidential politics might not have been irrelevant, either: Buchanan already knew, in the early days of October 1995, that the Louisiana caucuses the following February would prove an important face-off with Texas Senator Phil Gramm for leadership of the Republican right wing.

The press conference, held in one of the airport hotel conference rooms, had exactly four reporters by my count, including me, as well as one television camera. Patrick Buchanan was undaunted. He made his way among the rows of empty chairs to shake everyone's hand before delivering his spiel about the abomination of gambling; when a columnist from the local *Times-Picayune* didn't arrive until just as he was finishing, the candidate laughed good-naturedly, "Shall I do it again?" Answering questions on affirmative action and trade, he fluctuated between an earnest desire to be understood even by those who didn't agree with him, and the I-really-don't-give-a-flying-fuck recklessness of someone who had nothing to lose. In the meantime, Buchanan's conservative politics were no longer quite as philosophically predictable as they used to be. He was still the man who decried the ethnic dilution of America's natural white European identity, having stood before the 1992 Republican Convention calling for a cultural jihad, but he was also in the process of carving out the most radical policy on campaign reform of any candidate running. Besides opposing his own party's Medicare cuts in Congress, his position on economic issues like trade and jobs had tangentially aligned him with the likes of Jesse Jackson and Ralph Nader. "Not to mention," I mentioned, walking with him through the hotel lobby, "the recent anticorporate tinge of your campaign," a characterization to which I expected some unreconstructed capitalist impulse in him might take exception. Instead he nodded vigorously. There was a time, he explained, when the leaders of big business loved America. "Now what they love," he said bitterly, "is cold efficiency."

I liked this point enough that I couldn't bring myself to suggest that maybe the leaders of big business once loved America because they owned it, and one always loves what one owns, and now they meant to own the world and didn't have much love left for something as quaint as America. Which was, after all, I said, "always a state of mind to begin with."

"Stop right there," Buchanan interrupted, polite but exasperated. By now we were sitting in the lobby waiting for his campaign van, an aide having been sent off for a soda-with-lime that never appeared. "That's where I disagree with you. Everyone always says, 'America is an idea.' America is not an idea. It's a country with traditions, a culture, a language. I mean, *I don't speak Gaelic.*"

And that was when I finally understood the true crux of the coming cataclysm. It was so simple. "So in other words, after all of it, after abortion and race and trade and jobs and welfare and immigration and O. J., what this campaign is really about is . . . the meaning of America."

"That," the man whispered, looking me right in the eye, "is exactly what this campaign is about."

Originally the plan had been that I would ride with Buchanan in his van to Baton Rouge, where I would engage him in many philosophical meditations on matters including gambling, race, conservatism, corporations, political reform, Bill Clinton, Bob Dole, Colin Powell, Abraham Lincoln, slavery, original sin, the Verdict, creole strippers, and the egregiously belated admission of the Velvet Underground to the Rock and Roll Hall of Fame. But once the press conference broke up, it became clear the campaign was having second thoughts about me, and was in fact denying they had ever agreed to an interview at all, as though I had come all the way to New Orleans just to wave to Pat's van as it rolled by. To be fair, Buchanan himself seemed more open to it. I probably made a mistake in not flattering him a little with the truth of why I was there, of why I had come all the way to James Carville's home state to find Buchanan rather than chase after Dole or Gramm: ever since I had gotten the *Rolling Stone* job, I had been amusing or alarming various people with the ridiculous prediction that Buchanan would win the New Hampshire Primary, still six months away.

As it happened this prophesy—which, though considered rash by my editors, I committed to print anyway for all the world to see—was based less on shrewd political insight than a combination of sheer math and my common sense being overwhelmed by my sense of metaphor, something to which I've always been too prone. Buchanan had run in the 1992 Republican primaries against George Bush, of course, stunning both the incumbent and the political world at large by receiving thirty-seven percent of the vote in New Hampshire; and while this was interpreted by virtually everyone at the time as a protest against the way Bush was handling the presidency and the nation's economy, my own feeling was that, given the rabid nature of the Republican Right, about two-thirds of the Buchanan support might well be solid Pat vote, a protest not just against Bush but the state of America and the universe in general. Moreover Buchanan had in 1992—and would have again in 1996—the support of New Hampshire's poisonous right-wing newspaper the *Manchester Union-Leader*. The *Union-Leader*'s considerable power was almost purely negative, which is to say it wouldn't necessarily get many votes for Buchanan but that a relentless rain of ferocious headlines at Bob Dole's expense, week after week and month on end, could seriously erode Dole's support, not rock-solid to begin with. If Buchanan had a core constituency in the range of twenty to twenty-five percent of the Republicans in New Hampshire, in an eight or ten man race that would be formidable, if not ultimately successful.

I confess that the analytical clarity of this is largely retrospective. The truth was that I was more impressed by something that, even in the fall of 1995, could not have been more clear, and that had to do with who Buchanan was, what he had to say, and how he was already lighting all the fuses of the campaign. Instinctively, in a way I barely understood myself, I believed Buchanan was the only one speaking to what this campaign was about, and the only one likely to speak to it in 1996, particularly with the exit of Colin Powell, whose very candidacy could not have helped being about anything *but* the meaning of America. Whatever one thought of Buchanan, he wasn't a phony like Gramm or a nihilist like Newt Gingrich. If he wasn't the Anti-Christ of American politics, as some would have it, if he wasn't necessarily a fascist (because Buchanan had more humor than anyone else running, and I've never known a fascist or communist who had a sense of humor worth a damn), he was certainly the Anti-Lincoln, someone for whom the second half of the Second Inaugural must have sounded like, well, Gaelic. There wasn't a lot of "with malice toward none, with charity for all" in Buchanan's rhetoric. And the very notion of union, which was literally a holy covenant for Lincoln, a Divine Mission, something much bigger than a mere political or social construct, was contradicted by the narrowness of how Buchanan defined a country whose traditions and culture and language he valued more than the passionate idea of it.

"You know," I finally felt compelled to ask, "there was a time when Goldwater conservatism was about a love of freedom, whereas now it seems Buchanan conservatism is about a love of authority." Unless I missed a subliminal message in his response, he didn't deny it. He talked about the decomposition of society since the Sixties, about the "pollution of the popular culture," and while it might have disturbed Pat Buchanan to be described as the Anti-Lincoln, my fear was that it wouldn't disturb him at all, given his romantic nostalgia for kamikaze Confederate generals and his enthusiasm for flying the Confederate flag over South Carolina's state capitol. And the question I was going to ask him before he cut me off to board the van for Baton Rouge was whether he worried, even as he spoke to his own uncompromising vision of America, that he made it more and more impossible for other people to hold on to their own dreams of America, and he was thereby killing America, scalding word by scalding word.

13

When I saw him again forty-eight hours later, it was at another press conference, this time in Manchester, New Hampshire. He was scheduled, along with nine other declared Republican candidates for the presidency, to participate in what had been generally described as the first debate of the election, but which the local TV station putting on the event now hastened to rechristen a "forum" when it became clear that any interaction between the contenders would be discouraged at all cost.

From the window of my Holiday Inn, located near an intersection of a highway and a river, Manchester appeared to be something more than a town and less than a city, its panorama of old brick-red buildings abutting the hills of autumn-red trees. Presidential politics are a cottage industry in New Hampshire—but for presidential politics, there's really not much point to there even being a New Hampshire—and high above Elm Street, which was as close to a facsimile of Main Street as America was likely to spit up in the Nineties, allowing for the pizza joints that occupy every three or four addresses, was a billboard that read: "Running for President? WELCOME TO NEW HAMPSHIRE! Now, what are *you* going to do about balancing the budget?" Still, national CNN coverage or no, even the cheerleading newsreaders on WMUR-TV, who plugged the forum all the night and afternoon before, had to admit the primary was still an awfully long way away; and the day of the forum brought more a sense of inexorable obligation than real excitement. Lamar Alexander of Tennessee, a self-proclaimed political renegade who in fact had had a long career in and out of Washington, including as secretary of education (a department he was now proposing to abolish), arrived for the big night walking up Elm as part of a publicity-seeking hike across the state; Bob Dole opted for an airplane. If it were possible for one man to fly in on two airplanes, Phil Gramm would have done it just to upstage Dole, so he flew in his swarm of senatorial sycophants instead, led by Texas Senator Kay Bailey Hutchison and New Hampshire Senator Robert Smith, all there to let the Senate majority leader know he wasn't even king of his own domain.

They arrived under the shadow of what was beginning to seem the nation's never-ending, ever-consuming obsession. Only hours before, NBC had announced a prime-time interview with O. J. Simpson, to take place on this very same night that Bob Dole was reassuring America his front-running candidacy wasn't imploding, and the other candidates were reassuring Bob Dole the nomination wasn't his just because he thought it should be. Every reporter in Manchester—which included all the big shots from the *New York Times* and *Newsweek* and *Washington Week in Review* and *USA Today* and Jim Lehrer *News Hour*—was thinking the same thing: "Say, can't we do this another time?" In response to which the Republicans feebly rationalized that the political junkies would be watching not O. J. but the forum, and they were the ones the party really wanted to reach anyway. I suppose they had half-convinced themselves of this when word came down during the Buchanan press conference that the Simpson interview had been canceled. Buchanan turned to his press aide and cracked, "Great job," and everybody laughed.

Buchanan had called the press conference to imply, in terms more oblique than usual, that if the party were to make an unseemly turn toward the center, he would pursue the nomination of a third party, including Ross Perot's Reform Party. The conference was held in an adjunct to my hotel called the Center of New Hampshire, in a much smaller room than the New Orleans fiasco; jammed with fifty or sixty snarling reporters and cameramen, it couldn't help looking packed on the evening news. Gazing around him as he arrived, Buchanan appeared almost abashed, as though having strolled into a masquerade where he might be exposed as an impostor at any moment. For much of his life, when he wasn't flacking for Reagan and Agnew, he had fashioned himself something of a journalist, so he knew a lot of these people; this time he didn't go around shaking everyone's hand, and his performance at the podium—including the trademark slashing karate chops—seemed more mechanical and self-conscious. I admit I was starting to wonder if I had overestimated Buchanan's significance in the scheme of things. It was true he was running second to Dole in the state polls, albeit "by a mile and a half," as one reporter put it during the press conference ("Better than fifth by a mile and a half," Buchanan laughed), and it was also true that he had just gotten the endorsement of the *Union-Leader*, as well as the benefit of whatever fury haunted the nights of its hate-throttled publisher, Nackey Loeb. But since arriving in New Hampshire I had become more impressed, probably just the way I was intended to be, by Phil Gramm's money.

It was in display all over Manchester. At the outset of his campaign the Texas senator had been given to bragging about his "ready cash" before someone must have explained to him that, even in politics, this seemed tacky; and at almost the very moment that Buchanan was holding his press conference, Gramm's glitzy glass campaign head-quarters on Elm was a bustle of activity, humming with campaign vol-unteers while TV cameras were unloaded from the vans in front, in sharp contrast to Buchanan's quiet storefront operation across the street and down the block. That night a Gramm bus waited at the curb outside my hotel while a rally in one of the hotel ballrooms was being filmed for a campaign commercial, pitiful little red-white-and-blue balloons drifting out through the double doors gasping for air. Gramm had to do a second take on the line, "I want to balance the national budget the way you balance your family budget," when the very well dressed audience laughed rather inappropriately.

Several blocks down the hill at the TV station, a mob of chanting Gramm partisans with their brand-new signs slowly overpowered an equally motivated Alexander mob. The street leading to the TV sta-tion was lined with more campaign signs, stuck in the ground as me-thodically as Christmas lights decorating a suburban tract, and it didn't take long to realize what was missing from this night in Man-chester: Manchester. There were no cars on the road or people on the sidewalks; it was presidential politics in a ghost town, with all the ghosts home before their television sets waiting in frenzied anticipa-tion of the "forum," or more likely the off-chance that O. J. Simpson would yet materialize amid the static. As a TV camera's eye floated over the Gramm and Alexander crowds, their canned fervor flickered to something almost real before reverting to a more perfunctory, robotic cheer once the gaze of the lens had passed. More balloons floated nightward into the beams of the kliegs. A large hot-air balloon with Dole's name attached was anchored to the ground, though whether it really would have gone anywhere unanchored, I couldn't tell. Between the competing Gramm and Alexander armies, stray Buchanan insurrectionists wandered here and there looking a little forlorn, and I found myself actually rooting for the old Anti-Lincoln, which convinced me I had so lost my bearings I nearly quit the job on the spot.

Later I came to my senses. Gramm's money was not going to beat Buchanan's message in New Hampshire, even if during the forum the messenger, stripped of his belligerent Irish charm, sounded just as harsh as his message really was—which was all the more startling when you considered that Buchanan was not necessarily the most conservative candidate in the race. Even discounting Gramm, zillionaire Steve Forbes espoused a sort of pure unfettered capitalism last seen around September 1929, and had been all over the Manchester airwaves the previous few days attacking Dole; and to the right of Forbes, Orange County Congressman Robert Dornan almost got through his whole speech without completely losing it in his usual fashion on the subject of Bill Clinton. He finally couldn't contain himself, sputtering in terms ("three-time draft-dodging adulterer") that could also be applied to Newt Gingrich. And then there was Alan Keyes, an interesting and articulate maniac who told the forum moderator his questions were "stupid." Protesting that the country had come to "define freedom in a corrupt and licentious way," Keyes did Buchanan better than Buchanan: "This campaign is not about what people *want* to hear," he concluded, "it's about what people *need* to hear."

If Keyes, a talk-radio host and former diplomat, was particularly conspicuous for his blackness, it was because in an America where Joe Christmas was suddenly everywhere, including the historical cross hairs of the Verdict and the Million Man March, the topic of race never came up at all. The Party of Lincoln would apparently not engage such a discussion. I was not shocked by this, or rather I was perhaps already jaded by shock, having had one that very afternoon when, strolling from one end of Elm to the other, I stopped slack-jawed to gaze on an exotic sight: a real live African-American crossing the street. I realized then I hadn't seen one in all my time in Manchester. I would see one other before I left, not counting a couple of reporters in the pressroom who may have found it even funnier than the rest of us when, at the outset of the forum, the lights suddenly went out and the candidates, who in fact were in isolation on one floor while the press was quarantined in front of a television set on another, found themselves in the dark. Suddenly there was not a single white Republican presidential candidate to be seen. Steve Merrill, governor of New Hampshire and a Dole supporter, had just finished bragging about the fact that the state has neither an income nor a sales tax, combatively posing the question, "But is this a state with low taxes and low services?" when the darkness answered, Yes.

There was a rumor later that the lights came back on, but I don't believe it. I'm quite sure I didn't notice any light at all, and I was still waiting to see the light after an hour and a half when the forum ended and all the spin maestros converged on us to spin, Gramm of course having bought himself the best spinners money could buy—all those Senate flunkies and seasoned consultants and prominent pollsters. Spinning for her brother to crowds of one or two was Bay Buchanan, the campaign's manager, who had stood a couple of people away from me during the forum radiating intensity and locking Forbes in a particularly frightening stare. It was right around then that I had the idea about kicking over the TV.

14

The TV was perched in the middle of the room, on a table, abandoned by everyone who had crowded around moments before. It was one of those crazy thoughts you get like sticking your finger in a fan or leaning too far over the railing on the top floor of a high building—totally compulsive and self-destructive, but there it was: I could lift my foot and, with one good push, over would go the table with the thirty-inch TV. I know this is pure melodrama, and I don't really believe I would have done it, even if the lonely Keyes spinner *was* trying frantically to latch on to someone, anyone, he could spin for. In another frame of mind I might have almost felt bad for him. But I wasn't in another frame of mind. "Looks like Alan Keyes won the debate tonight," he started in with me. "He was the only one to talk about social issues . . ." and at that moment I was either going to kick over the TV or just turn around and walk away, which was what I did. Within five seconds I heard him glom on to someone else behind me ("Looks like Alan Keyes won the debate tonight . . ."), like one of those guys in the airport trying to convert you, already a soulless little huckster at the age of twenty-two or whatever, and I'm sorry if that sounds harsh.

For God's sake, lighten up, I told myself outside in the Manchester night, putting as much distance as I could between me and the offensive banality of these men who wanted to be President, not to mention the one who already was President. Because everyone knew this country was in trouble, and none of these men was up to the job, the only consoling thought being that when Lincoln became President, almost everyone thought he was the least qualified man ever elected. In the fall of 1995 we were already a nation so sick on fear that we had no national faith left, no patience anymore for the hard business of being Americans; and there was no way one could trivialize this fear: it was the fear of salaries constantly going down instead of up, social guarantees ripped away rather than delivered, streets threatening rather than inviting our passage, diseases eluding rather than dutifully succumbing to our arrogant technology, one big fear of finally having to live moment to moment, which was something we used to be good at in this country, a long time ago. We weren't good at it anymore. And whereas in the great electoral crucibles of the past our fear had a gravitational center that existed in the moment, now the gravitational center of our fear was in the future. And the future used to be where all things American began, which meant that to be afraid of the future, we had become afraid of being Americans. Flying out of New Hampshire the next day I thought to myself, Well, hell, I can't write about *this* for the next year, I'll wind up two psychoses short of a postal worker or drooling in the corner of one of those nuthouses they're closing in L.A. In my mind I half-wrote my resignation letter. But then I wrote this instead, while outside my airplane window the autumnal red trees of Manchester burned like the angry red flames of Malibu.

15

America wearies of democracy. Thirty years after a war that wounded its heart, twenty years after a scandal that scarred its conscience, ten years after fiscal policies that ridiculed its sense of responsibility and fairness, the country has nearly exhausted the qualities by which democracy survives and flourishes. America feels at the end of its power, and the result is a hysteria of which we're barely conscious, a hysteria in which democracy appears as a spectacle of impotence and corruption. As Americans we have come to act more oppressed by freedom than exhilarated by it, more concerned with freedom *from* than freedom *to*. We divide between the vast and growing majority of us who—out of a sense of futility, confusion or indifference—are so disengaged from democracy we never vote at all, and those of us who vote not to thoughtfully resolve complicated issues but to express our rage.

History is clear that democracy cannot long navigate a sea of national rage. Untempered by rationale and open-mindedness, fury eventually consumes democracy rather than nourishes it, because it overwhelms our tolerance, our willingness to be reasonably informed, our determination to hold ourselves accountable for what we decide. Most important, it overwhelms our basic faith in democracy itself and our belief in the individual freedoms that are inviolate to the power of the majority, identified by the Declaration of Independence as endowed by God and codified by the first ten amendments to the Constitution. We display less and less patience with what we previously held to be unalienable, less and less patience with democracy's inherent inefficiency and the morass of conflicting interests that are read in democracy's results. We display less and less patience, in other words, with America.

A deep freeze has settled in the American soul. The nation gets meaner and more petty until rage is the only national passion left— and then it is anger not at those on top, which is the anger America was born of, but at those on the bottom, for whom America is supposed to be the last abiding dream. Increasingly we view individual freedom not as the fundament of collective freedom but as an affront to collective sensibility or security. We are encouraged by talk-show commentators to regard the most basic precepts of democracy as sentimental luxuries at best or, at worst, legalistic refuge for vicious criminals, social parasites and moral scum. We find indignant solace in the single greatest myth of the contemporary political landscape, which holds that the problem with the country is the government, the politicians and the process as a whole. This myth, that the process has grown hopelessly out of touch with what we really want and feel and need, is the opposite of the truth. The truth is that we are the problem with America. The process and politicians, the lobbyists and "special" interests—by which we mean any interest that doesn't pertain to us—reflect us all too perfectly; and we hate them for it.

From dismal campaign to dismal campaign we demand "change," and then give every indication of wanting nothing of the sort, and not having the slightest idea what we ever meant by it in the first place. Confronted with change that is truly profound or revolutionary, which is to say unavoidably painful and disorienting, we scurry back to the status quo that so infuriated us to begin with, and that not so long ago we claimed was unacceptable. From angry election to angry election we demand politicians tell us the truth, and then punish those who do. When they speak of unpleasant realities and tell us things must necessarily get harder before they get easier—Bob Dole on the subject of the deficit and Bruce Babbitt on taxes in the presidential campaign of 1988, Paul Tsongas on the economy in 1992, Warren Rudman and Bob Kerrey on entitlements, William Bennett and Jack Kemp on illegal immigration—we dismiss them at the polls or denounce them from the streets. From political season to political season we demand our problems be solved, and then make ruthlessly clear we expect someone else to pay the price. We say we want government to be smaller, but we never name government programs directly affecting us that we would be willing to forgo. People in the cities cry for cutting farm subsidies; people in the suburbs call for cutting inner-city programs. In the American politics of the mid-Nineties, welfare recipients were the sacrifice of choice, though the American economy allots to welfare only three percent of its budget.

To suggest we are hypocrites sounds elitist. It subverts the populism on which both the Right and Left capitalize, and offends the professed egalitarianism of a news media already cowed by accusations of liberal bias. At one level we're intelligent enough to understand our hypocrisy and that much of what we would like is irresponsible. Our common sense admits that national economic survival is not served by cutting taxes and not possible without addressing the three epic components that make up most of the national budget, which one segment or another of the public has declared sacrosanct: defense, Medicare, and Social Security. But if we despise ourselves for this hypocrisy, at another level we have convinced ourselves that we've earned our delusions. This is because we have secretly come to fear and resent that the American dream itself may be a delusion. This is the source of our rage, and of the rage that would devour democracy. It is a rage at ourselves, which we can barely stand to live with, but which is the only thing that seems to pump blood through the national heart anymore.

It is a rage at contradictions that confound and beset us. Though America won the Cold War we've grown spiritually lethargic: international triumph appears not to have so much consolidated our power as dissipated it and revealed its uselessness. Though the economy has improved we've grown financially insecure: indeed this "improvement" infuriates us because our own incomes stagnate or diminish and we feel likelier to lose our jobs than advance in them. Though crime statistics have dropped we've grown physically more vulnerable: it is the very nature of modern crime, rather than its numbers, that bends our darkest imagination—not just because crime has become more random and bizarre, but because it is now being committed by children for reasons they cannot even name, and which confirm that a six-year-old may be soul-dead and beyond redemption. Though our culture has mirrored our vicarious desires we've grown sensually alienated from ourselves: we glamorize the very violence we find so threatening, and no matter how far we place ourselves beyond AIDS's reach, a plague that equates the most primal life force with the ghastliest of deaths must infect not just the body but the national psyche.

All of these contradictions conspire to make democracy senseless, and all grow out of the biggest delusion of all, the delusion that most enrages us. This is the delusion of American innocence. A virtual cottage industry of social and cultural analysis has been built on this delusion, as one historical phenomenon after another—from the assassination of John Kennedy to the Vietnam War to Watergate to American hostages in Iran to O. J. Simpson hurtling down the L.A. freeways—is offered as the moment when the country "lost" its innocence. One of the Nineties' most successful motion pictures was about nothing less, its hero not only all the more noble but apparently all the more American for how dim-witted he is. In retrospect it will be ironic if democracy dies in such a delusion, that we never grew up enough to accept that America has never been innocent at all. It is not possible to call innocent a country where the original residents were systematically wiped out and the new tenants built a society in large part on the labor of people who were shipped over in chains from another continent in the hulls of boats. These original sins do not negate America's idealism and romanticism. But that such an idealistic and romantic country was created out of such profound transgressions is a more complicated paradox than we can entertain.

In this growing contradiction between our false innocence and our true idealism, the argument over the meaning of America is increasingly left to those who populate the extremes of anarchy and repression: radical liberal and radical conservative, obscenely poor and obscenely rich, the overdemanding and the ungenerous, the decadent and the narrow-minded, the casually promiscuous and the Stepford Virgins who peer out of advertisements as role models of "the new celibacy," and the two main political parties themselves, one representing incompetence and intellectual bankruptcy, the other bad faith and the iron hand. This pendulum of ever-widening extremes has been set in motion by the very democracy that would be sliced in two by it, and the middle ground where the questions of democracy are supposed to meet the answers is often a no-man's land where anyone who tries to occupy it risks being cut to ribbons. The current resident of the White House, for example.

Bill Clinton—or perhaps more precisely, the phenomenon of Clinton—is his own contradiction. A pallid political portrait of lefts (job training, student loans, tax credits for the poor, health care reform) and rights (crime, free trade, line-item veto, welfare reform), he became in the early years of his presidency the most curiously demonized figure in American politics since Richard Nixon, viscerally loathed by a third of the country and regarded with pitiful contempt by another third. Unlike with Nixon or Lyndon Johnson, Clinton's demonization was not about politics. Whatever baseness or vulgarity may eventually have been attributed to Nixon and Johnson, the roots of their controversy lay in politics at its most vivid: the anti-communism of the Forties and early Fifties, the civil rights struggle and Vietnam War of the Sixties and early Seventies. What was unsettling about the overwhelming rejection of Clinton in the 1994 congressional elections was the extent to which it was personal, and to which it demonstrated how Clinton's persona was the landscape across which America tried and failed to come to terms with the last quarter-century in general, and the Vietnam War in particular.

Far more than recent Cold War victory, which cannot be measured in any immediate terms but defense jobs lost, it is a generation-old Asian defeat, still brutally measured in lives lost, that traumatizes the country's memory. For those who have hated Clinton, nothing so characterizes him as his conduct as a student during the Vietnam War, and how that conduct was emblematic of the counterculture. Other matters, having to do with obscure real estate ventures or allegations of womanizing, are really peripheral. The Right that has hated Clinton for not serving in Vietnam has never similarly hated Dan Quayle or Newt Gingrich for the same. The difference is that Clinton's avoidance of military service remains a subtle restatement of the ongoing twenty-five-year argument that the war was bad, while Quayle's is a declaration that the war was noble. In the eyes of the Right, the hypocrisy of Quayle's position—his belief that it was a fine war for someone else to die in—does not discredit but rather absolves him. In contrast Clinton is the embodiment of something the country still cannot allow itself to believe: that it was an entirely useless war in which fifty-eight thousand Americans, not to mention countless Vietnamese, *died for nothing.*

Thus, in its first election of Clinton in 1992, the American democratic process resulted in a conclusion from which the country itself recoiled. This was compounded by Clinton's moral and political failure during the campaign to speak forcefully about his opposition to the war, though it was a discussion for which an economically preoccupied country had as little enthusiasm as Clinton, and for which it probably never would have rewarded him with election. Rather it rewarded him in part for obscuring the matter, and as a result Clinton could not later escape the nation's fixed sense of him as someone who always took the most politically expedient position on any issue and thus had no credibility, as opposed to Ronald Reagan, who was remembered as taking firm and even unpopular positions and therefore having a vision. This image of Clinton was so strong that people believed it even when it was plainly contradicted by the record. Having favored the inclusion of homosexuals in the military, having jettisoned a tax cut in favor of deficit reduction, having vigorously supported a trade agreement that was initially opposed by the country at large and his party in particular, having engaged sweeping health reform that was popular in the abstract but represented such a huge political gamble no other President had ever seriously tried to come to terms with it, and having put American dollars in Mexico and American troops in Haiti and Bosnia when everyone was against it, Clinton took more politically risky positions in three years than Reagan did in eight. Clinton was hated because, one, "he never does anything unpopular," and because, two, *everything* he did was unpopular.

In all the various subconscious messages from the nation to itself that Clinton's 1992 election represented, and for all the ways he was a metaphor for the deep-seated national conflicts we could stand to neither face nor finish, Clinton appeared in the first three years of his presidency to be American democracy's last futile and ineffectual gasp. He was neither visionary enough to transcend national rage nor depraved enough to exploit it; and because rage was exhilarating to an otherwise enervated nation, we were not willing to give it up to anyone who couldn't redeem or justify it. It didn't matter how often we were told by however many reliable sources that the national deficit had been reduced by half; national surveys showed we insisted on believing it had grown larger. It didn't matter how often we were presented the facts that less than one out of fifty of us had our taxes raised in the 1993 budget; we insisted on believing it was "the biggest tax increase in history." We insisted on our rage in the same way we insisted on our cynicism, because it was the last easy thing we knew how to feel, the last simple emotion we could understand, and the last from which we could still draw a sense of power, no matter how fraudulent it might be.

Every time the Left burned an American flag twenty-five years ago, every time the Left didn't simply criticize the government's policy in Vietnam but supported Asian guerrillas shooting and killing American soldiers, every time the Left reveled in America's humiliations, the ascent of the Right became inevitable. We can only conclude that an empowered Left might well have exploited a rage that razes democracy as surely as the Right did. Nevertheless, after the election of a moderately liberal Democrat to the presidency in 1992, the Right incessantly questioned not simply his policies or his character, but his very legitimacy. In Clinton's very first presidential speech to a joint session of Congress, Republicans openly *laughed* at him, something for which there was no precedent in modern memory. In remarks on the floor of the House, Dick Armey, the Texas Republican congressman who later became majority leader, taunted Democrats with references to Clinton as "*your* President"—this following his description of the First Lady as a Marxist. Former Marine Colonel Oliver North said that Clinton was not his commander-in-chief, and the chairman of the Senate Foreign Relations Committee, Jesse Helms, suggested that the country's military might happily do the President harm, given the opportunity. The Republican Speaker of the House repeatedly claimed the Clinton White House was a bacchanal of drugs, and radio commentator Rush Limbaugh hinted—and Jerry Falwell openly charged—that Clinton had people murdered.

In the shortest and meanest terms, all of this might be viewed as "merely" a partisan effort to destroy Clinton at any cost. It was worse. Questioning Clinton's legitimacy, the leading spokesmen for the Right insidiously questioned the legitimacy of democracy itself. They spoke of Clinton's election as a kind of foreign coup—an insinuation made by Gingrich in ever bolder variations on Republican chairman Rich Bond's comments in 1992 about "real" Americans, and Interior Secretary James Watt's jocularity of the early Eighties that there are two kinds of people, Americans and liberals. If Clinton's presidency was the product of the democratic process and that product was illegitimate, then the process that produced it was by definition illegitimate; in essence, the Right argued that any democracy that produces a Clinton presidency invalidates itself. This was more than just ruthless partisan politics, more than "the same old thing" political opponents had been doing to each other for years. No one in a more turbulent America questioned the legitimacy of Nixon's election in 1968, when he received a percentage of the vote similar to Clinton's. Indeed, we hadn't seen anything quite like it since the election of 1860 when half the country considered intolerable any democracy that would produce the likes of Lincoln (who received a smaller percentage than either Nixon or Clinton).

Over the last quarter-century, perhaps in response to the latent totalitarianism of the Left in the late Sixties, the Right transformed itself accordingly. It moved far beyond Reaganism, not to mention the libertarianism of Barry Goldwater. It still gave lip service to the principle of individual freedom unfettered by the power of centralized government, but it was difficult to remember when a contemporary conservative spokesman of significance energetically, heatedly championed the rights of the criminally accused, for instance, or an individual's freedom to express an unpopular, even arguably anti-American thought. In fact, it was difficult to remember when any significant conservative spokesman last championed any specific individual freedom other than freedom from taxes or the freedom to own a gun. Since the administration of Richard Nixon, the true priorities of the Right were not liberty but authority, not singularity but conformity. Gingrich's celebration of the "normal American," as opposed to the presumably abnormal President, was not impetuous but calculated. At both the leadership and grassroots level, the country's new majority party that emerged out of the 1994 congressional elections was energized and funded and driven by people who believed that many of their fellow Americans were not real Americans, not normal Americans, but the Enemy. In the name of righteousness or patriotism or Jesus or America, these people were loyal to a vision of the country that was not pluralistic and democratic, but intensely religious or ideological or both.

In the last years of the Twentieth Century, the rest of America would eventually have to choose whether to abdicate to such people the meaning of America, if not out of rage then inertia. Thomas Jefferson never envisioned America as either a religious or an ideological country; in the Nineties he would have been a misfit, sharing with the Right its hatred of high taxes, heavy government regulation and gargantuan bureaucracy, and supporting the general divestiture of power from the federal government to the states, and sharing with the Left its hostility to religious zealots, oversized military budgets and gargantuan corporations, while belonging to the American Civil Liberties Union and generally encouraging Americans to be as abnormal as possible. Certainly no one would find Jefferson very normal, an aging eccentric widower with a vaguely scandalous past shuffling around in his shabby clothes in his strange house with all its weird inventions, on top of a remote foggy Virginia hill. But no one would have to wonder if he really believed in democracy, or have to ask whether he believed in it more than his own power.

The grand arrogance of America was always that it would dictate its own terms to history rather than the other way around. Again and again the Twentieth Century tried to say no to democracy, again and again America answered: yes. The final American irony would be if, at the end of the century with no foes left, having vanquished all who laid siege to democracy, this country now turned to finish the job. If it succeeded, it would be because America forgot that ultimately democracy cannot be translated in terms of the material things it allows us to acquire, that it was always supposed to be dangerous, idealistic but not innocent, and forged of as many passions as there are voices, among which there is only one common rage, and that is the rage for justice.

16

I had spent the summer of 1995 recovering from pneumonia and was just beginning to figure out what to do next, when the phone call came from out of the blue. "What we want," the features editor at *Rolling Stone* said, "is a novelist who will write about the 1996 presidential campaign as though it were a novel." I admit that when the magazine flew me to New York to talk about it, I assumed the job was in the bag. "Oh, it's all set," the editor agreed, "but, uh . . . Jann can be . . . *difficult* . . . so we thought maybe he should just meet you," and two weeks later, ten minutes into my interview with the magazine's owner and publisher, I realized I didn't necessarily have the job at all.

Sitting on the other side of a huge empty desk, Jann Wenner kept narrowing his eyes at me in a way I think was supposed to suggest uncanny shrewdness but was really a desperate hope that if he squinted long and hard enough I might turn into R. W. Apple. He considered the *New York Times* the magazine's only serious competition on the campaign trail. "Who are your contacts at the White House?" he demanded to know, and in my vaguest manner I tried to explain I didn't have any contacts at the White House, that actually I didn't have any contacts anywhere. Though among my fiction I had published a book about politics and one piece or another for various publications over the years, including Wenner's arch-rival the *New York Times*, I wasn't a reporter and had never been one; I wanted to write not so much about the campaign itself, I explained, as about a year in the inner life of the country during the campaign.

He visibly shuddered. I think he had horrible visions of me dispatching bulletins between cow milkings from Midwest farmhouses in the middle of January, living with the Olsen family for a week and getting the pulse of the land, so to speak; and if there was one thing he most certainly was not interested in, Wenner made clear then and there, it was what *ordinary* people thought about this campaign. In the meantime a hundred more important matters distracted him. As our interview unfolded a certain routine developed, during which he would ask various questions about this and that—my contacts at the White House and some such—and just as I would begin to whimper some snively non-answer he would grab the telephone and start barking directives to various rock stars across the land about the upcoming Rock and Roll Hall of Fame concert, or start madly scribbling something completely unrelated to what we were talking about, just to let me know he was so beset by brainstorms he literally couldn't sit still. Others would assure me later that I should consider myself fortunate he actually looked in my general direction every once in a while rather than conduct the entire interview with his gaze cast grandly over Sixth Avenue. On the advice of one of Wenner's former writers I brought him a copy of one of my early novels, which he commanded me to sign and whereupon I scrawled some feverish inscription "with respect and admiration"—handwritten evidence of complete ass-kissing obsequiousness on my part now fully documented and preserved for posterity in the future Jann Wenner Memorial Library. In his own puckish fashion he was charming. But it was only another ten minutes into the interview when I realized with an almost audible gasp that he didn't have a clue who he was; he didn't seem to know, I later told an editor at another magazine, if he wanted to be on the cutting edge of American journalism or invited to dinner at the White House. "Oh, he knows," the editor answered, "he knows exactly which one he wants. He just likes to pretend to himself that he still wants the other one."

17

Given such a realization, there's really no one but myself to blame for what happened. But I had been reading *Rolling Stone* almost from the outset of its publishing life, starting in college in 1969 and for the next five or six years when it was arguably the best magazine in America; it was harder to say which was more brilliant, Wenner's instincts or the stable of writers those instincts attracted. Actually, I had my own sketchy history with the magazine: around 1976, when it was relocating from San Francisco to New York, the managing editor at the time, Ben Fong-Torres, had called to ask if I was interested in a job. This meant me relocating too, of course, and since I had just spent a year bouncing around Europe and the States and was only beginning to settle back down in L.A., I declined. Ten years later I actually wrote a cover story on Whoopi Goldberg, something none of the current editors now seemed to realize, including Wenner. For one reason or another it didn't seem important enough to bring up.

If *Rolling Stone*'s glory days were far behind it, Wenner having lost his feel for the zeitgeist back around the time of punk rock, I still couldn't help pretending it was the magazine of legend. So Jann and I were an odd pair—him pretending he was the *New York Times*, me pretending he was *Rolling Stone*. Stymied by our interview and momentarily considering shipping me off to Colorado to consult "the Sage of Woody Creek," by which I assumed he meant Hunter Thompson, Wenner instead hustled me down to Washington, D.C., where I spent a day with the magazine's national affairs correspondent, William Greider. Greider was a newsman of the old school, once with the *Washington Post*, who back around the beginning of the Eighties found himself, much to his own astonishment and that of his colleagues, writing about politics for a rock and roll magazine. Now he had taken a leave from *Rolling Stone* to finish a book about the world economy. Extraordinarily gracious, he advised me at length on how to run interference for Wenner's identity crisis, though he never put it that way and never would; he was extremely loyal to Wenner, who had earned that loyalty by generously supporting Greider over the years, standing by him through lean times. Wenner took the veteran newsman's counsel seriously, and since I finally got the job, Greider must have told him some reasonably positive things about me. I would like to think he isn't sorry now.

I went back to Los Angeles and wrote Wenner a letter, including a thousand words about why he should hire me, and concluding with several hundred about why he should not. "If you want a traditional reporter," I told him, "almost anyone could do it better than I." This probably bewildered him all the more. Another three weeks passed before I was hired officially, albeit with the admonition, from Jann's right-hand man, that *Rolling Stone* was a "reality-based publication," by which he meant that, all that earlier business about covering the campaign like a novel notwithstanding, I couldn't just make everything up.

18

So I wondered if *Rolling Stone* wasn't testing my mettle perhaps when the magazine's travel department kept booking me into cheap little hotels like the dump in Washington called the Governors' House, which first lost my reservation and then gave me a room with no heat. "Is it really so cold?" the manager at the front desk purred malevolently on the telephone, frosty little clouds floating across my eyes every time I exhaled. A stream of maids, janitors and various maintenance personnel filed through the room to hold their hands up to the vent and confirm that, indeed, there did not seem to be any heat coming from it. The manager promised me the room would warm up "very soon," by which he meant, it occurred to me around four in the morning, May.

By Orlando, though, I decided it wasn't *Rolling Stone* behind the Freeze-Out but the Republicans. It was cold in Orlando too; the temperature that morning had dropped to just above freezing and, checking into the Peabody Hotel, which certainly appeared to be a step or two up from the Governors' House, I discovered . . . no heat. Not only was there no heat but the air conditioner was on: this was Florida, right? "You need to adjust the thermostat," the front desk clerk explained patiently. I assured her that at this point in my life I generally understood the principle of thermostats. An hour later they finally sent up a guy to dismantle the heater, reassemble it and guarantee me everything was perfect, and after yet another hour, at two in the morning with the temperature still plummeting, I decided two hotel rooms without heat in two cities a thousand miles apart was just a little too much of a coincidence. That was when it dawned on me that the command center for the Bob Dole for President campaign was on the floor right above mine, in all likelihood the room above mine, where snickering Dole operatives at this moment were siphoning off my heat, throwing switches and twisting gas pipes and ejaculating into the Orlando night warm plumes of tropical balminess, that would rightfully be mine in a Bob Doleless America.

19

Orlando is a city where the air is perfumed as though by a decadent, synthetic flower, and the water in the hotel fountains smells like a menthol cigarette. Taking your shower in the morning you smell it in the steam that rises around you, and the water that comes from the tap in your room tastes of it. Huge neon silhouettes of Mickey Mouse greet your arrival at the airport, where an unctuous voice on the monorail bids you a good stay. Orlando has Disney World and Epcot Center and Universal Studio, Sea World and Wet 'N' Wild and Busch Gardens, Cypress Gardens and Gatorland and Pleasure Island and the Mystery Fun House and Pirates Mini Golf. The newest attraction is Splendid China, in which the world's largest and most impossible country has been miniaturized for an afternoon visit. So artificial as to be a geographical abstraction, Orlando is a landscape against which philosophical abstractions of politics and even spirituality trivialize and debase themselves; if there is nowhere else in the world where moral righteousness has become as equated with materialism and leisure as it has in America—to be poor and without a vacation is to be a sinner—no American city is as much in the business of leisure as Orlando, unless it's Las Vegas, which is more honest about its notions of sin and salvation.

Like a city in a bubble, Orlando aspires to be scrupulously protected from the toxicity of Real Life, so the weekend before Thanksgiving 1995, when the temperature dropped to just above freezing, the cold seemed not just rude but anarchic. As though the bubble had ruptured somewhere either so high in the sky or so close to the ground that no one could see the crack, other anarchic elements besides the cold were slipping through as well: in a small, stark conference room of the Peabody, two ministers and a conservative Republican member of the Lake County school board were warning darkly of an "immoral street gang . . . trying to take over the psyche of the land." They were speaking not of drug lords or urban gangstas or even decadent welfare-state liberals but the Christian Coalition, a political organization that believes Jesus was the first Republican. At that very moment the Coalition was holding a rally only a few miles away, proceeding with its plan to take over if not the psyche of the land then at least the Republican Party, which was proceeding with its own plan to take over the country, as is entirely fair in politics.

The three had names the Christian Coalition could only envy. One of the ministers, Jim Armstrong, was a tall, soft-spoken uncle figure who conveyed understanding even at his most confrontational. The prim, intense young woman who opened the press conference was the Reverend Marni Harmony, a Unitarian, which the Christian Coalition would hardly count as a religion at all. Randy Wiseman was burly and gregarious, and a year before had run for the local school board against an even more conservative Republican; he described the vaguely terrorist tactics—the scurrilous mailers, the threatening anonymous phone calls—that the Religious Right had used to harass him first politically and then personally. He was impressive not for what he said but because his politics and his Christianity presumably gave him some credibility on the issue, and it probably says more about my suspicious nature than anything else that I found myself wondering if he was really as conservative or Republican as all that. On the other hand, in Orlando, Florida, on this particular weekend, it didn't seem likely he could really be anything else.

Because there were a lot of Republicans in Orlando this weekend, and anywhere you saw more than half a dozen of them in one place, one was probably running for President. None was hanging out in dreary hotel rooms with anxious Unitarians; the crack in Orlando's bubble hadn't let in that much anarchy yet. All were making their pilgrimage to the Christian Coalition rally, which certainly could not be confined to a conference room, having instead assumed the space—and perhaps, it hoped, the innocence—of an elementary school, where much groveling for the blessing of the Coalition's chief enforcer, Ralph Reed, was in order. I don't think the Christian heretics at the Peabody press conference, even someone with the name of Marni Harmony, were naive enough to think they were going to draw the sort of crowd Ralph Reed did, let alone all those aspiring presidents; rather the plan was probably to deprive the Coalition of an extra sixty seconds on the local TV news by offering a rebuttal. A couple of cameras did show up, so they might have succeeded but for Shelby Cox.

The matter of little Shelby Cox was one more bit of anarchy that had slipped into the city and slithered up its streets a couple of nights earlier. By the evidence of the videotape that all the news stations played over and over, she was a lovely bedbug of a kid, four years old; the film showed her running on the beach, in her trailer home mugging for the video camera, always smiling. She had been missing two days and now people were dredging the nearby river for her body, while praying she had just wandered off somewhere and would show up any minute. The night I arrived in Orlando a new burst of hope came with word that a surveillance camera in a department store had caught sight of a girl who looked like her, being led by a mysterious young woman on a shopping spree who nervously bolted when she realized she was being filmed. Shelby Cox so dominated the news that the Christian Coalition rally got about sixty seconds, the claims of Jim Armstrong and Marni Harmony and Randy Wiseman to their fair share of the airwaves thus reduced to about ten seconds if they were lucky. As far as I could tell, though it's possible it flashed by so fast I registered it only subliminally, the thirty-four hundred Republicans who happened to be descending on the city got almost no airtime at all.

20

This had to have been a shock to Jeb Bush, George's son and head of Florida's Republicans, who had convinced the national Republican Party as well as the national media that this convergence was significant, all empirical evidence to the contrary. A mock convention and straw poll of delegates who had been chosen by lottery, Presidency III, as it was grandly called, vaguely suggesting either a Hollywood megasequel if you're a Democrat or a rich man's yacht if you're a Republican, had succeeded in persuading everyone that it was nothing less than the ritual opening of the 1996 campaign, in the same way Presidencies I and II, also in Florida, had portended the elections of Ronald Reagan and George Bush—though any number of other states could claim to have been as prophetic.

Not a single real delegate was chosen in Orlando for the National Republican Convention in San Diego the following August. That business would be left to Super Tuesday in March, when Florida was scheduled to hold a real primary, along with a lot of other southern states. All the Orlando bash could offer was a perfect example of why it was absurd to be covering a presidential election a full year before it happened—that plus a showcase of all the presidential candidates of the post-Colin Powell Era of Republican Candidacies, the Colin Powell Era having lasted three weeks. A strong showing in Orlando, whatever people decided that was, might mean a vague new clout, some fleeting new exposure, and perhaps even a dollar return on the various candidates' investments in the event, which in the case of Senators Dole and Gramm and Governor Alexander were lavish right down to the Godiva chocolates and ballroom dance lessons intended to seduce any delegates whose hearts were still up for grabs.

While Dole's campaign headquarters was on the floor of the Peabody right above my own, the mezzanine level had been taken over by Alexander. The first day of the convention he serenaded a ballroom full of potential converts as they stormed his buffet tables; playing piano no better, but perhaps no worse, than Bill Clinton played saxophone, Alexander was accompanied by Crystal Gayle and Ray Stevens as they performed witty anti-Clinton versions of "Your Cheatin' Heart" and "What'd I Say" ("Tell your ma/tell your pa/gonna send you back to Arkansas"). The crowd was so moved it gave Stevens a standing ovation, which he chose not to reward with an encore; "Ahab the Arab" might have seemed a little undignified even to a room of slightly stupefied Republicans, and I guess "Mr. Businessman," Stevens' faux-protest Sixties hit recorded back when he found counterculture sentiments more profitable, was out of the question. After the entertainment, when Alexander finally got around to his speech asking the audience for its support, the delegates headed for the exits in droves, except for those too sated to budge.

In the Virtual America of Orlando, Presidency III was the Virtual Republican Campaign. Like China it was reduced to its most concentrated form of inauthenticity. On the first day of the convention Phil Gramm flew in from Washington and drove straight from the airport to the brand-new Omni-Rosen Hotel just so he could stroll down a vast hallway the architects might have liked to imagine was a kind of Orlando Versailles, if you replaced the palace mirrors with pasta joints and croissant shops. Then he got back in his car, drove back to his plane, and flew back to Washington, all for the five seconds that might show up on the local news that night, Shelby Cox be damned. A mile away the Dole campaign set up "Camp Bob" and "Kiddie Camp Bob," with clowns, jugglers, face painters, stiltwalkers and dixieland bands. Even the antiseptic new convention center where Presidency III would be held got you going in circles like an amusement park funhouse; at the press office I picked up a schedule and map showing that the highly touted, nationally televised candidates' "debate" to be hosted the first evening by Larry King would be held in Hall A. But following the signs to Hall A for half an hour, I kept finding myself back where I started. "Oh, there is no Hall A," the nice old lady at the information desk laughed when I asked her about it. "Hall A has been turned into Hall F, I guess," she conceded, "it's a little confusing."

I might have assumed this was just another trick by the Republicans to throw me off the track if, prowling the empty innards of the convention center, I hadn't kept bumping into Pete Wilson. The first couple times I thought he was just some drunk who stumbled in from one of the hotel bars, his face pasty with exhaustion and his tie slightly askew; he had that desiccated look of someone whose life has taken a very bad turn and he can no longer quite bear to face the world. I came around a corner and there he was. We kind of danced around each other, each trying to get out of the other's way. "Uh, sorry," I mumbled. Wilson grunted desolately in response. It really wasn't until the next time we crossed paths that I actually realized who he was, bumping into walls and appearing very disoriented, and I couldn't imagine what he was doing here; he *was* the governor of California after all, a fairly demanding job; and he hadn't been running for President for at least a couple of months now, his own once hugely hyped presidential campaign having already ended in a strangled cry of irrelevance. So there wasn't much point to him even being at Presidency III.

Only then did I understand, with some horror, what had happened. Only then did I understand that in fact Pete Wilson was lost in the convention center like I was, and that moreover he had been here for weeks, since before his campaign collapsed, futilely searching for Hall A and not having gotten the news yet that he was not going to be President next year or any other year and that his political life was for all intents and purposes over. On my next go-round, now looking for Hall F, I came upon him one last time. Someone had taken mercy on him and stuck him in front of a TV camera where, well, you couldn't exactly say he came to life, but he was a little more animated, for a dead man. Nothing gets the embalming fluid coursing through the veins of a political corpse like a little TV coverage, and after a while I couldn't stand to watch anymore, so I left.

21

In an obscure Fifties novel called *In Milton Lumky Territory*, Skip Stevens is a young salesman wandering the byways of America. He is not much different from what one might imagine a young Pete Wilson was once like, ordinary and uninteresting in his Americanism except for his dreams which, as with the glorious intangibility of all dreams, are the only thing that make him vaguely original. Does anyone doubt that, life taking an only slightly different direction, Pete Wilson could have wound up a traveling salesman? Indeed Skip is a contemporary of Pete Wilson's, about the same age Wilson would have been in 1959, involved with an older woman as Wilson was with his first wife, with all the maternal implications. There would seem to be something about a certain kind of Republican—Wilson, Gingrich, Nixon—that leads them to marry their mothers.

In Milton Lumky Territory is Philip K. Dick's great lost novel; it was only finally published in England in 1985, and has never been published in this country at all. At the end of the book Skip rents a room in Boise, Idaho. He's had an interesting week: having met Susan Faine, an older divorcée looking for someone to save her small office-supplies business, he found himself—within a matter of days—married and the manager of Susan's business, driving madly across the country in search of a warehouse of typewriters. When Skip made the disastrous decision to buy the typewriters, the business immediately unraveled, and the marriage with it; Susan, still the owner of the business, has just fired him. It also happens Susan was Skip's teacher in the fifth grade, something neither of them realized until the affair passed the sexual and psychological rubicon, at which point they discovered that time had only barely mitigated the loathsome recollection she had of him, and the terror he felt of her. One day in the fifth grade Susan assigned Skip to write a paper about a trip to New York. "I never have been there," the eleven-year-old boy told the twenty-one-year-old teacher, who answered witheringly, "Couldn't you pretend?" Now broke and ruined, lying on the rented bed for which he's spent his last twenty bucks, Skip slips back into his memory of this incident—except that instead of writing about a trip to New York that never happened, the eleven-year-old merges with the man on the bed to "remember" the rest of his life with Susan Faine, in which all his initial hopes and instincts about love, marriage, and business have been borne out, and the couple move to Denver where they run an even bigger and more successful enterprise.

The last chapter of *In Milton Lumky Territory* is this reverie of the future. For a reverie, however, it is remarkably without euphoria, annotated with pretend-triumphs that are banal and pretend-tragedies that are inconsequential—an alternate history of the rest of Skip's life related with the same numb calm as the events that brought him to this moment of stunning failure. It is, in short, an American reverie, postwar and war's unblemished triumph, post-nuclear and the nuclear age's primal tragedy. It is the reverie of an American who has forgotten who he is, in a country that has forgotten what it is and, for the moment, likes it that way, if "like" isn't an altogether too intense word for it. The novel ends in the middle of this fantasy, with Skip and Susan and their little girl (who doesn't really exist, of course) sitting in their Denver house quietly watching a movie about submarines on television, the desolation of both the rented bed, and reality, far behind all of them.

22

In Frank Sinatra's 1957 version of "There's No You," the singer is similarly suspended at the intersection of dream, memory and a sorrow so profound it is beyond bitterness, verging on something that is almost rhapsody. Cut at around the same time Phil Dick was beginning to write *In Milton Lumky Territory*, "There's No You" is possibly Sinatra's greatest recording: written in another American time altogether, and now slowed by Sinatra to the speed of rapture, the song can't help recalling Gatsby more than Lumky, when American dreams were so ephemeral as to be unforgettable, and so unabashedly foolish as to be heroic. "How softly they're sighing," the singer sings of the trees, "for summer is dying," and when he sings it he sighs it, conveying the kind of heartbreak that women are more courageous about expressing than men. In the sigh of the trees he watches the dream blow away, and in Sinatra's post-nuclear interpretation of pre-nuclear romanticism America hurtles into the intersection of dream, memory and sorrow, and crashes into itself, lured by whatever the dream was: money, power, Ava Gardner.

In my Orlando hotel room I opened a national magazine to an astounding photo captioned "Three Caballeros," showing the now tottering Sinatra with Bruce Springsteen and Bob Dylan. "The Chairman of the Board, the Boss and the Bob," the photo clarified, in case the rest of America was as floored as I was. It was an update of the Sinatra Rat Pack, with Springsteen as Peter Lawford and Dylan as Joey Bishop, waiting to be joined by Willie Nelson's Dean Martin and Michael Jackson's Sammy Davis, although who would have thought even ten years ago that Sammy Davis would come to seem less freakish and more soulful than Michael Jackson? In the photo Sinatra, on the brink of his ninth decade, typically appeared the most assured; Springsteen, another New Jersey Italian, was some odd mix of haunted and knowing; and Dylan, the Minnesota Jew, was the odd man out. The magazine item went on to explain that two nights before a huge television tribute was taped in Los Angeles, Sinatra and his wife had a more private affair, at which "the guest list, a short one, included Dylan, Springsteen and longtime Sinatra friends Steve Lawrence and Eydie Gorme. After dessert, the five singers gathered around the piano for impromptu renditions of 'It Had to Be You' and 'All or Nothing at All,'" with, the reporter insisted, Gorme haranguing Dylan to sing louder. Two nights later Dylan would perform for the television audience his own "Restless Farewell"—a slightly less-satisfied "My Way"—and Springsteen would do a stark, harrowing "Angel Eyes" alone on guitar. At the end of this national celebration for an American mobster who also happened to be the greatest popular singer of the Twentieth Century, a "We Are the World"–style hodgepodge of performers dragged the old man up on stage to finish off, once and for all, "New York, New York," where he hit the last note with such aplomb and bravura, and handed the mike over to

Tony Bennett with such swagger, that he didn't even have to say it out loud: *You see? That's how it's done.* Inescapable was the sense that he had just sung the last public note of his life.

23

"Are you sure?" another reporter narrowed his eyes the next day when I told him about Pete Wilson wandering the convention center. "Maybe you're confused," he said. "Didn't you just come from Disney World? Maybe you were still on one of the rides."

"There is not," I seethed, "a Pete Wilson Ride at Disney World." We were in the Peabody mezzanine waiting to see Lamar Alexander. A wan figure of no discernible personality, with a high forehead and thinning hair that made him look like an academic even as he wanted to be a Republican tough guy, albeit a Republican tough guy without the rough edges, which just confused the image all the more, Alexander had struck on the amusing strategy of running for President as a veritable babe in the woods of beastly politics, though of course he had been in politics at both a federal and state level for many years—"Long enough," went his standard joke, "to be inoculated but not infected." His governorship was relatively moderate as Republicanism went these days, though he would just as soon have kept that a secret between the 250 million of us, at least until he won the nomination; the federal department he stewarded—education—was one all the right-wingers now wanted to close down, including Alexander himself, though he didn't seem to feel that way at the time he was running it. One of his opponents, the irrepressibly berserk Robert Dornan, was circulating Orlando suggesting that when he became President he would happily appoint Alexander secretary of education again, just so he could torch the agency the way he should have done the first time he had the chance.

At any rate Alexander was staking a great deal on Presidency III. Hoping at one point to place third in the straw poll, the Alexander campaign was now sufficiently caught up in its own excitement to dream openly of finishing second. People were running all over the hotel in the horrible red-and-black flannel shirts that Alexander had made the campaign uniform, and the bright crimson banners hanging above the mezzanine and ballroom shouted, a little desperately, "Lamar! Lamar! Lamar!" As possible Republican nominees went, Lamar was a little unlikely. Obscure southern governors running for President might have sounded like a good idea if you were a Democrat, but it really wasn't Republican style; in Orlando, however, Alexander's vapidness had its own logic, rendering him the Virtual Candidate, a holographic image you could pass your hand through, or maybe even a principle or idea you particularly cherished. Given the Sane Man/Crazy Man Theory of presidential politics, one couldn't rule him out completely. The Sane Man/Crazy Man Theory had been explained to me over margaritas in an L.A. Tex-Mex restaurant a few weeks before by novelist and essayist Michael Ventura. Put succinctly, this theory says: the sanest candidate wins the nomination, the craziest candidate wins the election. "The crazy guy wins the nomination," I had repeated, my brain awash in tequila, "the sane guy—"

"No, no, no," Ventura shook his head, "the *sane* guy wins the nomination . . ."

". . . the *crazy* guy wins the election."

"Look at the record," he said, laying it out for me. Sure enough, as far as I could see, this theory had never been wrong. In 1992, when George Bush ran against Pat Buchanan on the Republican side and Clinton against Jerry Brown for the Democrats, the "sane" guys won the nominations only for the cracker son of an abusive drunk stepfather and hedonistic horse-betting mother to take the election. In 1988, while the tediously stable Michael Dukakis survived a megalomaniacal Jesse Jackson in the Democratic contest, Bush ambushed the clearly unhinged Bob Dole for the Republican nomination and then babbled wanton gibberish at flag factories all the way to triumph in November. Walter Mondale, altogether too well-adjusted for American politics, beat preternatural loose-cannon Gary Hart in 1984 for the Democratic nomination only to lose the general election to the reality-challenged Ronald Reagan, who four years earlier beat Jimmy Carter after Carter fought back an existentially flipped-out Edward

Kennedy. Carter versus Ford in 1976, Nixon versus McGovern in 1972, Nixon versus Humphrey in 1968 . . . thirty years later, did anyone now doubt that, initial appearances to the contrary, Lyndon Johnson was always screwier than Barry Goldwater in 1964? "All right, all right!" I cried miserably as Ventura ticked off the examples. The combination of the Sane Man/Crazy Man Theory and Cuervo Gold was more than I could stand.

"Sometimes it's a tough call," Ventura allowed. In a race involving two undisputed psychotics like Kennedy and Nixon in 1960, for example, the degrees of sanity between them were as pointless to calibrate as they were impossible, which only left people arguing for decades whether the winner really lost and the loser really won. At any rate, applying the Sane Man/Crazy Man Theory to the Republicans in 1996, Lamar Alexander looked pretty good: Dole was a brooding paranoiac, Buchanan an inspired sociopath, and while it might not be fair or exactly accurate to say Gramm was crazy, when a man has a hole where his soul is supposed to be, it suggests a madness almost too profound to measure, except perhaps by the sort of relentlessly sadistic demeanor that Gramm exhibited on a round-the-clock basis. Which left Alexander, since anyone boring enough that he had to wear a flannel shirt and slap an exclamation point after his name to make himself interesting was either sane to the point of inertia, with an id as flat as the Mojave, or so metaphysically, bone-chillingly demented as to evoke the Void and a universe utterly bled dry of God and hope.

I didn't have the heart to broach this last possibility with Bob and Herman. Bob and Herman were both Alexander supporters who had just met in Orlando and were already fast friends. Herman was large and ruddy, in his late forties, "very conservative" by his own characterization; Bob was in his mid- to late sixties and had once run for assemblyman in upstate New York. They were not bigots or Christian fascists or heartless, money-consumed authoritarians, but men who genuinely felt the government had gotten far too powerful for America's good—about as American a notion as one could have. Now, with bracing, good-humored enthusiasm, they wanted to do something about it. Neither man, Bob's failed run for political office notwithstanding, was a political creature by profession; both argued that people had to stop blaming politicians and take responsibility for their country. "Everyone keeps saying the process is broken," said Bob. "But you can't fix it in Washington. You have to fix it in the cities, in the counties . . . from the bottom up, not the top down."

"You know," Herman said, "I really haven't run into a lot of zealots here. The guys who want to feed old ladies dog food."

The only thing I didn't understand after talking to Bob and Herman was exactly why they were for Alexander. I wasn't sure they understood, either. Herman liked the way Alexander said the government couldn't do everything and everyone had to learn to manage their own lives, but all the Republican candidates were saying this in one way or another, many far more vividly; for that matter, the Democrat in the White House was saying the same thing. This was a point of philosophical argument that conservatives had long since won. Bob had been leaning toward Colin Powell before Powell's withdrawal; Herman was somehow propelled to Alexander when he couldn't decide between Dole and Gramm. Perhaps without realizing it, Bob and Herman had intuitively stumbled into the quagmire of the Sane Man/Crazy Man Theory, which on the one hand suggested that, as the sanest candidate, Alexander was the party's most logical nominee, an argument undercut on the other hand by the most commonly stated reason for Alexander's support, that he had the best chance of beating Bill Clinton.

Because it was already becoming very clear, a year before the election, that if the theory was true and it was the craziest man who would go on to win in November 1996, then Bill Clinton, the Sybil of American politics, might have it in the bag after all. After three years of revealing one facet or another of a severe multiple-personality disorder, including Campaigner-in-Chief Bill, Therapist-Laureate Bill, National-Self-Flagellant Bill, and Gladhander-in-Obsequiam Bill, the most deeply hidden, recessive identity of all had recently emerged to, by all appearances, take possession of the Clinton consciousness. This personality was called: President of the United States. In clear defiance of his image as the most utterly poll-driven political animal since the President before him, President Bill was not only sending troops to Bosnia on a matter of principle—even as every poll screamed he risked nothing less than his presidency itself—but he was also engaged in a battle with the Republican Congress over the budget, during which he was heard to say things like, "If the people don't agree with me, they're entitled to a new President." It was a statement so flabbergastingly out of character, so contrary to everything we had come to believe about him, that I almost fell off the bed in my hotel room when I saw it on television.

24

While Herman insisted there really weren't many zealots in Orlando, a good third of the delegates were fellow travelers if not outright card-carrying members of the Religious Right, which partly accounted for why attendance at the Larry King debate was a little light. The Christian Coalition rally at the Westridge Elementary School was still in full swing, even if all the presidential candidates were by now at the convention center—except those stuck in the Sodom of Washington, D.C., where Presidency III was being upstaged yet again, not by missing little girls but the government itself. This very week, amid a budget battle that produced some of the bitterest ideological invective since the Sixties, the affairs of state had ground to a halt; for many of the delegates this seemed like something less than a catastrophe. They cheered raucously at every mention of the government's coma.

In the meantime the debate was shrinking by the moment. When I had peered into Hall F that afternoon, five chairs had been up on the stage; by broadcast time there were four. The other participants, all members of the United States Congress, were to beam in from the Capitol, floating above the convention on the huge monitors that bookended the stage. Even so, there was some question about whether Dole was going to participate at all, via satellite or any other way; one minute the word was that he was in, the next he was out. As the front-runner with the most to lose, it certainly made sense that he would try to weasel out of the whole thing—at least until it made contrary sense that weaseling out of the whole thing wouldn't look so hot. There was widespread speculation, not entirely unfounded, that he was intentionally scheduling a Senate vote on the budget at just the moment the debate was taking place; but when everyone caught on to *that* ruse, the timing of the vote changed. So up until the debate began, it wasn't at all clear Dole would be part of it.

The delegates approached the debate with conflicting feelings of excitement and scorn for the media event they were part of. They somehow sensed that maybe the patronizing Larry King wasn't one of them, something he confirmed at one of the rowdier moments when, like a teacher calling a class to order, he cried out, "Decorum!" As the debate began, the only thing he really wanted to talk about was not the candidates who were running but the one who wasn't, asking the others if they would put General Powell in their cabinet. Alexander assured Larry he would. Buchanan, seated right next to Alexander, not only wouldn't, but promised that his entire cabinet would be right-to-life. Bob Dornan, who a year later would go on to lose his congressional seat to a completely unknown Hispanic woman and make quite a spectacle of himself in the process, now argued with King at length about the correct pronunciation of "Colin." When the Great Beam-In came following the budget vote, of course it was Phil Gramm who rushed from the Senate chamber to get on TV first, with an expression on his face like he was on the verge of a giggle-fit. He sidestepped the Powell question, launching into his usual pitch with most of his favorite lines, about doing "the Lord's work in the Devil's city" and how all the people who were collecting welfare and "riding in the wagon" now had to get out of the wagon and help push. Gramm was born on a military base at the government's expense and went to school on a government loan, and one way or another benefited from government aid his entire life, so presumably his idea of getting out of the wagon and helping to push was for the rest of us to make him President of the United States. Soon the stray anarchy loose in Orlando wreaked havoc on the technology, and the sound of the transmission from Washington went slightly out of sync with the picture, everyone's lips moving to the wrong syllables, though in Gramm's case you couldn't really tell anything was out of the ordinary.

By the straw poll the next night, the candidates were in a frenzied contest to see who could throw the rawest meat to the ravenous delegates, among whom the Buchanan supporters betrayed the most bloodlust in their cheers. Stretching from one end of the hall to the other, a forest of delegation signs marked all the state's counties—Gulf, Indian River, DeSota, Sarasota, Puttnam, Liberty, the mighty Dade. Saint Johns bragged of its mere twelve percent Democratic registration, while Nassau took special pride in "skinning its alligators in the summer and its Yankees in the winter." Lafayette County had exactly one delegate: "Lafayette," he would later announce in the roll call, "unanimously casts its one vote for Bob Dole," to which the convention cheered wildly, not for Dole but the defiant unanimity. During the speeches Alexander got off a good crack about Clinton being the first President in history who felt compelled "to work out his midlife crisis in public," and Dornan promised to impeach the President if he sent soldiers to Bosnia, as of course Clinton would soon enough. Buchanan was at something less than full throttle, occasionally bellowing one of his vintage vows of destruction ("If I am the Republican nominee, I will take that hollow man apart!"), though his assault seemed to wilt in a Florida climate that really didn't favor such Hun-like exuberance. Or maybe it was just that he knew Alan Keyes was up next.

One might have expected Buchanan to be Jerry Lee Lewis to Keyes' Chuck Berry, recalling the famous story of the Fifties concert when both Lewis and Berry were on the same bill. Lewis, incensed he had to open for Berry, scorched the audience with a version of "Whole Lotta Shakin' Goin' On" before setting his piano on fire, stalking off the stage and snarling at Berry "Top *that*," along with a very bad name that Mark Fuhrman would appreciate. Buchanan did not set the podium on fire, though he did enter and exit the convention to John Mellencamp's "R.O.C.K. in the U.S.A." Then Keyes came on. A former State Department and U.N. official who now ruled his little part of the right wing's talk-radio empire, he was the least known man running for President, and his entrance received little applause. As his black face loomed Oz-like over the convention on the giant monitors, his strategy apparently was to insult the audience into supporting him, calling the delegates patsies for a media that refused to take him seriously—"not," he said, "because they don't like me, but because they don't like you." He was still incensed at how Larry King had spent half the debate the previous night talking about Powell, and now Keyes tore into the general as the kind of black man the white media loved because the white media created him. He ridiculed the Republican Party, and by inference the assembled delegates, for having bought into this: You say you want a revolution, declared Keyes, but I am the true revolutionary, the one who understands that the real problem with America is spiritual, the decimation of "the marriage-based, two-parent family," the holocaust of abortion, the fraud of affirmative action. "I am an abolitionist!" he thundered. Just as he would have fought to free the slaves a hundred and fifty years ago, he had now come to free the Republicans.

The audience became prostrate with excitement. The more they cheered, the more Keyes humiliated them; the more disdain he radiated, the more they cheered. Frantically waving his arms for them to shut up, Keyes kept shouting over their applause, "Wait, wait!" as though to say they hadn't even heard the good stuff yet, as though on the one hand his ego held their applause in contempt, but on the other hand his message was genuinely more important to him than any petty adoration. When his allotted time ran out and he wasn't finished, the convention officials turned off the microphone, and the audience howled in protest. Keyes didn't move; minutes passed. Music blared over the speakers. Dislodged not an inch Keyes went right on screaming into the music, and though no one could hear a word he said, the cheering just got louder and louder until the mike finally came back on, as though he had transformed his voice back into sound through nothing more or less than his own sheer will and perhaps God's. The crowd roared. They roared for a lot of reasons, perhaps the simplest of which was that Keyes was the first real thing that had happened in Orlando, unless you wanted to count two lonely ministers and a school board member in a Peabody conference room the day before; they roared for the chime of his words and the authenticity of his righteous fervor, and it was for the danger of Keyes that the delegates roared too, and for the way he was one of them, not in spite of his blackness but, in a very improbable way, because of it. Like all the true believers among the Christian Coalition, not Ralph Reed and Pat Robertson but the ordinary people they exploited whose social and spiritual anguish was deep and heartfelt, Keyes was a fellow outcast, another American nomad, and it was not just his words that wore that status but his face, the black face and the white blinding words.

After Keyes finished and left the stage, I rushed out into the open convention center to find him. He was hurrying away in the wake of the sensation he had created, lingering for a moment among a crowd of stunned new admirers, and it was touching, actually: these were not wealthy retirees responding to the novelty of a black arch-conservative, congratulating themselves on the fact that he was OK with them even if, no getting around it, he certainly was mighty black-looking. Rather these were old white men in frayed shirts and faded pants with the cuffs rolled too high, so genuinely moved by Keyes' moral appeal and electric presence that they came up shyly to shake his hand and then didn't let go, pumping his hand over and over, not finding the words. Just as shyly, Keyes thanked them in return. The alchemy for this kind of connection was complicated almost beyond expression or literal understanding. As with Colin Powell, at some level an America marked by the original sin of slavery longed for a black prophet to save it; and to call such a longing phony or sentimental would only betray a lack of imagination or poetry, even as the notion was so paradoxical as to border on the biblical, like Jesus saving the Jews for a world of Christianity.

25

After Keyes got everyone so excited the Republican Party decided it better get a grip on things, which is another way of saying they brought on Richard Lugar. Sure enough, the Indiana senator hadn't reached the lectern before everyone made a beeline for the restrooms outside in order to get back before the vote, during which the doors would be locked and no one would be allowed in or out of the hall. Seated near the back of the convention, I could hear delegates outside who had lingered a little too long over the urinals banging on the doors, howling in rage. To no avail: the doors stayed closed almost two hours, until the free bottles of drinking water that the Alexander campaign handed out earlier took their toll and the delegates trapped inside the hall were clawing at the walls to get out, threatening to crawl off into the corners and relieve themselves. "I guess," Jeb Bush finally succumbed to the wisdom of so many bulging Republican bladders, "we should open the doors now and let people go to the bathroom."

As for the results of the vote, let's see, I know I have them here somewhere. Dole got thirty-three percent, Gramm twenty-six, Alexander twenty-three, Buchanan nine and Keyes an entirely spontaneous eight; had his microphone not been shut off, who knows how far he would have gone. Dornan, Forbes and Lugar got one percent between them. Arlen Specter, the senator from Pennsylvania and the sole pro-choice Republican running, received exactly zero votes, technically because he had failed to show up and therefore any votes for him would not have been counted, though it wasn't clear there would have been any votes to count even if he had shown up, which is why he didn't. In a few days he would pull his hat out of the ring and throw the towel in its place. By the quantum physics of presidential politics, if one candidate did not do as well as expected, it followed that someone else must have done better—so only some Einsteinian lapse could account for how it was that *all* of the candidates somehow fell short of expectations, with the exception of Keyes, whose eight percent would not seem to have compensated for so much disappointment. Orlando, then, turned out to be the microcosm it meant to be, though perhaps more accurately than it might have wished, of an America underwhelmed by the election before it.

The day after the straw poll I wandered through the debris of the convention center as everything was being dismantled, from the stage and podium to the tower of bleachers at the back where a bank of cameras had filmed the proceedings. Out in front of the center, correspondents were broadcasting live on the Sunday morning talk shows.

Finally about to leave, I was stunned to hear come over the intercom, in the middle of all the slick generic country pop that had been playing for three days, Bruce Springsteen's "Youngstown," a history of the United States in less than four minutes, written among the smokestacks of northeastern Ohio where once "they made the cannonballs that helped the Union win the war." A hundred and twenty years and four or five wars later, the man still stoking the Youngstown furnaces starts to wonder why: "Now sir," he says to the boss man, "you tell me the world is changed/Once I made you rich, rich enough to forget my name." Youngstown was the other side of the American metaphor from Orlando, and hearing the song now I couldn't be sure whether some stray Orlando subversive had programmed it as a perverse coda to what happened here, or whether it was just one of those random acts of vandalism that metaphors commit now and then. Or whether the song had come not over the intercom at all but through the crack in the Orlando bubble, the last bit of wild randomness before the fissure sealed itself. The fissure in the country, from which the song had come in the first place, would not heal as quickly.

On the way to the airport I kept my eyes peeled for Pete Wilson by the roadside, holding a sign that read WILL GOVERN FOR FOOD, or selling "Powell-Wilson 2000" buttons instead of pencils. At the main terminal, walking past the neon Mickeys, I saw the morning paper; the headline read TOWN MOURNS SHELBY COX. Her body had been found in a shack about fifty feet from her trailer, where the eighteen-year-old boy who lived next door had hidden it after murdering her. Even in Orlando, the Virtual America with the Virtual Politics, Real Life had its due sooner or later. Sometimes, if one was lucky, it was just a Bruce Springsteen song. But sometimes it was worse.

26

I heard Springsteen sing "Youngstown" again a week later in Los Angeles. He performed at the Wiltern, a beautiful old converted movie house down on Western Avenue and Wilshire Boulevard. It was one of the rare times in twenty years I had seen him in concert when he seemed not so sure of himself, though thinking about it afterward I realized maybe he hadn't been sure of himself for a while. Was it since he turned forty—the same year I turned forty? Was it since his first marriage fell apart—as my own marriage was falling apart? Was it since the moment his greatest fame passed him by, or since he became famous in the first place? Unlike "There's No You" or *In Milton Lumky Territory*, Springsteen's most recent album, *The Ghost of Tom Joad*, was not an act of obsessed memory; oddly such an act came closer to the beginning of his career, with a record in the late Seventies called *Darkness on the Edge of Town*. In those days Springsteen, so transparently a young man of destiny, lived in the past and the future at once—the past that he made sure everyone understood he had savagely cut loose forever, the future that he made sure everyone understood was his to take on whatever terms he chose. Few of us have such futures offered us. For all the hugeness of his dreams and his determination to live them out, the power of Springsteen's songs often came down to the realization that audacity has its limits, and that part of his responsibility as an artist to his audience was to be audacious for the rest of us. If he was inevitably alienated by both the past and the future, his new songs were about Americans alienated from the present. He didn't share much with the destitute and forsaken Americans he was singing about now except that alienation; and the essence of Springsteen's alienation—the illusions that have to do with happiness and fulfillment, and the confusion of purpose that is a result—would only have struck his audience as a luxury, something he would have been the first to acknowledge.

27

He had always been a prisoner, once the self-proclaimed prisoner of rock and later the prisoner of love. But as the Seventies turned into the Eighties and the Eighties fell away to the Nineties, he became mostly the prisoner of his own audience and impact; a control freak who commandeered his career early on from the dictates of managers and record executives, he nonetheless couldn't control the rapt devotion of a congregation to whom he imparted faith above all else, and who received that faith with an intensity and dedication a notch or two this side of Scientology. People who hated Springsteen did so for two reasons, both of which were the same on the face of it but actually contradicted each other. First, they thought he was too good to be true, which is to say they found him unabashedly and irrefutably idealistic in a snotty age that was way too cool for such idealism. Second, they thought he was too good to be true, which is to say they considered him a phony whose artistic conscience, apparently alone among rock stars, could not afford his being rich and famous. People who shrugged off the gall of a very wealthy John Lennon singing "Imagine" or "Working Class Hero" found Springsteen's elevation in socioeconomic status hypocritical, perhaps irredeemable. By the lights of his songs in the Nineties, Springsteen may have thought they had a point.

The Springsteen audience had taken its own hits over the years, their possessiveness of Springsteen most shaken in the mid-Eighties by an influx of less worthy apostles. These included the instant Malibu converts who arrived at his concerts thirty minutes late and left forty minutes early, and the proles who thought the 1984 song "Born in the USA" was jingoism, a willful misunderstanding reinforced at the time by no less than an American President running for reelection. This was sacrilege to a hardcore faithful that embraced Springsteen with hope in an earlier era distinctive for its hopelessness. Maybe you had to be there. I was, waiting nearly an hour in a parked car in Redondo Beach on New Year's Eve 1974 for the radio DJ to identify the singer of a song called "Incident on 57th Street." If his music of that time later sounded uneven or sometimes dated, the more striking thing about Springsteen in the Seventies was how he was completely relevant and utterly anomalous at once, by way of a passion on the one hand that matched the punk moment, and a romanticism on the other hand that defied the postmodern moment. Co-writing "Because the

Night" with punk magdalene Patti Smith, he was just street enough, and his negotiations vis-à-vis the aesthetic politics of the time just canny enough, for him to sidestep the punk putsch of 1976 and 1977 while mounting his own stormy guerrilla march across the American shadowlands in his 1978 concert tour. His best song of the decade, "Thunder Road," flung down the gauntlet in a gesture so defiantly pure of heart that it endured wildly different interpretations in hundreds of performances over the years; years later you could pretty much divide the world into those who were still swept up by it, and those who probably never were in the first place.

By the end of the Seventies, Springsteen's vision sounded exhausted. The endgame of what he could do was already in sight, particularly in the midst of the punk ethic that held rock and roll wasn't about careers but rather blurts of venom and meaning. That in the aftermath of this supposed exhaustion he produced his two best albums, 1980's *The River* and the 1987 autopsy of his own romanticism called *Tunnel of Love*, pushing the scope of his music beyond its early assault on his own spiritual resignation, seemed an act of will as much as talent; that in doing so he also became a star among the hipper ironists on the scene, Michael and Madonna and Prince, seemed a fluke as much as an inevitability. One couldn't be sure whether the fact that alone among these prima donnas he actually had something to say helped or hurt. But the tension of Springsteen's most interesting music was that even as he wouldn't break faith with the audience that had kept faith with him over the years, he showed signs of feeling constrained by the contract. The audience's bond with Springsteen was obviously more than musical, it was uncomfortably messianic, an escalation of the artist-audience relationships of the Sixties that were both profoundly personal and communal, when the identity of an artist was more than image and something that could only be called presence, and in which the audience always wound up taking more from the artist than it returned, unless you think mass adoration and millions of dollars are a big deal. Bob Dylan found such a relationship intolerable almost from the beginning. Springsteen, being less subject to the turbulences of genius and a nicer guy, was patient a little longer. Then he fired his band. Then he fired us.

Only rank sentimentality—to which Springsteen's audience was no stranger—diverted one from the conclusion that both were necessary. To what extent Springsteen the writer had edited his riskier impulses to what his E Street Band could play, only he could say; what was certain was that the sound of the band was so much a part of the Springsteen presence he finally needed to jettison it, if not to launch any personal revolutions then at least to strip himself down. I'm not sure he could bear anymore the burden of making records that changed people's lives. As it had for many Americans, for Springsteen the Nineties had become a chasm called the American Dream, but he found himself on the other side of that chasm, stranded from the audience that brought him to that point, cut off by the Dream from America itself. Having fulfilled the great American promise of self-invention, he had also fulfilled the great American secret of self-isolation: and as both the promise and the secret were the same, so were the glory and the madness. The other two caballeros, Sinatra and Dylan, presumably knew about the promise and the secret too, not to mention glory and madness, and had also found themselves on the other side of the divide. But whereas for Sinatra part of the American Dream's appeal was its very tawdriness, and whereas Dylan was always opportunistic enough to see the Dream in terms of its practical uses, Springsteen deeply believed in the Dream, and therefore the betrayal implicit in its promise was more poignant.

At the Wiltern in L.A. those waning autumn days of 1995, playing with no other musicians, he was even more utterly alone than the empty stage could convey. In the process of firing us, firing the old band, then firing the new band with whom he had momentarily replaced the superior one, he had in the process fired his manifest sense of self-purpose, by which he had held audiences so spellbound for so many years as the greatest live performer in the history of rock and roll, making the usual allowances for James Brown and Otis Redding, of course. He was now literally advising his audiences to behave themselves during his songs. Naturally he was funny and good-natured about it, but it couldn't help sounding a little uptight, he couldn't help sounding a little terrified that he was out in no-man's land without his vaunted musical army and without the fervor of his multitudes, which was vanishing just a little more slowly than his record sales. The younger, more romantic Springsteen would have made such solitude into its own melodrama. Now the evidence of his new songs was that, in his isolation, Springsteen had grown enough to see such melodrama as cheap, when the real drama of the country around him was exacting a huge toll in a thousand unseen daily scenes.

The new songs, about tramps and hobos and immigrants and railroad ghosts wandering the tracks of history and memory that ran from the Thirties to the Nineties, from the America that once heard the prairie songs of its promise to an America that now heard only the asphalt hiss of its secrets, were Springsteen's reach back across the chasm. And if the only thing the singer really had in common anymore with the lives he was singing about was alienation, then as a result the songs were only intermittently successful, even as their good faith and courage were never in question. "Now a life of leisure and a pirate's treasure don't make much for tragedy," he had sung at the outset of the Nineties, "but it's a sad man, my friend, who's living in his own skin, and can't stand the company." Springsteen knows himself too well and, the grandeur of past ambitions to the contrary, has too much perspective to be a phony; I've always assumed that when the legendary producer John Hammond, who also discovered Billie Holiday, Bob Dylan and Aretha Franklin, said Springsteen had more integrity than any other artist he'd ever known, he knew what he was talking about. If the heroism Springsteen's audience once thrust upon him had become more existential than romantic, if he was no longer the prisoner of rock or even of a new adult love that set him free, he was still the Dream's willing prisoner, embodying its promise and raging at its secrets. Whatever the ravages of heroism and success, love and adulthood, alienation and America, he was still possessed of the American conviction that, in a country that has always refused to be the prisoner of history, he was not destiny's prisoner but rather destiny was his.

28

"My God," my friend Ventura groaned into his tequila, "Erickson's gone and gotten infatuated with America again. She's winked at him from across the room and now he's going to follow that diseased hooker down whatever dark alley she wanders into." I had come home for the holidays to catch my breath from three months on the campaign trail and to deliver my second piece to *Rolling Stone*, after Jann Wenner had reluctantly accepted and published the first. Viv and I spent New Year's Day 1996 with her family near the banks of Lake Michigan. There was no confusion about winter now: this wasn't the dislocated winter of late summer or early fall but the winter of dead winter, and climbing northward along the Michigan shore it stripped the trees and deluged the countryside, the houses becoming fewer, farther from view, haunted, hunkered down.

One afternoon driving in the snow I heard Ralph Reed on the radio. As Reed would have it, the snow was God's idea of a joke, hitting hardest on the day that—two weeks after Congress shut it down in its ongoing battle of the budget with the White House—the federal government was scheduled to sputter back into business. A blizzard so apocalyptic as to be out of the Book of Revelation buried the country's capital, closing the government again; and that this coincided with an appeals court ruling unfavorable to the President of the United States in a pending sexual harassment case, not to mention the First Lady buried up to her neck in questions about a real estate scandal and the botched 1993 firing of seven workers in the White House travel office, made it the best day the Republicans had had in a while. So one could hardly blame Reed's giddiness. Phoning in from his home in Chesapeake, Virginia, to a Religious Right radio station that advertised videos about how the death of Clinton adviser Vince Foster wasn't really a suicide, Reed couldn't help laughing about all the snow. "The Lord certainly has a sense of humor," he said. The moderator of the show thought it was pretty darned humorous himself.

The snow didn't seem like a joke to the rest of the country, more God's punishment, though Reed might have liked that interpretation just as well. People in Washington certainly didn't think it was funny a week later when I got there: Elizabeth Dole, for one, probably didn't think it was so funny, sitting in her D.C. townhouse nursing a busted wrist after a treacherous slip on the ice; and my cab driver for another certainly didn't think it was funny, raving at the snow-clogged streets in his path. "It's jammed! jammed! jammed!" he cried in frustration at the traffic, pounding his steering wheel as he tried to make his way across town. I had an appointment at a right-wing TV station behind Union Station where, safe from the snow outside, everyone I met was in distinctly better spirits. The network bustled with activity and more employees—over a hundred—than the small building could contain, or even the one next to it that the network had just taken over. The media director, a former newspaper reporter who now hosted a program on the network called "Capitol Watch," gave me a tour through the winding labyrinthine halls that led down one set of stairs and up another, from the lobby to the newsrooms to the glassy sound booths and three studios, a fourth located in the congressional office of Tom DeLay, the very conservative House Republican Whip. I was greeted by many pleasant people who insisted their operation was open to all political points of view, even as the media guy breezily characterized the audience as "conservative populist. People who aren't too happy about free trade, don't like to be taxed and," he laughed, "want Washington to go away."

Well, it seemed all right to me. I had been working on my cynicism lately, hoping that at the very least I might hone it into an expression of healthy skepticism rather than a professionally snotty attitude. There were, to be sure, a lot of pretty conservative shows on this station, including an hour by the Christian Coalition; "Straight Talk" with Gary Bauer, head of the Christian conservative Family Research Council; an ongoing series hosted by Accuracy in Media, a group obsessed with how all the news is written by liberals; "Full Disclosure," a conservative-alternative "60 Minutes" investigating yet again all those "unanswered questions" about the Vince Foster suicide, and "On Target with the NRA." But a lot of the other shows looked harmless enough, aimed at financial investors and military history buffs and train enthusiasts. The program that was taping when I got there, "American Family," concerned nothing more provocative than parents and kids learning how to use a personal computer together. Listening in on the half-hour recount of the news headlines I didn't sense any subliminal KILL CLINTON codes flashing across my brain synapses, and when the advertising director explained plans to sell chunks of time to candidates during the coming election, for political "long-form" ads of the sort Ross Perot used so effectively in 1992, I asked her point-blank if a liberal Democrat could buy half an hour of prime time as easily as a conservative Republican. "Absolutely," she answered.

So all in all it didn't seem so scary. The station wasn't run by pod Republicans from Mars; they were all friendly and cooperative, in what was by all appearances a largely secular enterprise. If the lines between Christian and Republican agendas were blurred, that just made it a true microcosm of the cultural conservative universe; the founder of the network, Paul Weyrich, having been one of the political architects fifteen years earlier of Jerry Falwell's Moral Majority, was a one-man switchboard for cross-wiring political and religious and social concerns, and he worked with a take-no-prisoners ferocity to make those concerns synonymous. Along with Gary Bauer he was also one of the organizers of the Republican Right press conference that helped run Colin Powell out of the presidential race before he got in. I had had an interview scheduled with Weyrich that I arrived to find was canceled, but as it happened Weyrich's own show, "Direct Line," was next up after "American Family," so, feeling calmer about things, I sat down to watch. The opening moments were devoted to a blistering attack on Republican congressmen who had, as far as Weyrich was concerned, caved in to the President on the budget battle by agreeing to raise the nation's debt ceiling. After a few minutes of that, however, he got down to the night's real order of business, which was a court ruling in Hawaii allowing the legal marriage of gay couples.

Weyrich's guest was an earnest young man named Tom Kilgannon from the Christian Broadcasting Network. Kilgannon was explaining how an obscure provision of the United States Constitution would make this Hawaii case tantamount to the law of the land—in the same way, he said, that the driver's license of one state is honored in another. In Tom's words this case was "the crown jewel of the homosexual movement." Even on the TV screen both Weyrich's and Kilgannon's mortification was palpable; Kilgannon appeared stricken by the prospect of an America exploding with gay marriages, while Weyrich just got madder and madder about the whole thing. The program took phone calls, which the switchboard operator assured me were not screened, and they started coming in now, all the callers quite upset. They decried the way an alternative lifestyle was being "imposed" on the rest of the country, "infringing," as Kilgannon would have it, "on the religious beliefs of the rest of us." I admit I wasn't exactly clear how other people's marriages were infringing on my beliefs, unless the courts were going to start forcing everyone into gay marriages, and I was reasonably certain no one had forced Tom Kilgannon into a gay marriage, since it happened that the young woman sitting just feet from me, with whom I'd been talking, was his wife. A very sweet, bright woman, Meg now worked for a conservative senior-citizens political action group and had once been with a public relations firm representing an organization called MediaResearch, where people sat around counting how many Clinton jokes Jay Leno told as opposed to how many George Bush jokes. Meg was understandably less concerned with what Tom was saying than how he was coming across on television. I tried to assure her he was doing fine.

We chatted and joked awhile and I finally left, the cold winter air blowing my hypocrisy back in my face no sooner than I was outside the door. Returning to Union Station, the Capitol gleaming in the night like a chiseled ice palace, I wondered if it was a complete moral failure on my part not to have taken Meg by the shoulders, looked her in the eye and told her, in as calm a voice as I could manage, "Meg, you seem like a very nice woman, but now you must listen to me carefully: *your husband isn't making any sense at all.*" I felt like I had been some sort of spy, not only with Meg but all the other nice people at the network, except Paul Weyrich himself, of course, who knew better. To Weyrich I wasn't a spy, I was the Enemy, and you probably are too.

29

You probably are too because, well, at this point the odds just sort of favor it. After all, if Bill Clinton—a bland figure in the political scheme of things, not to mention a regular churchgoer for whom religion has played probably a greater part in his personal life than any President in modern times, with the exception of Jimmy Carter—if Bill Clinton is so dark a force as to inspire even the righteous to bear false witness against him time and again, what with outlandish charges of murder, then it just seems likely that, whoever you are and whatever you believe, you're the Enemy too. Throw down this book and check out the hair growing on the back of your hands if you don't think so.

Weyrich knew this, which was why he wouldn't talk to me. Ralph Reed knew this too, which was why he also wouldn't talk to me; Pat Robertson, the figurehead of the Christian Coalition, knew; and at the Republican Convention in 1992 Patrick Buchanan knew, declaring war on a nation of degenerates. In the estimation of seasoned journalists and politicians, Buchanan's manifesto was an electoral public relations disaster that marked the end of whatever chances George Bush ever had of getting reelected; but history may not come to see it that way. Rather history may come to view the Buchanan speech as more comparable to the speech Barry Goldwater gave to the 1960 Republican Convention that nominated Richard Nixon the first time, in which Goldwater put the party on notice that a conservative tide was coming and would demand its due. Following the congressional elections of 1994, Ralph Reed laid claim to his share of the triumph: by his estimates a third of the voters who went to the polls had been evangelical Christians largely responsible for the massive Republican victory, with Catholics going Republican for the first time ever in an off-year election. And in the next election, Reed had told the guy on the radio amidst all the mirth about the weather, Evangelicals would be the base vote and Catholics would be the swing vote.

By 1996, in a country where the vast majority of people considered themselves religious, the Religious Right had moved beyond its poor-white, Bible-Belt stereotype to include lawyers and doctors and business executives linked not just by Sunday church services but fax machines and computers and satellite dishes. Their influence in present presidential politics was inarguable. Bob Dole's campaign manager openly and bluntly admitted that any Republican candidate without the support of the Religious Right could pretty much forget about the party's nomination, because these were the activists who would dominate the primary race, raising money and getting themselves and others to the polls. For all the charges of extremism that he would come to level at Buchanan in the primaries, not long after launching his campaign in early 1995 Dole gave a highly publicized speech about the decadence of popular culture that was simply a marginally calmer, sanitized version of Buchanan's '92 convention frolic, clearing it with Religious Right leaders such as Reed and Gary Bauer before he gave it. And in the months leading up to the New Hampshire Primary it was impossible to tune out the language of cultural conservatism, at least until it gave way to the language of flat taxes; every candidate had television and radio ads talking about "values" and "principles" and how if you believed the American family was sacred, and that it was under assault by Washington, Phil Gramm was your man.

Republican professionals might have dreaded a repeat of the '92 Buchanan spectacle at the upcoming San Diego convention, but to someone like Bauer the real threat was exactly the opposite. "The odds are overwhelming," he told me in early January, "that I will support Bob Dole if he's the Republican nominee. But that's with the caveat that if the party at the convention takes a walk on a number of issues, particularly abortion, that I think are important, not only I but a lot of other people could wind up doing something else. Though I'm not sure what that would be." As far as Bauer and his allies were concerned, "taking a walk" would include the nomination of a pro-choice vice presidential candidate, not good news to whatever aspirations might be held in that regard by New Jersey's Governor Christine Whitman, or Pete Wilson of California or William Weld of Massachusetts, or, most pertinently, Colin Powell. Balancing the ticket on the issue of abortion made no more sense to Bauer than balancing the ticket on the issue of taxes; and in the still young campaign Pat Buchanan was already drooling in public over the prospect of leading a very large contingent of howling, betrayed right-wingers out of San Diego and into third-party martyrdom, sweeping the Republican Party to righteous oblivion with them. "I don't know if the Republicans realize it or not," Bauer hinted darkly, "but they have a real high-risk convention coming up, in which they could do incredible damage to themselves."

I had not looked forward to talking with Bauer. A one-time family issues adviser to Ronald Reagan, Bauer knew I was the Enemy perhaps better than anyone, and I knew he knew; and it was perfectly all right with me if God's white heaven shat a whole new Rockies' worth of snow between L.A. and D.C. just so I wouldn't have to talk to Bauer or Reed or any of them. In an atmosphere of political demonization they were as much my favorite demons as I supposed I was theirs, though I was a pretty far cry from the wild drug-taking homosexual they liked to make videos about for their fund-raising. On television Bauer was a particularly pinched presence, his face frozen into the rigor mortis of an unforgiving soul; by all accounts he was the most unyielding of the Religious Right leaders, if nowhere as down and dirty as Jerry Falwell. As far as Bauer was concerned even Ralph Reed was a sellout. When Reed laid out the Christian Coalition's agenda in 1995, ten points called the Contract with the American Family that conspicuously tried to finesse the issue of abortion, Bauer blasted him in the same way he blasted values-maven William Bennett a few months later for talking up a Powell presidency.

For all that, however, I was confused by another side of Bauer's reputation, which was as someone who knew how to talk to the Enemy, even reach whatever point of conciliation could be reached without compromising in the slightest. From Bauer's standpoint, talking to me was, if anything, only a measure of his purity; in his Washington office, among the sanguine calm of his books and family photos, he was relaxed, cordial and perfectly capable of expressing grudging respect for a genuine philosophical difference. What he didn't respect, what most offended him even as he cast a hard eye over the realities of the coming election, was the natural opportunism of politics. Whatever else was true of Bauer's all-consuming fixation with the moral state of America, it wasn't opportunistic. The son of Democratic blue collar parents including an alcoholic father, growing up in Kentucky across the river from Cincinnati at a time when organized crime literally ran the city—"gambling, prostitution . . . Frank Sinatra used to come in and entertain"—he watched families fall apart when fathers never made it home with their paychecks. The young Bauer became a Republican ("to my family's horror"), his first political enthusiasm for the presidential quest of Barry Goldwater in 1964. But even at the age of eighteen he found Goldwater a little suspect, more libertarian than a true moral crusader, so that thirty years later when Goldwater started warning the GOP that the Religious Right was taking over, it sort of confirmed what Bauer had figured all along.

That Barry Goldwater wasn't pure enough for Bauer wasn't surprising; that anyone could ever have been perhaps was. For Bauer and the rest of the Religious Right, Ronald Reagan was a political John the Baptist if not Jesus, roguish early days of cheating on Jane Wyman and bonking starlets notwithstanding. This had more to do with Reagan's personality and timing than his policies. Reagan emerged as the leader of American conservatism just when the Sixties were starting to strike some people as a lot of spoiled children having entirely too much fun; so when, as governor of California, he denounced the student revolts that shook the state's colleges, even while he was signing one of the country's most liberal abortion laws, he spoke for a livid America in more dramatic and convincing terms than Richard Nixon or Spiro Agnew. Of course, Reagan proved in his presidency to be as much a fair-weather friend of salient cultural issues like abortion as Bob Dole, but this didn't seem to diminish his aura, perhaps because defeating communism was seen as a legitimately higher calling than anything else. "Whoever inherits the Reagan mantle down the road," Bauer now said almost wistfully, "is going to be a very powerful figure in the Republican Party for years to come. It probably won't happen," he added, "in 1996."

It was telling that at the outset of the 1996 campaign, Gary Bauer's most forceful blow was not an endorsement of any of the candidates running but the anti-endorsement of one who wasn't. In the most frenzied autumn days of Powellmania, Bauer sent out six thousand faxes to activists and journalists ripping Powell, and then held his breath wondering if he had in the process ripped apart his own power base of a quarter-million Family Research Council members. He got all of a dozen negative letters. In the meantime, however, Christian conservatives had yet to coalesce behind any single candidate the way they did behind Pat Robertson in 1988, or even in the way they gave to Buchanan in 1992 their hearts if not exactly their imprimatur. Instead the Religious Right was promiscuously favoring with its affections Buchanan, Gramm (regarded with skepticism if only because his anti-abortion position seemed about as heartfelt as everything else about him), Alan Keyes and even Dole, who attracted the resigned interest of religious conservatives less averse to political reality and winning elections, and who therefore scored valuable endorsements from the heads of the Christian Coalition in caucus and primary states like Iowa and South Carolina. Dole, of course, was exactly the sort of person Bauer meant when he talked about political opportunism. "I'm deeply suspicious," as Bauer put it, without exactly using Dole's name, "of someone who seems to be doing a wind-check every morning on an issue like abortion. If on something that profound you're willing to make these fine gradations of movement in order to deal with the latest poll, then it seems to me on almost every other issue you're going to be totally unreliable."

"So who do you miss most among those not running?" I asked.

"Good question," he said, almost as though he had never even considered the matter. "I guess before my recent disagreements with Bill Bennett," he smiled ruefully, "I was enthusiastic about him getting into the race. But I'm not so sure anymore it would have been that great of a thing—if he would have done the same thing as a candidate that he's done on the sidelines the last couple of months." Like his disillusionment with Barry Goldwater, Bauer's answer revealed how little it took for even a kindred spirit to tumble from whatever he viewed as grace: just months before, Bennett had been a patron saint of the Cultural Right, national warlord against drugs under Reagan and author of the best-selling *Book of Values*; now, one fuckup and he was *out*. Yet rigid as his parameters of acceptable moral and political behavior were, Bauer was right about his central thesis. There *was* a spiritual crisis in America; everyone of any depth at all knew it; and addressing the Foreign Press Club in Washington a couple of months before I met him, speaking of how one could "measure a nation by how many of its children cry themselves to sleep at night," Bauer was eloquent. "I believe that on through 1996," he said, "and into the next century, this is going to be the great debate in America. It's going to be a debate about liberty and how you use it, the relationship of liberty to virtue, and it's going to be a debate about the simple question of how it is that free men and women live their lives."

30

Of course, whatever constitutes your American spiritual crisis—a country, for instance, that defines itself by the worth of what it owns rather than the price of what it believes—may be different from Gary Bauer's, which is basically an America that likes sex too much. If Bauer put the issue more squarely than any of the men running for President, he also contributed significantly to the nation's greatest and most destructive internal dynamic: hostility to any sort of moral nuance, and a determination to cast all issues in terms of moral extremes that could not possibly allow for the commonality from which nations are built. Whether this national characteristic was borne out of a frontier mentality that couldn't help but view existence in brutal life-and-death terms, or whether it goes back farther, to the colonization of the land by religious fanatics, at once persecuted and persecuting, probably doesn't matter. It is bitterly ironic, if that's really the word, that for hundreds of years, before and after its founding, the country tried so badly to finesse the one issue of American history for which there were no moral nuances, the one issue that more than any other demanded clear moral accounting, which was the importation of people from another continent for the sole purpose of being beasts of burden.

In 1996 it was also ironic—well, no, given America's failure on slavery it was probably fitting—that the issue now rotting Millennial America's faith more than any other was one as profound as slavery, and yet unanswerable in the way that slavery could and had to be answered. This was the question of when human tissue assumes its own soul, which is to say when a subdivision of cells in a woman's womb ceases to be part of her and becomes its own entity in the eyes of God. Since no one on the planet knows the answer to this, it said everything about America's arrogance that the country was filled with people who claimed they did. Moreover, as clearly as there had to be an answer to when the life of the soul begins, it was as clear that, barring some collective epiphany or visitation of divine insight, we would probably never know it, and were doomed to futilely continue trying to know the unknowable. In other words, a social dilemma rooted to a fundamentally metaphysical concern demanded a political resolution, which in typical American fashion apparently meant reducing the matter to childlike notions of "choice" and "murder."

Led and organized by people determined to shut off within themselves any deep spiritual consideration of the issue because it was politically expedient to do so, the "pro-choice" faction was the more intellectually dishonest, going back to the United States Supreme Court's ruling on abortion in 1973. The constitutional right to an abortion is synthetic in almost any sense of the word—a right clearly determined by men rather than self-evidently endowed by God, to use Jefferson's language from the Declaration of Independence. This isn't to say that the freedom to have an abortion might not be one worth formulating by society; most formulated freedoms, after all, are not expressly established by the Bill of Rights, which is why the Ninth Amendment was written, stating that the government cannot presume an individual right doesn't exist simply because it isn't so expressly established. But the Supreme Court's equation in 1973 of a right to privacy with a right to an abortion had less to do with legal logic than what liberals at the time considered the unfolding political necessity of putting the Constitution on the side of abortion, the dubious integrity of such an argument be damned. Even more specious were the subsequent constitutional arguments that committed the government to subsidizing abortions for those women who could not afford them, in order that such women were "guaranteed" their constitutional freedom. It could well be that the government should subsidize abortions for poor women, if there were a national consensus to do so; but the leaders of the pro-choice movement had no faith in such a consensus—for good reason: there was none—and thus used the Constitution toward their ends in an argument not unlike suggesting that because the First Amendment recognizes a man's right to a free press, the government is obligated to buy him a newspaper, or because the Second Amendment recognizes a man's right to bear arms, the government is obligated to buy him a gun.

The paradox for the pro-choice movement was that over the course of twenty years its political victories had in some ways only undercut its moral authority. This was true even as most people accepted that, before some mysterious and undefined moment when the benefit of doubt on behalf of the mother must accede to that on behalf of the fetus, a decision to abort a fetus was something to be resolved at the intersection of a woman's conscience and medical circumstances, the whispers of God perhaps thrown in for good measure. The public was more reasonable than either of the extremes driving the discussion. But as was seen in a controversy over late-term or "partial birth" abortions, which involved the ghastly execution—there was no other word—of fetuses that for all intents and purposes were brought to term, by early 1996 the pro-choice movement had lost confidence in its ability to mount even a medical case for its position, let alone a moral one; reflexively, then, it fell back on a political one, as it had done so often over the preceding twenty years, absurdly contending that to ban late-term abortions would open the door to banning all abortions. Thus in the mid-Nineties, because the public simply didn't want to talk about abortion at all, therefore refusing to seize the argument back from the extremes, that argument was defined by those who would outlaw all abortion, beginning virtually at the moment of conception, and those who would permit all abortion, up until virtually the moment of birth.

Whether the absolutism of the second precipitated or answered the absolutism of the first really didn't matter anymore. For that matter the ancient constitutional point-counterpoint of the original *Roe v. Wade* decision probably didn't matter much anymore either; a Supreme Court Justice honest enough to vote against *Roe v. Wade* in 1973 might just as honestly vote against overturning it in 1996, reasoning that while there was never really a constitutional right to an abortion in 1973, by 1996 there had become one—an integral thread woven into the fabric of freedom over the course of a generation. What had come to matter more in 1996 was that the intellectual bankruptcy of the pro-choice movement was more than matched by the rife and indisputable meanness that characterized the "pro-life" movement, whose self-righteousness seemed to range from the merely vicious to the proudly violent. Randall Terry, the leader of Operation Rescue, an organization covertly dedicated, in all its voluptuous notions of self-martyrdom, to terrorizing women and murdering doctors, was as monstrous a figure as the contemporary American political scene had produced, his true interest not the lives of the "unborn" but his own power. At the outset of the 1996 presidential campaign, as the Religious Right had become the single most influential and relentless political force in the country, the heart of the pro-life movement had calcified into something hard and ungenerous, not a speck of Christian love or forgiveness to be seen in it anywhere. With its smug supposition that the very experience of abortion was something a woman could ever be cavalier about—"just another form of birth control"—at its core the pro-life movement was not really about saving fetuses. At its core it was about middle-aged men punishing young women for having sex.

Sexually, America is the most twisted country west of Islam. Most prominently among the nations of the West it recoils from the biological reality that, around the age of twelve, a human being becomes a sexual adult, that nature does not regard menstruating daughters and hormonally charged sons as children. America's peculiar fanaticism regarding its "innocence," not to mention the puritanism of the country's beginnings, insists on a sexuality that is less biological than religious—and since most religion is largely about life's relationship to death, this is to say that at some subconscious level America regards sexuality not as a life force but a death force. From the perspective of the so-called Moral Right, the metaphoric implications of AIDS could not be more joyously clear. The likes of Gary Bauer, to be congratulated for putting the issue of America's spiritual crisis so squarely, also perpetuated the brutal division of America's sexual nature between license and repression, a healthy middle ground of sexual conduct apparently as unfathomable and forbidden as a middle-ground policy on abortion. In 1994, around the time Republicans were rampaging their way across the political landscape into Congress, a survey revealing that virtually a third of Americans had no sex life whatsoever was greeted with a national sigh of relief. The abstinence "movement," urging not just teenagers but anyone outside marriage to disavow sex, was advertised in *Rolling Stone* as "the new revolution"; and on afternoon talk shows, thirty-year-old virgins were the new heroes, no one suggesting that it might not be entirely normal for a thirty-year-old man or woman never to have had sex. Nor did anyone propose that people marrying their sexual blind-dates did not honor the institution of marriage but rather insulted its seriousness, treating it like a child's fairy tale. In the country's totalitarian demand for absolutes, the center was collapsing not only politically and economically but sensually; the new abstinence campaign was not simply a "moral" or religious movement but a political one, the sensual meaning of America defined more and more by the promiscuous and the celibate who shared only a growing sensual alienation. And while both promiscuity and celibacy were increasingly vehement responses to each other, they were also responses to the Sexual Revolution of a generation before, implicit arguments that the revolution was a fraud. It was the only thing about which both extremes were right.

31

I will tell you this much. I am forty-six years old, a heterosexual who has never considered a homosexual experience or felt a homosexual attraction, but who can remember two dreams homoerotic enough in nature to have unsettled me at the time, though not so much as to shake my understanding of who I am. I have not slept with so many women that I can't count them all, but more than I can count off the top of my head. I've never picked up a woman in a bar or spent the night with anyone whose name I've forgotten, or awakened with someone I didn't recognize. My sex life began late, after I started college, and has been characterized largely by stretches of monogamy (including a failed two-year marriage) that were occasionally interrupted by more hectic interludes. Such interludes often came from an ache of the heart as much as the body.

That's enough of that. Beyond this, whatever I could say about my sexuality in this context would either not interest you or would interest you for the wrong reasons. It seems important to have said this much only because, in the sexual shadowlands of the Nineties, commentary converges with confession. "We have reached the dead end of sensuality," a friend of mine declared recently, by which he meant, whether he knew it or not: *I* have reached the dead end of *my* sensuality. It is one thing to write about politics with the pretension of objectivity because, however we might view the political landscape from different vantage points, it is territory we all traverse in common. But sex is the secret country, of secret borders crossed with secret passwords. There are no common sexual experiences, though some might bear similarity to others; ultimately each experience is unique, by virtue of not only each singular psyche but its singular collision with yet another singular psyche. I might profess to address here the meaning of sexuality in our time. But what I really address is the meaning of myself.

We have reached the dead end of sensuality, my friend said, and it was a statement both true enough to repeat and false enough to refute. Looked at another way, sex is—after the Cold War and in the age of AIDS—the last subversive act. In an America that lusts for conformity and the iron hand, sex still lies just beyond authority's reach, where it is still capable of severing the Moment from both past and future, which is to say from both history and prophecy, memory and expectation. The only other thing that so vividly engages our imaginations anymore is technology; if sex is the last subversive act, technology is the only faith remaining after politics and religion have betrayed us. Now, like commentary and confession, technology and sex converge as virtual sex and cybersex, on CD-ROM and the Internet, until a vague new sexual gestalt infiltrates the labyrinth of all our libidos, including those of us who stay the hell away from the Internet. (I do not go on-line with America because I do not want America on-line with me.) Sex is technologized, technology is sensualized. The result has a cold sheen, a clockwork hum. But even having taken on this new forbidding form, sex still appears to offer the last door to revelation.

I live, as do others of my generation, in the shadow I cast over my own life long ago. In the late Sixties and early Seventies, the Sexual Revolution liberated sex of consequence. It liberated sex of consequences social and biological, and presumed to liberate it of those emotional and psychological as well. The ideals of the Sexual Revolution were utopian and transcendent; the rock and roll of the time, also utopian and transcendent, had a lot to do with this. We were utopian enough to believe that there was no difference between our sexual ideals and our sexual identities, and that the first could transform the second, that human sexuality could be liberated of its darkest impulses. It was this aquarian vision that argued, for instance, that rape is "not an act of sex but violence." To say rape has nothing to do with sex is like saying bank robbery has nothing to do with money. Rape is an act of violence *and* sex. Sex is what distinguishes rape from a mugging. But it is the legacy of sexual utopianism that forces us to divorce something as ugly and unacceptable as rape from something as powerful and irresistible as sex.

In the early Nineties the sensually alienated, the repressed and the licentious, came to recognize and respond to the darkness of sex that utopians denied: obsession, possession, voyeurism, exhibitionism, domination, submission. Now in the shadowlands of the Nineties teenage girls were screaming "I want to fuck you like an animal" at Nine Inch Nails concerts, and women ruminated openly and impatiently in the pages of *Future Sex* magazine about the caprices of the penis. Artists, novelists, filmmakers and songwriters didn't so much challenge as simply ignore phony distinctions between "erotica" and pornography; the recesses of sensuality—its physical desecrations, its psychic mortifications—were ritualized by sex shops, S&M clubs, fetish balls. This verged on sexual anarchism, of course. What other response to sexual totalitarianism was likely? And while like any anarchism it danced on the edge of nihilism and a numb degradation, it was also the price of the subversive act that pursued freedom; and if the more extreme forms of this anarchism seemed about self-obliteration, that was a kind of transcendence in itself. Having already been writ large by a virus only the Millennium could have invented, the "little death" the French refer to when they speak of the orgasm became part of the new sexual iconography, which included the mutilation of erogenous zones: pierced lips, pierced tongues, pierced nipples, pierced labia, pierced genitalia.

To piously assume such acts only debased or deadened one's existence was to miss their profundity. People danced at the abyss' edge not just because they felt the self-destructive urge to tumble over but because they also felt reaffirmed, revitalized, even resurrected by the gamble and danger. The pull of the abyss only grew stronger as Midnight 2000 grew nearer; even among people who considered themselves altogether too rational to attribute any more meaning to the Millennium than they would to any other New Year's Eve, there still existed a subconscious expectation that the transition from this thousand years to the next must be momentous, that it must necessarily be the end of something that was never really understood and the beginning of something that cannot yet be known. This expectation might be accompanied by both the secret hope that, just beyond midnight, the Millennium's virus will vanish completely, in a twinkling, and by the primal dread that an apocalyptic wave of black semen will sweep us all away.

By stripping sex of its consequences, we utopians nearly made it inconsequential. It was a naiveté on our part that was as peculiarly American as repression. Sometime around 1982 AIDS began to change all that, though if it hadn't been AIDS it would have been some other unimaginable serpent, coiling up the tree of sensuality. To those of us old enough to remember what sex was like twenty years ago, AIDS still seems an aberration: "Sex can kill you!" we exclaim to others and ourselves, astonished. But in fact it was our own age, the age of sex-without-consequence, that was the aberration. Until not so long ago sex could always kill you. Until very recently sex was always mortally consequential. For most of history, syphilis was nearly as fatal as it was common, and childbirth always an extremely risky proposition. Both the New Decadents and the New Celibates of the Nineties determined to reacknowledge sex's consequences, and only in a country as paradoxical as America, born of revolution but constantly denying its revolutionary identity, born of passionate men and women but constantly denying its passion, could sexual aberrants become the spokesmen for the sexual norm that was lost in the limbo between them. At the Millennium, the world will divide into those who love sex more than they fear death, and vice versa.

All right. I will make one more confession. One night some years ago, in another decade during the brief dusk between utopia and shadowland, I was seduced on the telephone by an anonymous woman. The telephone rang, I answered, and her overture was so immediate and blunt that I was either going to succumb or hang up. She described herself for me sentence by sentence like a stripper revealing herself thread by thread—her blond hair, her breasts—though this self-portrait may have been as much a fiction as a stripper's dance. When we finished she asked if I was all right, because I think I must have sounded a little discombobulated. And this outburst of empathy is what I'll always remember most about the experience; I think she was as surprised by it as I. For nights afterward I racked my brain trying to figure out if she was someone I knew, only to conclude she was indeed a stranger, in a rendezvous as random as seven numbers tapped on a telephone. Some months later I moved to another apartment. A couple of months after that I was back at the old place one afternoon, collecting some things I had left behind, when I heard a message come through on the phone machine downstairs, in a voice I recognized immediately. "Where do you go and what do you do," she said, "when you're never home?"

I don't know what this means. I suppose sex is the last subversive act because we don't always have to figure out what it means. It may be the only thing anymore that we don't have to figure out the meaning of, and while once I was more prone to contemplate such things, I'm smart enough now not to. That's my excuse, anyway. For some reason having as much to do with commentary as confession, it seems important to add here that at forty-six this ex-utopian's life, sexual and otherwise, is happier than it was at thirty-six or twenty-six; and it also seems important to point out that, assuming evil neither completely vanishes nor completely sweeps us away, the weirdness on this side of the Millennium may be replaced on the other side by a giddy release, a collective whoop of relief and joy in which the shadowlands are met by a new break of dawn. If we must contemplate the meaning of sex, there is always love, of course: I haven't forgotten about love. I don't think anyone ever does. The "moralists" who claim we're falling into a cesspool of sex without love show how little they understand either one. The galoots at Hooters checking out the waitresses, the fourteen-year-old girls crying back to Trent Reznor, are, in some fashion as quaint as it is disturbing, in love. The Twentieth Century never accepted this. The Twenty-First might.

As for my affair on the telephone, it was my one undeniable moment of true Nineties Sex, coming even before the Nineties did. It was my most memorable mating of technology and imagination, and perhaps my most subversive act of self-obliteration, since in its aftermath I've come to wonder whether it happened at all. And telling you about it now may be my last chance to distinguish between commentary and confession, though I'll only know for sure at 11:59 on the thirty-first of December 1999, when I'll be sitting by the telephone, waiting for it to ring.

32

In the throes of a spiritual crisis, a nation is doomed to be disappointed by democracy. Even the national consensus of an election cannot address a collective trauma of the spirit, and even the most profound of elections is always an uneasy truce between the political and spiritual. In a totalitarian state where mind control is the order of the day, an intense spirituality, collectively shared by many people, can become a blow for freedom because it reaches deeper than the mind, to the soul where neither police nor government can go. But in a democracy that exists by breathing the cross-breezes of pluralism and tolerance, the natural political expression of a single-minded spirituality is often either anarchy or authoritarianism. In my conversation with Gary Bauer, his lamest answer was the most important, when I asked if he considered the guiding text of America to be the Constitution or the New Testament. There's no question, he told me, that the guiding text for Christian Americans is the New Testament. The founding documents for the United States might be the Constitution and the Declaration of Independence, "but while they are not in and of themselves religious documents," said Bauer, "they were written by religious men and they do reflect, broadly speaking, a Judeo-Christian value system."

As he undoubtedly realized, his answer sidestepped what he must consider the Constitution's most embarrassing lapse: its specific and unmistakable instruction that the country isn't supposed to have a guiding religious text. With the fearsome exception of Sam Adams, the people who founded the country—Washington, Madison, Franklin, Paine, John Adams—were, while often men of deep spiritual feeling, not devoutly religious; they were as impressed by the Enlightenment as they were by the Scriptures. If Thomas Jefferson and Abraham Lincoln are the two great iconic visionaries of American history, in that they addressed more powerfully and insightfully than anyone else the meaning of America, the fact is that Lincoln was a Christian of only a very vague sort (for which he was attacked in the presidential election of 1860), and Jefferson was not any sort of

Christian at all (for which he was attacked in the presidential election of 1800). While passionately admiring Jesus as one of the great moral philosophers of all time, Jefferson accepted Jesus as neither a divine figure nor a personal savior, and had as little use for the Gary Bauers of the late Eighteenth Century as they had for him. Jefferson's God was an ambiguous supreme being who created the universe and then left it to men to sort out the particulars—a Creator who endows each of us with unalienable rights, including the right to tell Bauer to take his grim self-righteousness and stuff it.

For the better part of a decade, however, Bauer and Christian conservatives were a lot more effective at telling the pagans among us to stuff it. If they had the culture on the run, it was for a number of reasons: first, when liberal Presidents tried to speak to the country's spiritual crisis, the result was a lot of mush about "funks" and "malaises" (a word Jimmy Carter never actually used, but that's neither here nor there), because their liberal nature was loath to sound judgmental. Conservatives, on the other hand, were perfectly comfortable using the rhetoric of judgment, which galvanized their message and their sense of mission. Second, what goes around comes around: in the Sixties the clergy of the Left were very happy to cast the debates over civil rights and Vietnam in religious and moral terms; and in the presidential election of 1960, questions about John Kennedy's Catholicism, and how it might inform his conduct of the presidency, were condemned out of hand by liberals as just bigotry, when in fact the structure and orthodoxy of the Catholic Church made such questions entirely valid, at least until Kennedy addressed them. Now confronted with comparable questions in 1996, the Religious Right sheathed its bully tactics in the same indignant protests of religious persecution. The religion that was its political sword was as well its political shield. On the offense, politics and religion were joined; on the defense the two miraculously separated, the profanity of the one hidden behind the sanctity of the other.

Third, liberals played into the hands of the Religious Right by ridiculing as square, narrow-minded hysteria the very real panic of parents who felt they were losing control of their children to an ever-debased popular culture. In the process this elitism condescended not only to the parents but to the culture as well; for forty years a lot of us said rock and roll could change our lives, and now we were not only denying it but insisting on its inconsequentiality when it suited our political purposes. It's not possible to believe in an art that lifts some people's minds and ennobles their spirits without also acknowledging that sometimes the very same art can corrupt other people's thinking and poison their souls. At some point over the last twenty years we came to see a culture of consequentiality as more dreadful than invigorating. The Left may have found it satisfying or useful to pretend the enemy was Jesse Helms or William Rehnquist, but these were simply political opportunists making the most of a moment, taking advantage of the fact that the American audience had no patience anymore for being affronted by art, and that American artists who staked their position as outlaws on the margins of society often seemed to have some philosophical difficulty accepting the fact that society wasn't obligated to embrace their revolutions let alone subsidize them. The furor at the outset of the decade over the National Endowment for the Arts was not a matter of censorship, as the Left would have it; the government wasn't making a decision to repress art but rather not to finance it. That repression was undoubtedly Jesse Helms' intention in attacking the NEA didn't erase the distinction.

Naturally the Right, being the Right, successfully used the distinction to attack contemporary culture as a whole. "There's no consensus in America anymore on what is art and what is not," wrote Reagan and Bush speechwriter Peggy Noonan at the height of the NEA controversy. "A century ago it was generally agreed that Whitman and Dickinson were art." A century ago no one agreed on any such thing. Walt Whitman was considered radical and obscene by virtually all of mainstream America and the literary establishment; the secretary of the interior condemned *Leaves of Grass* as immoral and fired Whitman from his civil service job for writing it. There has never been any such consensus except in Noonan's dreams. At one time or another in the last twenty years, in one library or another across America, such a "consensus" has seen fit to ban the likes of *The Adventures of Huckleberry Finn, The Great Gatsby, A Farewell to Arms,*

As I Lay Dying, *The Grapes of Wrath* and *Invisible Man*, for reasons that variously offended both the Left and the Right. At one time or another in the last hundred and twenty years, for one reason or another having to do with politics or aesthetics or morality or all three, the cultural establishment has had no use for Walt Whitman or Mark Twain or D. W. Griffith or Louis Armstrong or Isadora Duncan or Mae West or Langston Hughes or Robert Johnson or Henry Miller or Cole Porter or Billie Holiday or Orson Welles or Jackson Pollock or William Burroughs or Charlie Parker or Little Richard or Elvis Presley or James Baldwin or Sylvia Plath or Thomas Pynchon or Janis Joplin or Martin Scorsese or Patti Smith or Chuck D or Kurt Cobain— all American nomads both possessed by their country's dangerous fever and estranged from their country by that fever. The notion of being part of some respectable consensus would have made any of them throw up. The failure of the Left, not to mention artists themselves, to accept the responsibility for that fever even as they claimed the right to burn freely with it became so transparent it hardly took a Christian fanatic to see and exploit it.

Most happily for the Religious Right, though, in its war on American culture and American thought, and in terms of the sheer power politics by which it conducted that war, was that in the deepest recesses of its soul it was unburdened by a tiresome affection for democracy. In its righteous wrath it hated democracy's messiest promise: that at the rubicon of freedom the Bill of Rights represents, the values of the majority must accede to those irritating unalienable rights that God, seized by some subversive impulse, gave each of us. This allowed Paul Weyrich and the guests on his TV show to turn definitions of freedom inside out, so that who you married and how you conducted your private life somehow became an infringement upon their beliefs, in the same way that in 1995 Ralph Reed's proposed refinement of the Constitution, a "Religious Equality Amendment," would slyly sabotage the First Amendment by invading public life with more and more religious ritual and symbolism, relegating freedom of worship to the rule of the many rather than the conscience of the one. The Religious Right's constant and insidious implication that democracy invalidated itself when it elected someone like Bill Clinton—not merely a bad President but a false one—was willful constitutional heresy in the name of Christian devotion, an extortion note from God as delivered by his most fervent messengers, that Christianity and democracy were by nature at odds and not long to endure together on the same planet.

It may be that the only thing that could ever finally stop the Religious Right was the Religious Right. Growing ever larger and more powerful, in 1996 it began to show the first signs of cracking like a fake diamond, and if the chisel was Colin Powell's quasi-candidacy, the hammer was the movement's own success. A year after its greatest political triumph, the midterm election of 1994, the Religious Right had become bigger than a single spokesman or point of view could control; about as monolithic as Eurocommunism, its ever-fragmented leadership was splayed across a spectrum that extended from the two-fisted intellectualism of William Bennett (who in a flash of either expediency or wisdom was now suggesting that the crusade against abortion might better be left to moral persuasion than law) to the gonzo terrorism of Randall Terry, whose bloodlust in the name of the unborn had a psychotic ecstasy about it. If Bauer did not endorse a presidential candidate because none was quite unsullied enough for him, Ralph Reed—who even Clinton adviser George Stephanopoulos admiringly called "a pro"—had reasons altogether shrewder and more hardheaded. He knew Republicans were reaching the point where they might come to consider Christian conservatives in the same terms Democrats viewed African-Americans, as voters who not only had nowhere else to go in November but were potentially more trouble than they were worth. "At best," as political analyst Kevin Phillips put it to me, "they're a slight net minus for the Republicans, in that they push the party too far to the right and throw Bob Dole off balance in the process. The Religious Right is worth something if you don't have to make a lot of concessions to get them, which of course you always do." In other words, Reed's Christian Coalition had become paralyzed by its new power: finally large enough to bear some responsibility for Dole's ultimate defeat in 1996, in a way that it wasn't quite formidable enough in 1992 to bear the blame for Bush's; yet if it mobilized behind someone who then faltered, its influence would falter with him, in the same way the Moral Majority faltered with Pat Robertson in the late Eighties.

The populist in me always wanted to believe the leaders of the movement were exploiting followers who were as good-hearted as they were frightened. I didn't doubt for a moment this was largely true in 1988, when Robertson ran for President, but in the winter of 1996 one could feel the leaders riding the whirlwind of their followers' fury and trying desperately to contain it. In a startling new book Reed actually suggested homosexuals should be treated with love and mercy, and admonished right-wingers who called Clinton a murderer: "When a pro-life leader says that to vote for Clinton is to vote against God . . . [this] reflects poorly on the gospel and on our faith." Maybe this was just a cynical tactic on Reed's part, but in a world where, more and more, communication begets power, it hardly mattered. And in the days before the New Hampshire Primary, at a snowbound Christian Coalition rally, my jaw dropped when crazy, gutsy Alan Keyes transformed great cheers to stony silence by telling the audience they could not politically impose their views on the nation but must bring the nation around through passionate and compelling spiritual and philosophical argument. In the final analysis, he said, much as Lincoln suggested a hundred and thirty-three years before in his address at Gettysburg, the guiding text of America was not the New Testament *or* the Constitution but the Declaration of Independence, with its assertion of unalienable freedom including the right, Keyes implied, to be wrong. The applause that accompanied his exit was tepid to say the most. Some months later, after a piece I wrote on the Religious Right ran in *Rolling Stone*, I got some letters from Christian foot soldiers as creepy as they were senseless; at their core was rage and resentment. "Please try to listen," sneered one, though exactly to what or to whom she didn't say. But that wasn't what was unsettling. What was unsettling was the little smiley faces in the letters' margins, and the assurances at the end of Jesus' love, utterly at odds with the true tone of the letters, as though wrapping the vitriol in a phony benevolence would somehow make it Christian. In short, a Christianity of etiquette rather than the heart.

In Los Angeles and later in Washington, I had talked on the telephone with one of the leaders of a state chapter of the Christian Coalition. At first John wasn't entirely sure I was the Enemy or not, and he was gun-shy as I tried to arrange a meeting with him and several of the followers. He was being protective for the most part, which I appreciated: he didn't want his rank and file submitted to the mockery of some hip, snide New York magazine. I tried to reassure him without conning him. The one thing I could promise was that I wasn't going to make fun of ordinary people working for something they sincerely believed in, whatever I might happen to think of it. Rather endearingly, John asked if *Rolling Stone* would run his photograph. "I always wanted to be in *Rolling Stone*," he said, a longtime fan of Jimmy Page's guitar if not, presumably, sharing Page's appetite for young nubiles and Aleister Crowley's black magick.

"You know," he tried to explain on the phone, "all the other political constituencies ask something from the government. We're the only one that doesn't ask anything. All we ask is that the government leave us alone." I confessed surprise to this. I told him I was under the impression that the Christian Coalition had a moral agenda that it expected the state to translate into policy. "I'm sure there are some who do expect that," he allowed, "but most of us think the church should just be the cultural center of the country, while the government is the political center." He did describe contemporary American society variously as "aggressively secular" and "atheistic." I finally convinced him that he should be a part of my story and, setting a time and a place, urged him to bring along that photo and I'd at least pass it along to the editor. But I didn't bat an eye when, forty-eight hours before our interview, John left a message on my phone machine canceling. Some "business" had come up: "I hope," he said plaintively, "you won't be mad at me." He didn't offer to reschedule. Maybe he decided I was the Enemy after all, as much as he didn't want to think so.

Still, I did mention John in the piece I filed, alluding to my frustrated efforts in meeting him. When a fact-checker from the magazine called him later to verify the quotes, he became upset, protesting that our conversations had been "off the record." I assured my editor that if our discussions were off the record, it was news to me, and after conferring with the company lawyers *Rolling Stone* rejected John's contention on the grounds that he was, after all, a public figure, the head of a state chapter of a very powerful national political organization. Thinking about it in the shower, though, I felt bad. I suspected John had realized the outraged reaction he would get from Coalition higher-ups after talking to me, and panicked; and it had never been my intention to get someone in trouble, particularly for trying to be candid. I could also see how he might have made the assumption, mistaken though it was, that what he said was off the record, given that we had been negotiating an interview; and while I thought he ought to be more careful about such things, I certainly hadn't meant to mislead or entrap him. So I called my editor back and suggested, not as something we were legally bound to do but should do in good faith, that we leave out John's last name and the name of the state of his particular Coalition chapter. John greeted this news first with satisfaction and then, some hours later, the threat of a lawsuit, which we ignored.

So after all that, the question I wanted to ask John I had to ask Gary Bauer instead. I saved it for last. "Do you think Bill Clinton is evil?" I said.

Bauer fairly reeled in his chair. "Wow," he said quietly. Later I counted off twenty full seconds on my tape before he even began to stumble into an answer. "I guess . . . I guess I would tend to define an individual as evil who is knowingly doing wrong, so, no, I would not describe Bill Clinton as evil. I would describe him as misguided, a hopeless liberal, and I think both he and his wife have an ethical blind spot. But I wouldn't describe him as any more evil than any of the rest of us. We're all fallen men and women, and I certainly will have much to answer for," Bauer laughed, "before the week's out. I think it's a mistake in the political process to suggest that someone is evil, unless he really is, which is possible in a democracy as well as anywhere else."

"You really had to think about that answer, though."

"I wanted to think about it," he admitted, "because I get mad enough at Clinton to start thinking of him in those terms, and there may even be times across the dinner table with my wife when I've used the word. But if I really reflect on it, it's not the appropriate way to describe somebody who, at the end of the day, is a political opponent, and whose vision for the country is, I think, wrong, but well within the realm of the kind of disagreements that men and women of good faith can have in a democracy." And with that, Gary Bauer succumbed to the better angels of his nature.

"So I asked Bauer if Clinton is evil," I told George Stephanopoulos a few days later. We were sitting in the West Wing of the White House as the sun broke through outside, knolls of brown snow from the previous week's blizzard melting into a dirty deluge that might wash Washington away once and for all—the God of Ralph Reed having his jollies again. "Evil!" Stephanopoulos exclaimed, perhaps only slightly less astonished than Bauer by my question. "He didn't actually say yes, did he?"

"He mustered every fiber of his being to say no."

"Those guys say no on the face of it," Stephanopoulos murmured. "But every message they send out says yes."

Walking back up Pennsylvania Avenue later, dodging the city's new rivers, I kept my eyes peeled for Jesus, on the off-chance he had come back after all, hanging out in the seat of men's corruptible power. But I couldn't be sure I'd recognize him. He might not be the old bleeding-heart Jesus anymore; he might be the Republican Jesus, altogether more efficient with his love and not wasting it on the sort of scum he squandered it on two thousand years ago—homeless riffraff and un-wed teenage mothers and dying homosexuals. It wasn't the Republicans' fault if Jesus had his priorities wrong, living with the trash while disdaining the respectable and even brandishing a whip. The new Jesus lives with the respectable and takes his whip to the trash. "Verily I say unto you," he may have told his followers once, "in as much as you have done it unto one of the least of these, my brethren, you have done it unto me." But two thousand years later the new Jesus, buffed to a gleaming new rectitude, is as likely to answer in the delirious words Randall Terry once used when implicitly exhorting his followers to murder abortion doctors. "Let a wave of hatred," he cried, "roll over you."

33

I had the admittedly peculiar idea to skip the New Hampshire Primary altogether. I realized, of course, that this would make for rather unconventional campaign coverage, but every other newspaper and magazine would be writing about New Hampshire, and by the time my piece appeared America would not want to hear another word of it. So I proposed bypassing the event for the Arizona or South Carolina primaries of the following week, after the dust had settled in New England and when there might be something more interesting to see, that others in their exhaustion might miss.

Naturally my editors at *Rolling Stone* were aghast at this, and dispatched me to New Hampshire immediately before I had any more such crackpot notions. I arrived in Manchester in mid-February when the rest of the media was still in Iowa for the caucus there. New Hampshire seemed even more a ghost state than it had months before on the night of the first Republican debate; the moment the Iowa contest was resolved, however, the media descended by the thousands, filling every motel and hotel up and down the Everett Turnpike from one end of the Revolution's cradle to the other, and at that point New Hampshire became something else, not a real place exactly but more like a studio lot with backstage streets and facades that people who looked just like real New Hampshirites went in and out of, as though they lived there.

By now it had become obvious that my position at the magazine was deteriorating. Asked to do a complete rewrite of my second story, I had sweated out a new version while on the road covering the Dole campaign, only for Jann Wenner to decide he never really wanted to do this particular piece in the first place. Upon his rejection of my revision just as the magazine was going to press, the editors asked me to come up with an entirely different story in forty-eight hours; of course, no one had to say out loud that my job was on the line. So I sat down to my desk between seven o'clock and midnight one extremely caffeinated Friday evening and knocked out six thousand words on Bob Dole, which I turned in the next day and the magazine printed.

Fanciful notions of a novelist covering the campaign like a novel had pretty much vanished at this point, assuming they ever really existed beyond their first inspiration. There was presently a frantic if unstated effort by the other editors to reinvent me as something resembling—as much as possible—the *New York Times* reporter Wenner really wanted all along, with much interviewing and quoting and statisticizing and only whatever imagination could be cleverly disguised in a political insight, and as little insinuation as possible of a narrative point of view, which is to say a narrator, which is to say me. Hired as one kind of writer I was now expected to be a rather different sort of writer. I wasn't sure who I hated more, the magazine for supposing my literary identity was so malleable, or myself for becoming increasingly miserable and petulant in a job that, after all, no one was putting a gun to my head and making me do.

Though people I talked to kept comparing Wenner to the character of the Hollywood producer in the movie *Swimming With Sharks*, I was reminded more of the old *Twilight Zone* episode where an entire household is held in the terrified thrall of a sullenly berserk little kid, who turns everyone that displeases him into puppets and banishes them out to the family cornfield. The office of *Rolling Stone* was a field of swaying, stricken puppets, with a demonic little Jann Wenner chasing me up and down the rows of corn as I fled in terror. The lower-echelon editors at the magazine had a strategy for survival, which was never to ascend too high in the scheme of things; once your head poked up above the lethal sightline, it was only a matter of time before Jann shot it off with his pop gun. It was routine for Wenner to lure people to the magazine from other jobs only to summarily fire them eight, ten, twelve months later when he suddenly woke one morning to one of his visionary outbursts—"Less politics! More naked TV stars!"—or to fire music editors for running Hootie and the Blowfish reviews not sufficiently enthusiastic to please the advertisers.

Soon the editors devised a Trojan Horse tactic for getting my stories past Jann, which was to frontload them with as much straight reportage as possible and hope this would placate his *New York Times* fantasies just long enough until the limits of his notoriously short attention span kicked in, as well as his fiercely predictable habit of never reading anything all the way through. This, of course, made the pieces a little schizophrenic. One also had to editorially negotiate the minefield of Wenner's ever fragile sense of himself, particularly given his personal life as it was being documented by the gossip columnists at the time—a hypersensitivity that, in one of my ongoing father-son conversations with Bill Greider, finally exhausted his patience. "Oh for Christ's sake," he exploded, in a completely exasperated tone that said stop-whining-and-be-a-pro, "just do what you're going to do and don't worry about Jann." On the one hand this advice was unrealistic, offered by one of the only people whose relationship with Wenner was such that he could follow it. But on the other hand it was also the only advice that made any sense at all, because trying to anticipate Wenner's whims would only make a person as crazy as he was.

By New Hampshire a certain editorial version of the Stockholm Syndrome had set in. Since there was no percentage in being frustrated with Jann, the editors at the magazine directed their frustrations more and more at me; exchanges as to the nature and intent of the coverage became ever more testy. Other reporters on the campaign trail kept asking me if I was having fun, a question that always put me in a bind, because I wasn't nearly a good enough liar to get away with saying yes, but saying no sounded churlish and self-pitying. I was by now so flummoxed by the whole thing that I couldn't be sure how much of it was the magazine's fault and how much of it was just a spoiled temperamental novelist wanting to have his own way. Things reached critical mass when Wenner approved my fourth piece only on the condition that I cut the climactic passage where the story came together. "Jann," my editor explained acidly when I asked why, "does not give reasons," and since the ordered cut made as little sense to her and the other editors as it did to me, objective editorial guidance was out of the question. Besides, it didn't matter why: far away and from on high in his Aspen ski lodge, Wenner was adamant. I hung up the phone, lay on my bed half an hour staring at the ceiling, and called my editor back. "No," I said.

"Oh," she sighed, frayed and weary from months of shuttle diplomacy between two egomaniacs. That was when I found out the situation was even more serious than I knew: she had come to the end of her own rope with Wenner, and would be leaving *Rolling Stone* within the next several months. So now my only real constituency at the magazine was gone, unless you counted Greider. I was a little tormented by the thought that, since she was the one who had the bright idea of hiring me in the first place, I had somehow cost her her job. "Well," I said, "I guess this is the moment of truth."

And then nothing happened. Over the next few days I waited for the phone to ring with the news that Wenner had killed the story and fired me too, but the call never came; the piece ran as I wrote it, completely intact with the section Wenner had ordered cut. I was assured by everyone that my position at the magazine had actually solidified, if anything—that Wenner had resolved to continue with me back when I pounded out six thousand words on Bob Dole in five hours on a Friday night. Not so far down deep inside, I knew this was nonsense. I found it curious, and perhaps indicative of how Wenner wielded power, keeping those who worked for him dazed and confused and off-center, that anyone could really suppose for two seconds that I could defy Wenner in the manner I had and not pay for it sooner or later. In the end I don't know whether Wenner ran the piece just because his attention span was so short he forgot about it, or because the magazine was about to go to press and he didn't have a choice, or because he thought he was being Orson Welles to my Joseph Cotten and so, out of some cockeyed notion of his own integrity, published the story the way I wanted it before making the next move. Because if you've seen the film, you know what happened to Joseph Cotten afterward.

34

One afternoon outside Manchester I left a Dole rally early so I could beat the candidate's four-wheel-drive motorcade to the next press conference, which was being held at City Hall. The mayor of Manchester was falling in with the rest of the state's Republican honchos and endorsing the senator. I got to City Hall and situated myself, and then went to find the men's room, which was occupied, four or five guys in dark suits patiently waiting in line outside. After a few minutes I began rattling the doorknob: "Jesus, did this guy fall in?" I muttered. The other men stared at me blankly. Afraid I was going to miss Dole's press conference altogether I started rapping rudely on the door, when it finally opened and Bob Dole stood there glowering at me.

Of course, in a similar situation any journalist worth his salt would have seized the opportunity to ask an incisive question or two. Didn't the Sage of Woody Creek become a legend interviewing George McGovern over a urinal? Instead I fled, mortified, sitting through Dole's whole press conference unrelieved. A few days later, after following Steve Forbes all over town, I was back at my hotel having dinner in my room; finishing the meal and setting the tray outside the door, I looked up to see Forbes all by himself walking down the hall right toward me, to the room where he was staying—right next to mine. Every leap year it was like this in New Hampshire, would-be presidents under your feet like rats; on the day Dole went to the state capitol to file the papers officially declaring his candidacy, he practically knocked over Hillary Clinton coming out. She had just filed for her husband and in the meantime was greatly irritating Dole with comments to the press about how the Republican budget would throw four million poor kids off the Medicaid rolls. You bumped into faux presidents in hallways and bathrooms in defiance of all expectation and physics; I'm still trying to figure out how Dole got to that men's room before I did. I imagine Manchester as a labyrinth of subterranean expressways running from this men's room to that rally, from this hotel hallway to that campaign headquarters.

With a little more than a million people, almost all of whom live at the bottom of the state, New Hampshire might be as representative of America as it wants, if it only had a hundred thousand or so black people. Economically ravaged in the recession of 1992, it made George Bush feel the full brunt of its wrath; things were getting better now in 1996, with unemployment down. But many of the new jobs were not good ones by anyone's account, and there were still empty storefronts on Elm Street, the main drag that runs through Manchester. The people of the state were not rich, perhaps not even sophisticated by the narcissistic, shallow standards of sophistication that New Yorkers and Los Angelenos pretend to; but they were very impressive in their political engagement, they paid close and cool attention to potential presidents; and whether the country ever considered itself to have conferred such a task, New Hampshire felt a national responsibility to screen out the duds and speak both to and for America, both from and to its next President. Everyone from cabbies to veterans to students to professors offered an opinion. ("Nice fella, Pat Buchanan," the doorman at my Holiday Inn assured me, "oh yeah.") It's a conservative state, pockets of it bordering on the rabid. I was having breakfast in my room one morning when I noticed something written on the back of the little label on my tea bag: "The UN—a site for sore allies." The next tea bag said, "Life is a tragedy for those who feel, a comedy for those who think." One started his day in New Hampshire with these little pearls of right-wing wisdom, like the messages in venomous fortune cookies. The last tea bag was the chiller. "A good scare," it hissed, "is worth more than good advice."

Nevertheless, particularly given the state's conservatism, there was some reflection of the national mood in the way that even here the tide had recently turned in Bill Clinton's favor. For all the attention paid in 1995 to Dole, Buchanan, Newt Gingrich and Colin Powell, the secret political story of 1995 was how, so imperceptibly no one noticed, Clinton had come back: "He's *trying*," one of my cabbies insisted, shaking his head, "it's those guys in Congress . . ." New Hampshire, it must be noted, could be enormously volatile politically for a state whose personality seemed so otherwise stolid; after months of stasis a campaign could literally rearrange itself in the last few days before the vote. Bill Clinton, Pat Buchanan, George Bush, Gary Hart, Jimmy Carter, George McGovern, Eugene McCarthy, going back through New Hampshire primaries all the way to 1968—all of these men won real or moral victories in the final week, sometimes in the final hours, thus transforming the country in ways large or small, and most doing it not by anything so glitzy or ephemeral as force of personality but rather by force of principle or vision.

Because the state took its primary very seriously, there was a great deal of foolishness in 1996 about other primaries—specifically those in Louisiana and Delaware—trying to elbow their way into the same week of the calendar or even earlier, sullying the seven-day afterglow of New Hampshire's mad passionate coitus with history. The whole Republican process had gone haywire, in a manner to match the party's ongoing ideological trauma, with states leapfrogging each other to move their contests up for maximum influence. At this rate one expected the primaries for the year 2000 to start before the 1996 campaign finished. New Hampshire believed it *owned* its place in the schedule, while candidates not doing especially well in New Hampshire, such as Senator Gramm, were happy to encourage Louisiana's debauchery—though Louisiana would turn out to be the worst thing that ever happened to Gramm. Before Louisiana, on a Dole campaign train called the "Balanced Budget Express," I ran into New Hampshire's Governor Steve Merrill who looked me right in the eye and, without any provocation on my part, said, "Phil Gramm is making a big mistake if he thinks New Hampshire shouldn't have the first primary in the nation." Of course Merrill was dead right, even if it was in a fashion he didn't anticipate.

One is hard-pressed to imagine anything in life as completely satisfying as the pallor of political death on Phil Gramm's face, so when his presidential hopes expired so quickly I couldn't help feeling history had cheated New Hampshire in general and me in particular. A legend even among his own Senate colleagues for his venality and viciousness, the Texan had begun his campaign for the presidency a year before in a blaze of money and brazenness; but by the final week before the New Hampshire Primary he was roadkill on the campaign highway, and one could only content oneself with the spectacle of vultures like myself picking over his carcass. At a press conference in the Center of New Hampshire Holiday Inn in Manchester on the day following the Iowa caucus, the rumor swept the room that Gramm would be out of the race within twenty-four hours; as it happened the press conference was in the very ballroom where the big splashy Gramm campaign rally had taken place the night of the first Manchester debate back in October, and now the hundreds of us assembled in the ballroom awaited the appearance of the very man who nailed Gramm's coffin shut, and who in those early October days had been holding his own press conferences in little rooms off to the other side of the hotel, then attended by a mere twenty or thirty reporters. Now Pat Buchanan needed a ballroom the size of an old Phil Gramm rally to hold all the reporters who had just awakened fifteen hours before, a thousand miles away in Des Moines, to the unsettling prospect that maybe the real story of the campaign was not Gramm, not Forbes, maybe not even Robert Dole, but Buchanan, who had run within three percentage points of winning Iowa and had outpolled a lot of people who outspent and outorganized him over the course of many months.

When Buchanan entered to scattered applause, flanked by his perpetually stunned wife Shelley and psycho sister and campaign manager Bay, he immediately framed the present political situation in terms admittedly self-serving but not far off the mark. Hoarse but elated, he made it clear that in the coming week he would continue to elaborate on a new theme—"a conservatism of the heart," he called it, no doubt formulating it as such to take the very rough edges off what even mainstream conservatives considered a rather scary version of their ideology, and also somehow codifying the evolving quirks of his own increasingly eccentric version of that ideology, with its leftist notions about free trade, corporate greed and what he scathingly referred to as the "turbo-charged, go-go economy." He decried "the arid, bookish conservatism of the think tanks." Not so long before, the notion of Pat Buchanan, Humanist, would have seemed a little nutty even in this bizarre electoral season; you knew things had gotten twisted when you found yourself cheering lustily for Buchanan to shellack Gramm even as you were already booking a seat on the midnight flight to Amsterdam for the night of November 5, 1996, in the apocalyptic event that he should actually become President. "The Republican Party is becoming the Buchanan party," he declared now, Bay nodding maniacally and Shelley appearing as stupefied at the prospect as the rest of us. "More and more people are coming to believe that Pat Buchanan can be the next President of the United States. And," he added with a chuckle, "I'm coming to believe it too."

The room, with its odd science-fiction light fixtures framed by weird tubular crystals, was teeming with many press superstars I hadn't seen at the other Buchanan press conferences. Only CNN's Bruce Morton had been at the one in October; now the *Washington Post*'s David Broder was there, PBS's Margaret Warner, Walter Shapiro of *Esquire* and *USA Today*, Tom Oliphant of the *Boston Globe*, the *Wall Street Journal*'s Al Hunt in a very spiffy purple ski jacket, and political analyst Michael Barone anxiously grabbing passersby and exclaiming, "I never said Dole was dead! I said Phil Gramm was dead!" Rudely interrupting a woman at the hotel's front desk in order to get directions to the conference, I turned to find the interruptee was Cokie Roberts. The ballroom was divided by a barricade of lights and cameras and microphones, the whole media overload short-circuiting whatever rationality conductors kept my darkest imaginings in check: a mysterious beige curtain running the length of one wall rustled ominously as though any moment it would open to reveal the Free Timothy McVeigh Brigade with automatics, mowing down all the liberal press's elite along with the flotsam like myself. Forty-eight hours later, with revelations of the Buchanan campaign's ties to white supremacists popping like flashbulbs, this hallucination wouldn't seem quite so paranoid. A young dark-haired woman in black cowboy boots standing to the side taking notes bore the most unmistakable resemblance to Heidi Fleiss, but that certainly didn't seem right—Heidi Fleiss covering the 1996 presidential campaign? For *Penthouse*, perhaps? The Playboy TV channel?—and I had almost discounted the possibility when I saw her glance meet the candidate's, and the memory of a night of ecstasy flashed across his eyes.

After Buchanan left, it all broke up. The press superstars hobnobbed with the other superstars while the riffraff rushed to the phones, checking his or her insights with everyone else around him and alarmed when they didn't synchronize. This wisdom-by-consensus was a disease of the national media, and as proof I give you Exhibit A: me. Having felt for months, on the basis of no empirical evidence whatsoever, that Buchanan was the Real Story of the Republican race for the presidency, I had been losing my nerve in recent weeks, instincts giving way to polls and other people's instincts. Now going into the final stretch and confronted with the most confounding New Hampshire Primary in memory, the press was desperately trying to pin the Real Story down even as the narrative line was shooting off in four or five directions. "I wouldn't write off Forbes yet," Walter Shapiro whispered to me, in large part because the press was doing exactly that, just a few weeks after Forbes had burned through *Time* and *Newsweek* covers like Sherman through the South.

To many the Real Story was now Lamar Alexander. Other than Dole he was the only candidate that any reasonable person could believe had a chance of actually being nominated in San Diego, and for the media the story of a campaign must always be about who is going to win and who is going to lose. The consensus was that Buchanan's appeal was ultimately limited. But there was still the more complicated story, which had been true at least six months, that while he would never be President, Buchanan remained the candidate speaking to that persistent nag of a question, the Meaning of America, and in a more narrow sense the meaning of the Republican Party. The most unsettling thing about all the brash claims he made at this press conference was how many of them were true. The Republican Party *was* a Buchanan party now, and particularly because the party would never nominate him for President, it would have to deal with him some other way: where Dole was the Resignation Candidate, where Alexander was the Remaindered Candidate, Buchanan was the Candidate of Ramification.

35

It may have just been the weather getting to him, the snowbanks of New Hampshire glittering like broken glass in the background. It *was* cold, no getting around it, and trying to set up a shot at an outdoor Dole rally in Concord, the cameraman next to me finally erupted. "Move the sign!" he screamed at some dim New Hampshire citizen braving the winter to see a future President and holding a Dole banner right in the camera's line of view. I looked at the cameraman and he looked back at me as if to say, What's the matter with that person? What would happen if everyone started walking around with signs? There would be no camera shots, there would be no news footage, and you know what that would mean? *There would be no TV.* Shit, you might as well cancel the election.

In the 1992 primary, when his political career was on the rocks, buffeted by the tides and currents of draft dodging and Gennifer Flowers, Bill Clinton campaigned dawn to dusk, at cafes in the mornings and bowling alleys in the afternoons and people's potluck dinners in the evening, climbing into vans at the end of the day and coughing up blood from a throat ravaged by pleading. Afterward a survey determined that one out of every four people in New Hampshire had personally met him, a statistic that happened to correspond almost exactly to how many people voted for him. By 1996 this tradition of what was called retail politics, in which the candidate personally made his case to the citizenry, had begun to change irrevocably. "For months it's completely retail, when television's paying no attention at all," Jonathan Alter told me, "and then that changes completely in the last week." Alter, writing about politics and the media for *Newsweek*, was arguing that the televisionization of New Hampshire had really been happening since at least 1988, but he had to admit that in 1996 it had taken a quantum lurch. New Hampshire had finally, utterly succumbed to America's television culture with its twenty-four-hour news and twenty-four-hour airwave talk and all the mutated twenty-four-hour bastardizations of the two; and while it was true that the citizenry was to some extent party to this—Democratic pollster Peter Hart said that pressing the remote control had replaced pressing the flesh; and it had been the public's positive response to Steve Forbes' TV blitzkrieg that forced the other candidates to answer in kind—it was also true that, in the last week before the vote, the public literally could not get close to a candidate for the press surrounding him. "A voter!" Lamar Alexander cried one day from inside his phalanx of reporters and cameramen, as though it were a UFO sighting. The voter in question had called out the governor's name and reached his hand through the crush. Alexander shook it, on the wild hope it was attached to a real person at the other end.

On Primary Day Minus Six, Five, Four, Three, we waited for the campaign to boil over into a frenzy of activity. The average reporter would spend the mornings on the phone trying to cajole daily schedules out of the various candidates, then wait for the faxes of those schedules in vain; after several such lost days I finally just drove into Manchester and physically presented myself at the various campaign headquarters. In sharp contrast to New Hampshire primaries past, in 1996 Buchanan rarely scheduled more than one event per news cycle, Alexander and Dole and Forbes rarely more than two, and a common peculiarity became instantly evident: the afternoon had vanished from the day. Invariably every campaign came to a halt by one o'clock and did not resume until nightfall, the afternoon left to constant "retooling"—filming ads and poring over polls and strategizing. By one o'clock the local TV stations had gotten their footage for the evening news and the political day was over, at least until the evening, when the new deadline was the morning news. Given a relative paucity of events to cover, each became that much more maniacal and that much more artificial, when Buchanan's one event of the day, for instance, turned out to be not a rally, not a handshaking stroll up Elm Street, not even a press conference, but the filming of a TV commercial, with TV news cameras filming Buchanan filming the ad. It was about that time that William Kristol of the conservative *Weekly Standard* started calling the campaign "postmodern," a suspiciously arty word coming from Dan Quayle's former chief of staff, but on the mark.

This year, this intensive distillation of the political news day coincided with several other processes of condensation. Add to the fact that the whole Republican race was collapsed into a few weeks, the idiosyncrasies of this particular campaign included an acknowledged front-runner at once anemic to the point of being blood-drained, but nevertheless the only candidate with the organization and resources to quickly consolidate his position, assuming he had a position to consolidate. Putting it in larger terms, in the middle of February the Republican universe shuddered between twin forces of gravity and entropy, where Bob Dole was either going to win, thereby restoring the scheme of things, or lose, the Republican universe imploding into a black hole. In the middle of this looming chaos was the media. The media had its own agenda in all this, of course, or more accurately any number of agendas, which produced any number of contradictions: on the one hand, as the Forbes phenomenon of January had proved, the press would have its Real Story even if it had to invent it. So, rooting for a story, one had to root against Dole. On the other hand, the press loved the aura of power and its own proximity to it, which meant rooting for Dole, in whom more than one reporter had made more than one kind of investment over the years.

By Primary Day Minus Four the consternation of such mixed feelings had just begun to sink in on the denizens of the Wayfarer Inn in Bedford. The Wayfarer was a press watering hole of legend, and had been for years; if you were covering the New Hampshire Primary you had to go to the Wayfarer, as much a scene for political writers as the Roxy on the Sunset Strip is for heavy metal rockers. Broder would stroll in wearing a lumberjack shirt and a turtleneck; Al Hunt in a spiffy turquoise shirt and CNN's Judy Woodruff, who happened to be Hunt's wife, held court at a large table with Eleanor Randolph of the *Los Angeles Times*; Jonathan Alter was slightly rumpled in a corner while Walter Shapiro was at the bar still in his coat and tie. Gloria Borger from *U.S. News and World Report* stood back to back with him, though whether either was aware of the other wasn't clear. Outside the window, across a little lagoon with a waterfall and bridge, CBS had taken over the convention center. Mixing with the press were pols and activists, guys from the Concord Coalition and Senator Bob Smith, a former shill for Gramm here to drink himself stupid after his man bombed so badly. The din was impossible to sort through and no one paid attention to any of the campaign coverage on the TV in the corner of the room except when a new political ad came on, at which point everyone grew completely quiet before lunging into a maelstrom of analysis as soon as the ad was over, dismissing it or concluding it would probably turn the whole campaign around. The Wayfarer was Meaning Central, where over Scotch and Stoli the most ludicrous thing, like Lamar Alexander not knowing the price of milk, became monumentally significant for twenty-four hours, and a hundred disparate meanings were frantically pummeled into two or three that everyone could agree on, or even One, the One of this particular season and this particular campaign year being: it was now or never for Robert Dole.

"It's now or never," Robert Dole was telling the students of St. Anselm College the next afternoon. Outside Cushing Center the snow was falling, the school basketball team was winning, finals were looming, and yet the kids were still there, every seat in the center full, signs that read BALANCE THE BUDGET NOW and WE WANT SOCIAL SECURITY WHEN WE GET OLD tacked onto the windows. Even Dole admitted he wasn't sure which were "real" signs and which the Dole for President campaign had cooked up. The Kansas senator was hitting his stride in his speech, telling the students that balancing the budget would mean lower interest on their loans for new houses or businesses, or for paying off the loans that were putting them through college, framing the budget issue very much in terms of their future, when he told them it was now or never, and though he meant it for them, not himself, if anyone in presidential politics was smart enough to know the score it was Dole. The day before the St. Anselm appearance I had caught up with Dole on the so-called Balanced Budget Express from Manchester to Concord, four or five cars of a slow train moving at about the speed of the rest of his campaign. Packed with media and Dole supporters and New Hampshire pols, the train snaked through the snow past shimmering riverbanks, white-clotted trees and pastel wood houses all so pristine the graffiti on the bridges was jarringly out of place; as a one-whistle-stop tour the Budget Express was as close to an old-fashioned campaign event as the crash of the Secret Millennium and the nova of cyberspace would ever again allow, not to mention temperatures of twenty-some-degrees-and-plummeting.

The train's leisurely pace seemed to sum up Dole's candidacy, as did its quaintness. A singing group of eight young women from the University of New Hampshire, dressed in torchy black dresses and calling themselves the New Hampshire Notables, were trying to rouse the assembled Doleful with a version of Steve Winwood's "Higher Love." They got one or two of the passengers to clap along. "It's good publicity for us," acknowledged Amy, speaking for the other Notables. "I can't say we're all Republicans, though." I followed the Notables from car to car until the lot of us cornered the candidate. Serenaded with what in the Sixties would have been called the "long" version of "Higher Love," verse after verse and chorus after chorus, the "In-a-Gadda-Da-Vida" of campaign songs, Dole looked only slightly less uncomfortable than when I stumbled into him emerging from the men's room; actually, truth be told, he looked happier coming out of the men's room. He smiled to the song and at the young women as long as he could, but after awhile you could see the tics in his cheekbones. Aides and reporters anxiously watched the Republican Senate leader self-consciously watch the young women sing to him; the idea was that in the twenty miles to Concord Dole was supposed to walk from one end of the train to the other shaking hands and saying hello to his supporters, but now the Notables were using up precious time as their higher and higher love scaled a veritable Mount Everest of rapture. Relieved applause exploded at the summit. The senator moved along. Reporters shot him questions as he passed. "Why do you think all these people are for you?" I mumbled, pretty lame as questions go, I'll grant you, but I wasn't at all sure he heard anyway.

"Mainstream conservative," he answered in the kind of rhetorical shorthand George Bush made familiar but which Dole had somehow mastered, if that was the word. "Known quantity, strong leader . . . Pretty nice train ride, isn't it?" he asked anyone and everyone. "Been a long time since I was on a train."

"The gravy train!" cried an older, distinguished-looking man next to me.

Dole considered this quite witty. "That's it," he answered, "the gravy train. It's the gravy train," he kept repeating, as he made his way down the car. On the gravy train it was the senator's self-described "known quantity" that seemed most pertinent to the passengers. Everyone indeed knew him, people well into their sixties and seventies who had been involved in state Republican politics forever, reaching out to take his hand and greet him like an old friend. There weren't a lot of young people on the gravy train, though to be fair it was a weekday, when many of them would have been working. One of the exceptions, Tim, wore a button that said "Veterans for Dole." Tim was in his early to mid-thirties, in the Marine Corps ten years until 1995; now he was riding the Balanced Budget Express with his two-year-old son, Connor. I assumed that for Tim, Dole's record as a wounded hero in World War II contrasted all too pointedly with the incumbent President's evasion of service during Vietnam. "Nah," Tim shook his head, "the first year Clinton was in office, the military was pretty horrified. . . ." But the military had made its uneasy peace with Clinton, Tim went on. Tim was for Dole "because I really believe the federal debt is a national security crisis, and while there have been scare tactics on both sides of the budget debate, Dole has been a calm voice in the storm." He pointed at Connor. "I think about his future."

The train was stifling. It sputtered the whole trip to Concord, occasionally stopping for moose on the tracks—"Braking for Hillary," one woman said, more Republican wit, and everyone laughed. Hillary Clinton was also campaigning in the state that day, even though the President was uncontested in the Democratic primary. No one was really in any rush to get to Concord; hot and jerky though the ride was, it was a relief from the cold outside, which even the natives found bitter. Everyone was having a pretty good time as the Balanced Budget Express finally staggered into the station where a welcoming crowd of a hundred or so waited, maybe more, with a real old-fashioned high school marching band, their kelly green uniforms and gold instruments glistening in the winter light. The media tumbled off the train, followed by the Doleful. Parents and kids in the crowd jumped up and down in place to keep warm; the remarks by Senator Judd Gregg, followed by those of Governor Merrill, were mercifully brief out of deference to the freeze. Then Dole came on. His "All right!" growl in response to the frigid cheers sounded like Earl Scheib, whose commercials on TV twenty years ago promised to paint any car any color for $29.95. Dole gave a short version of his usual New Hampshire speech, not so different from the one he would give to the students at St. Anselm the next day; the 1996 election wasn't about Bob Dole, he declared, it wasn't about Bill Clinton, "it's about you and our country. . . . President Clinton can't be trusted with our future. The principles of the conservative revolution must be continued, and they need a faithful leader. If our ideas are to change America, Republicans must elect someone who knows how to make change happen. I'm not afraid to lead. I know the way. . . . I'm proud to be on the Balanced Budget Express! Come on board, Mr. President, we'll save you a seat!"

Most of this was as stilted as it sounds, coming alive only when Dole obviously departed from the script, like the "we'll save you a seat" line. Few people watched or waved from the Concord windows; it was too cold for that. The streets were deserted and slick with ice. Still, the Senate majority leader seemed in good spirits as he walked from the railroad track to the middle of town. At the capitol building a winding caravan of supporters, reporters and bureaucrats clambered through a maze of old hallways lined with portraits of weird New England politicians and generals from the Nineteenth Century, with names like Noah Martin and Moody Currier, peering down from the walls and shuddering from the thundering passage of so many strange trespassers. Dole would vanish into one doorway only to reemerge from another on another floor, so there was a crazy scramble to figure out where he was going to appear next. Finally he didn't appear at all. On his way to a $250-per-plate fund-raising dinner that night in Bedford, he presumably opted for a balanced-budget limo, and the Balanced Budget Express returned to Manchester without him. But without Dole on it, it really wasn't the Balanced Budget

Express anymore, it wasn't even the gravy train, it was just The Train Back through the approaching storm that would sheathe New Hampshire with a new cover of snow before morning.

36

We do not need to take the train back through Bob Dole's life to figure out where along the track he thought being President was a good idea. There almost certainly was no stop marked Presidential Aspiration; the Aspiration boarded on the run, like a hobo hopping an empty car. It was now or never for Bob Dole more than anyone else in the presidential race of 1996, because he would either become President in his third effort in sixteen years, or it could be said with as much certainty as politics ever allows that he would never be President.

He often made a curious statement when talking about this. After losing the Republican nomination in 1988 he said, "I never expected to be running for President again. I assumed George Bush would be reelected in 1992." Subsequent logic breaks down. How would George Bush's reelection in 1992 have precluded Bob Dole's options in 1996? It said something about how destiny was a non sequitur for Bob Dole, a man who thought his life was over before it had barely begun, fifty years earlier; and his whole life had been a string of now-or-nevers ever since the moment that, as a poor boy far from his Dust Bowl home, he dragged his ravaged body, along with the body of a dead soldier he was trying to rescue, back into a foxhole on an Italian battlefield in the closing days of World War II. If nothing about his circumstances, political or otherwise, ever precluded another run for the presidency in 1996, what Dole meant when he said he never expected to make another such campaign was that he had made his peace with it, and perhaps with the fact that down deep he didn't care much about being President anymore. Certainly one could arrive at such a conclusion given the lethargy of his candidacy. Months later in the spring, when he resigned from the Senate, there was much blather in the media and among the political commentators that, having now committed himself fully to his presidential campaign, he seemed more at peace than he ever had before. This was nonsense. Dole was most at peace as a United States senator, and as Senate Republican leader. The truth was that, in Nixonian fashion, when Dole resigned from the Senate he made no peace at all. Rather he declared war on himself, war on the dreams he once held that had the temerity to die within him.

He looked old. I'm sorry. It's a graceless thing to say but, up close on the Balanced Budget Express, he looked his seventy-three years. Oh, certainly he looked a very fit seventy-three, but that was not the same thing as looking sixty-three, which he often did on television. Now in the presidential race of 1996 Dole campaigned from the Zone of a Perceived Age. This Zone began about eight feet away, and ended about twenty. It was an odd phenomenon, something about the light perhaps, but more than twenty feet away he appeared old and gray enough to fade into a sidewalk, and then when he moved within the twenty feet he lost ten years, and looked his best. Then, nearing closer, within about seven or eight feet, he looked old again, you really saw it and it shocked you a little, it actually made your heart sink—the hair thinning on top, the skin pulled tight around the features, and the tan that looked artificial, as though his face had been stained with a dye. In a way his politics were the same, his persona the same; they came to life when they were neither so far away as to be transparent nor so close as to appear withered, inviting neither close examination nor a distinct perspective. From this Zone he hoped to flourish. But neither the presidency, nor the campaign for it, were likely to honor such parameters for long.

Thus his position in the early months of the race might have been exactly the one he wanted to occupy: not so far ahead of his opponents as to make him a foregone conclusion, thereby inspiring a lethal complacency, but an extremely healthy distance. In New Hampshire his most threatening competitors were at once the unlikeliest—a right-wing commentator and a rich guy with nothing better to do, each striking their particular sparks not off their experience or winning personalities but their ideas. Dole, of course, was now a man of all experience and almost no ideas, and a personality more tortured than winning, though it had mellowed over time. He was the Walking Wounded of American presidential politics, a dark scar of a man slashing his way across the face of the country, resembling no one so much as his mentor, Richard Nixon, while neither as malevolent nor brilliant. Ripped by a bullet in the Second World War, his young robust body shriveled on the right, his right arm irreparable and the rest of him paralyzed for a year from the waist down, facing the life sentence of a three-quarter quadriplegic which he overcame with incontestable courage, he had been going to war with his fears and rage ever since, and it was on the train of that particular life that the hobo of Presidential Aspiration leapt somewhere along the way in the last half-century. First elected to Congress around the time Bill Clinton was a teenager bird-dogging southern babes in his pickup truck, Dole was the vice presidential nominee of the Republican Party in 1976 when, during a debate with Walter Mondale, he made a now-famous statement about all the dead men in Twentieth-Century wars that were started by "Democrat" presidents. "Including me," he almost seethed, to those of us pretending to hear the whispers of his soul.

In other words, for Dole politics was always personal, and becoming President was personal—and though the train of time presumably took him farther and farther away from fear and rage, the journey never stopped being intensely personal. If he had mellowed over the years, he also retained the potential for becoming publicly unhinged, as when he cried at a farewell testimonial to George Bush, a man he never even liked, or the funeral of Richard Nixon, a man for whom such pure grief was far too simple to be appropriate, or even on the night when a proposed amendment to the United States Constitution mandating a balanced budget went down to defeat—a sobering blow to Dole to be sure, since he led the fight for it, but perhaps not worth nearly breaking down before millions of people on television. Months after wrapping up the nomination, having made the decision to resign not just his leadership position in the Senate but his seat itself, he almost lost it again, and one wondered at the time if the sacrifice was really worth it, even if he won the presidency, worth it not just for us but for him. Dole was not a Man of Ideas like Pat Buchanan or Steve

Forbes, or even a Man of Sheer Ambition, like his other two main challengers for the nomination, Alexander and Gramm. He was a Man of Obsession. In this way he resembled not only Nixon but . . . Bill Clinton. God, the very idea must have made him nuts! Bill Clinton, whom he so openly despised. "All you have in politics is your word," Dole said contemptuously at one point during his press conference with the mayor of Manchester, and there was no doubt about the inference. "My style is to get things done, *his* style is to change his mind. My priority is to save the country. His is to get reelected."

Whatever his style or priorities, for the President of the United States politics was personal as well, and that was what the two shared. And if there were ways in which a Clinton-Dole race set up the interesting if obvious analogy to two other great rivals, Kennedy and Nixon, the comparison broke down once one transgressed the issues of style, because John Kennedy brought a killer's cold dispassion to the business of politics; it was Kennedy's brother Robert who made things personal. Even as early as New Hampshire one already realized that a Clinton-Dole battle might well come down to a matter of which spectacle we could most bear to watch and emotionally survive as a people: the dashed dream of one man versus the broken obsession of the other, both psyches so plugged into existential stakes of winning and losing that on election night the loser was as likely to throw himself off a building or pull an Uzi out from under his coat and massacre a room of sniveling sycophants as to graciously concede defeat. In 1992 Dole couldn't graciously concede to Bill Clinton even when it wasn't Dole who had run against him, appearing on television moments after Clinton's election not to ask the country to unite behind the new President following a difficult election but rather to remind the American people that Clinton had totaled up only forty-three percent of the vote, after all, therefore leaving it to Dole to represent the other fifty-seven. That Dole could actually be so bitter about the defeat of George Bush, a man he had rightly and openly called a liar when Bush savaged him in the New Hampshire Primary of 1988, perhaps revealed better than anything else what a strange piece of work the man from Kansas truly was.

Bush came close to losing it all to Dole in 1988, which was why he lied about Dole's record. In the tradition of Republican presidential politics, what was interesting about this was that the nomination should have been Bush's for the asking; that was the way the Republican Party worked. There was a corporate, hierarchical dynamic in the Republican Party that honored seniority and sheer endurance, by which one became chairman of the board through a long series of alternating humiliations and promotions. Every once in a great while a wild insurrectionist movement had its way with the GOP, but in modern history only Barry Goldwater's nomination in 1964 qualified, when Nelson Rockefeller, the governor of New York, had obviously been groomed for the party leadership by the party establishment. Nixon, Gerald Ford, Ronald Reagan, Bush: they were all, either institutionally or procedurally, Next in Line, vice presidents or previous challengers who had paid their dues; so in 1988, when the party briefly threatened in the Iowa caucus and early New Hampshire polls to skip over Bush and nominate Dole, it was a bit unseemly, if not downright un-Republican. Ironically Dole was then the Man of Ideas, his main idea not unlike the one he was running on this time: eliminating the federal deficit and balancing the federal budget. Yet now there was the feeling that the Balanced Budget Express was only a bandwagon Dole had opportunistically jumped on like a hundred other passing bandwagons he had jumped on of late, all heading rightward across the landscape as in one instance after another he reversed course on long-held positions: against the assault-weapons ban when he was once for it; against affirmative action when he was once for it; swearing a no-new-tax pledge when he once refused to, at great cost to his future and great credit to his integrity; accepting the support of gay Republicans and then rejecting it in order to please the Religious Right, then accepting it again when the publicity got so bad he had to blame his staff for the fuckup. In the meantime his position on abortion had become convoluted almost beyond comprehension: favoring a federal ban one day, opposing it the next, then favoring it again the next with dire exceptions, he tried to split hairs between the Religious Right and the political center ever more finely.

Before one New Hampshire group after another, Governor Merrill would give Dole as poignant and honorable an introduction as a President could hope for. "If you want to live in the land of the free," he told crowds, "you must also live in the home of the brave. And Bob Dole is a brave man." And if this was no longer true in political terms, it remained so in personal terms, for the man to whom politics was deeply personal. But of course this was also a fancier and more eloquent version of the Next-in-Line argument, an insistence on Dole as the Heir Presumptive; and what had to have been running through Dole's mind now was that eight years before, the party nearly discarded the Heir Presumptive, at Dole's instigation. What he must have feared now was that the current Men of Ideas would be more successful than he had been, because the Republican Party had changed in those eight years, having at once become ever more ideological while at the same time coming closer to being the country's majority party. The last time this particular combination derailed a political party was 1968 and 1972, when the competing pressures of majority representation on the one hand and ideological representation on the other fractured the Democrats, who in some respects never really put the pieces back together. Dole had the party's establishment solidly behind him with a majority of the nation's Republican governors supporting him as well as most of the New Hampshire party apparatus, and the Dole campaign war chest fat with contributions from Amway, Metromedia, and Time Warner and Walt Disney, two of the nefarious entertainment companies the senator ripped in his culture speech of spring 1995, not to mention other paragons of cultural virtue like tabloid king Rupert Murdoch, Las Vegas casino czar Steve Wynn, and the tobacco industry at large. But there was still the sinking feeling that all this that had once saved George Bush was not necessarily going to save Bob Dole now.

37

So James Carville lied when he said this was going to be the most interesting election of our political consciousness. Because by all rights it should have been, the country teetering on the edge of every kind of bankruptcy you could mention—but even journalistic self-interest wasn't so shameless that one could pretend this election could wind up anything more portentous than the greatest sweep-it-under-the-rug contest in memory, between two Men of Obsession obsessed about almost everything except what they actually believed, a moderate liberal and a moderate conservative who both shared, shall we say, a fundamental flexibility of moral and political vision.

On the other hand, one could not be so cynical as to ignore the fact that every once in a while, even in the midst of presidential politics at its most cynical, Bob Dole was spotted here and there around the country in the throes of statesmanship. Various crazies surrounding him to the contrary, and left to his own devices, it was obvious he preferred working out the 1995 budget with Bill Clinton to watching the country go up in ideological flames. And if the most potentially explosive issue of the winter was a peace in the Balkans that only America, lucky us, could enforce, assuming anyone could, in his own epilepsy of statesmanship Bill Clinton had dispatched troops while every poll screamed he risked nothing less than his presidency, and Bob Dole supported this dispatchment which no number of attached caveats would absolve him of if the policy went terribly awry. Bosnia was an issue that New Hampshire voters, like other Americans, were willing to wait and see about—which didn't mean they weren't deeply wary. Be all that as it may, I couldn't help supposing that, even with the freezing temperature and his lousy poll numbers, those rare moments in the campaign that actually found Dole in good humor had to do with the relief of finally rising to the occasion, after a year of sustained political whoring: Dole was simply feeling better about himself, his obsession having succumbed to his dignity and patriotism.

Because whatever else was true, Dole was not an insubstantial man. There was a moment in 1988 when, forged of honest ideas and hard-life experience, and disdainful of no-new-tax gimmicks, he was arguably the best President of the bunch we had to choose from. But that time was past now, as seemed evident when Dole stood before the students in Cushing Center at the Catholic liberal arts college St. Anselm and grazed a moment of connection with them when he said, "It's now or never. It's your century coming up. The next century is yours, you're the shareholders. You'll be the ones running the company called America—the rest of us will all be gone." An American baby born in 1996, he went on, would pay $160,000 in taxes just toward the interest on the national debt. Near the back of the hall, along the side, a big kid in a cap called out a question. "But what can you tell Generation X," he asked the senator, "that will give them faith again in the American system?"

Dole utterly unraveled. His answer barely contained his fury. "To be disenfranchised or frustrated or cynical," he replied, "well, you can sit on the sidelines if you want and complain . . ." but what his snarl really said was: *I went and lost an arm in the war for you, punk, that's what I've done. Who are you to be talking about lost faith?* His comments then disintegrated into a rambling discourse about the Voting Rights Act and term limits and how his wife, Elizabeth, a formidable figure in her own right who was once in Ronald Reagan's cabinet, would return to her job as president of the Red Cross if she became First Lady, and that would be a fine example to all the young women in the country. He made an odd joke about blood banks in the White House, and as the audience of students grew uneasy he switched to a whole different tone, partly defensive and partly apologetic: "I'm not perfect," Dole allowed, joking, "if you don't like me, at least take a look at Elizabeth. She's the best half of this campaign." Offstage a phone could be heard ringing. "That must be her calling now," he cracked, "to see if I'm working," which got a laugh. Finally he ended by desperately pointing out that, if elected, "we'd have a speaker named Newt and a President named Bob. We've never had a President named Bob before. How many Bobs are there in the audience?" Out of two hundred students, not a single one raised his hand. "I don't believe it," Dole muttered.

I ran over to the student who had asked the question. His name was Mike and he was a history major. "What did you think of his answer?" I asked.

"He didn't answer it," Mike said with disgust. "He just talked about all the things he's done and then made light of it. And that was it." A few minutes later I saw one of the younger Dole operatives wander over to Mike and start talking to him—a little damage control. They spoke for a while and, when the operative left, Mike turned to a friend and rolled his eyes.

All right, let's be fair. First, Mike was near the back of the room, partly obscured from Dole's sight by a pole, and Dole, peering into the lights, looked like maybe he couldn't really hear the question. Second, it was a question that sounded simple but was, at its heart, impossible. On the other hand, while Bill Clinton wasn't likely to have provided a very satisfactory answer either, one could imagine the President getting within striking distance of it, empathetic if not ultimately insightful, which was probably why when I asked one of St. Anselm's political science professors where the students' sympathies lay, he said, "Most of them would like Clinton to be good, even if down deep they suspect he's not." In which case the same generation that supported Clinton in 1992 hadn't completely relinquished its faith in him, tarnished and bruised and severely tested though that faith had been.

This would matter, because just as Bob Dole campaigned for the presidency from the Zone of a Perceived Age, the country would elect a President from the Zone of a Perceived Faith. We had become very careful with our faith, neither getting too close to it, where it looked old, nor too far from it, where it looked dead, but just the right distance, the distance we considered wise and tempered by experience. And to a certain extent we had earned the right to be cautious, after the litany of liars our history had offered up in the last thirty years, in one President after another. But this caution was also the way in which we kidded ourselves, by pretending it was only the liars who betrayed us rather than we who betrayed ourselves with all our contradictions, with the things we wanted and demanded and the things we weren't willing to give up even as we expected everyone else to give something up. If Clinton and Dole did balance the budget and bring peace to Bosnia, it would be with no real thanks to us. These great sweep-it-all-under-the-rug elections were our own doing, of course; we just elected these guys to do the sweeping. "Cautious" faith is another contradiction, if you haven't noticed: faith isn't supposed to be cautious, or tempered by experience. It's blind to caution and experience. It doesn't know zones, and it doesn't know now or never.

38

"Oliver's still ranting about you," Dr. Billy O'Forte said the last time I saw him. I used to work with Dr. Billy on a weekly newspaper in Los Angeles, where at one time or another we both reviewed movies; by Oliver he meant Oliver Stone, who had been unhappy with me ever since 1991 when I wrote a scathing piece on *JFK*, the most dishonest major American movie of the Nineties and one for which a number of otherwise honest and intelligent people made some perfectly flabbergasting excuses. "Who is that guy?" Stone cried when Billy, covering the 1992 Democratic Convention for the newspaper, bumped into him in New York. "I wonder," he sneered, "what it's like to be that filled with self-hatred and self-loathing," and now every time Dr. Billy saw Stone he was subject to the filmmaker's tirade about my self-hatred and self-loathing. Damned if I wasn't beginning to think Stone was right, though. By the time I reached New Hampshire I was practically screaming every time I looked in the mirror, so I had to figure it was only my Nixonian self-loathing that led me to conclude Stone's newest film, a phantasmagoric portrait of the thirty-seventh President, was his masterpiece.

Unfortunately, when *Nixon* came out many commentators still hadn't gotten over *JFK*, and transferred their indignation accordingly. In part because Stone has the sensibility of a totalitarian and the soul of a crybaby, his critics were unwilling to distinguish between the lie of a movie that purports to be a documentarian investigation of facts, even as it's predisposed to believe the facts it chooses to believe and make up the ones it can't otherwise account for, and the metaphorical liberties of a life interpreted on film, which may exaggerate some things or collapse certain dramatic points for the sake of narrative expediency, but still captures the essence of its subject: an American nomad caught in the vortex of his memories, as his life implodes. While Stone has never been the heavy thinker he thinks he is, *Nixon* instead benefits from his talents as an allegorist, and a command of film language that grows braver and more startling with every endeavor. It's only fair to also acknowledge that for a man so antagonistic to the subtleties of human affairs, Stone routinely gets terrific, complex performances from his actors, which can't be a complete accident, of course. *Nixon* is an epic psychodrama, which would seem to be a contradiction in terms, epics played out on exterior landscapes and psychodramas on interior ones; the only other example that comes quickly to mind is *Lawrence of Arabia*, in which psychodrama often gives way to epic of the more, well, epic sort, when T. E. Lawrence becomes too impenetrable to comprehend or convey.

Still, it wasn't until one morning in New Hampshire, several weeks after I had seen the movie, that I woke to the real revelation of *Nixon*. No dream forewarned me; I just opened my eyes and there it was: *Nixon* was not the sequel to *JFK* but rather *Kiss Me Deadly*, Robert Aldrich's 1955 film about a sleazy, nihilistic private eye named Mike Hammer in a sleazy, nihilistic town called Los Angeles, where the end of the world is just around the corner. Upon waking I realized that Dick Nixon was Mike Hammer's meek, once conjoined twin brother, separated only when Mike ripped himself loose from Dick in an explosion of blood and bone, incapable of bearing one more moment of Hannah Nixon's suffocating "saintly" love; by the time he was old enough to drink bourbon and fuck women, Mike Nixon had had enough of saints, including not only his mother but the sniveling pathetic sap attached to him at the spleen. He split Whittier for nearby L.A., changed his name to one that would bludgeon into oblivion once and for all any ties to his past, and lived out Dick's psychological yearnings for physical brawls more honest than politics and women somewhat on the looser and fleshier side of Patricia Ryan. *Kiss Me Deadly* is the first nuclear noir and perhaps the last as well, unless one counts Oliver Stone's *Nixon* itself, skirting as it does the radioactive incandescence of its predecessor forty years earlier. In the last scene of *Kiss Me Deadly*, Hammer finally blusters his way onto the end of the world, as Dick himself might have done elected to the presidency eight years too soon.

In the years after the war, in the late Forties and early Fifties, on the rare occasions Dick came home to Los Angeles from Washington, he used to drive the streets at night half-looking for Mike, thinking he might bump into him in one of the little bars off Hollywood Boulevard, drinking with his cheap actor pals. If he never thought of himself as an Angeleno, what Dick shared with both Mike and L.A. was the place's fundamental rootlessness and fragmentation, none of the parts of his identity quite connecting to the others, his personal identity in turn not quite connecting to the identity of place. Only such a profoundly alienated person could go on to be elected President of the United States and still believe deep in his soul that everyone hated him. People who are born in Los Angeles are different from those who come to it, because they're the only ones who have not chosen to be there; almost no one just winds up in Los Angeles. They choose to come to Los Angeles because their dreams and appetites are at once so huge and vague that it is the only destination that makes sense, since it is the city that, above all others, promises to provide them with what they want or, in case they don't know what they want, show them. It's only later people realize that, like New York, L.A. is run by people for whom denying other people their dreams is fun.

It was probably fitting, but cruel nonetheless, that Nixon would eventually be displaced at the center of American political life by another Angeleno, one of the very actor pals Mike drank bourbon with at Boardner's tavern on a little Hollywood sidestreet called Cherokee, who escaped to Los Angeles in the Thirties not long before Nixon, courtesy of the war, escaped from it. If the two most influential American Presidents of the last thirty years—the one who was born there and the one who came there—both defined their dreams in relation to Los Angeles, it was in entirely different ways; born on the edge of America in Yorba Linda, Nixon always seemed to yearn for America's heart, which he bitterly surmised was not to be found in his hometown, while Ronald Reagan, growing up in America's heartland, rushed to Los Angeles assuming that the real essence of the country was to be found in its fingertips. Reagan's political ascent began just as Nixon's career was between death and resurrection, at a time when Los Angeles was lurching from a self-image of Dreamland to one of Utopia, which wasn't the same thing. Dreamland was the movies, where the American subconscious translated itself into mass consciousness and together we could embrace or repress our dreams as a people. In the Depression of the Thirties and the war of the Forties, when the politics of the times insisted these were crises we shouldn't have to face alone, part of the magic of the movies was their reassurance that we didn't have to face our dreams alone either.

By the Sixties, though, Dreamland had succeeded in rendering our dreams so harmless they didn't have resonance for us anymore. The movies that were coming out of what was left of the old studio system—as opposed to filmmakers working in New York and London and Rome—were outdated even before they were made; musicals won a lot of Academy Awards in the Sixties. The new Utopian Los Angeles was created by aerospace, real estate and rock and roll, with the implicit suggestion that the subconscious was no longer something we had to get a grip on but something to be succumbed to. The old imagination was dead and the new imagination—born of the nuclear star that, twenty years before, was first sighted east of L.A. in New Mexico and then novaed west of L.A. over Japan—was without limits. Utopian L.A. gave back to the individual the individuality of the dark, along with the individuality of his pleasures, and offered a blank slate on which he could write his own soul, assuming he knew the vocabulary of the soul.

Nixon never knew the vocabulary of the soul. Rather he knew the vocabulary of America, and while he never had any use for Dreamland, and perhaps shared more with Utopian Los Angeles than his repression and rage would allow him to acknowledge, he understood how the rest of the United States was repulsed by what the new Los Angeles represented. So he became the candidate of American revulsion. He wasn't driving the streets of L.A. looking for Mike anymore. Coveting his missing conjoined twin's physical power and brutish toughness, and at the same time believing too much in his own weakness, he aspired to some political equivalent of that brutishness and relentlessness, and to a large extent achieved it. Rejected by California in the 1962 gubernatorial race, Nixon rejected L.A. while absorbing its lessons. The young public relations whizzes he recruited out of the University of Southern California not only taught him about the ephemeral nature of modern reality and how it could be manipulated, but became his own little private army of Mike Hammers, on the campaign trail and later in the White House. Later, of course, he was undone by Mike, both the Mike for whom he had an army of surrogates and the Mike to whom he gave his own political expression; if he didn't blow up the world in a blinding flash of civilization's insanity, he blew up his own life—and, as seen in *Nixon*, in the sharded lights and colors of the detonation were a thousand visions of what that life had been or might have been, at least at the point that the two might still be distinguished in the daze of his despair.

For Reagan, of course, the soundstages and back lots and publicity machines of Hollywood taught him about the ephemeral nature not of modern reality but modern memory, and how memory could be the agent not of the past but the future. If Los Angeles imparted to Nixon a radical vision of truth, and a conviction that it could be anything one chose to make it, it imparted to Reagan a radical vision of nostalgia, and a conviction that it could be anything one chose to remember. For Reagan the truth was rude, a source of cynicism. For Nixon nostalgia was pain, a function of madness. Opposite expressions of the Los Angeles psychosis, Nixon was *Kiss Me Deadly* and Reagan was *Singin' in the Rain*, Nixon was the Doors and Reagan was Jan and Dean. The paradox was that Los Angeles eventually led them, by their radically different routes, to the same place politically—although given the nature of the times, perhaps it was not so paradoxical. In the years that Nixon's career was peaking and Reagan's was beginning, when L.A.'s schizophrenia between Dreamland and Utopia was becoming socially manifest, the United States, which was always a place, went to war with America, which was always an idea, and the dividing line between the two seemed to run right down Sunset Boulevard, hippies to the north and police to the south, film executives at the east end and rocket scientists at the west. For Reagan this shift of the ground beneath his feet may have been a betrayal.

For Nixon it was just one more example, in case you really needed it, of what the world would do to you if it got the chance. As candidates of revulsion, their greatest triumph in the manipulation of truth and memory was how they portrayed themselves as the champions of liberty and individualism when what they really loved was authority and conformity. By 1968, of course, Utopia was all broken glass and plumes of smoke. Utopia's presidential candidate was assassinated in Los Angeles at the Ambassador Hotel, where the Coconut Grove once hosted the Oscars and Ronald Reagan danced with all the starlets Nixon would have despised because, reasonably, he assumed their pleasures were beyond his reach.

For those of us growing up in the nuclear-noir era, Richard Nixon was our most reliable point of political reference. His rise accompanied our childhood and his disgrace our coming of age; that disgrace seemed utterly peculiar not only to him but, somehow, to us as well. When he was buried in 1994 hail fell in Los Angeles, a blitzkrieg of ice hitting the ground just about the time Nixon's coffin did, en route from New York; so the meteorology of the man's death was as surreal as the funeral's lionization of him, which itself was as surreal as the way that, in life, he was demonized. The occasion of the funeral provided Bob Dole the stage for his most conspicuous outburst of vulnerability. Once part of one's life has become mangled and shattered, the rest becomes hard and untouchable except for that place where, with the slightest touch, the shell falls to pieces: Bob Dole wanted to be Mike Hammer too, once, and as a result became a man for whom life was such a secret that, by all accounts, even his wife could not be called a complete confidante. This, harsh as it is to say, had the effect of making his public weeping nearly grotesque, a violation by the rest of us. One recalls George Bush twisting uncomfortably in his chair to Dole's choked valediction to the defeated President at a Republican farewell dinner following the 1992 election—or maybe that was just Bush's conscience getting to him, after the way he had slandered Dole in the Republican race four years earlier. At Nixon's funeral, after crying for the departed President during his tribute to him, Dole nearly broke down yet again during a television interview with columnist

dread, for which there was no hard math. The two great idées fixes of New Hampshire politics had always been budgets and taxes, and at the outset of the '96 primary it wasn't much different; against the background of the ongoing debate in Washington over how to balance the national budget, New Hampshire was similarly galvanized. Out in force at Dole's St. Anselm speech was the Concord Coalition, a group committed to balancing the budget while trying to remain nonpartisan in the process. Relatively enthusiastic about Congress' new young zealous Republican freshmen, the Coalition nonetheless bluntly dismissed one of the centerpieces of the GOP budget plan—a huge tax cut that predominantly benefited the wealthy—while also disparaging a proposed $500-per-child tax deduction for families. "The irony, of course," one of the Coalition's organizers told me as we waited for Dole, "is that the child who earns his parents $500 will wind up paying for the interest on the debt that's created by that tax cut."

Soon, though, this new budget discipline provoked an identity crisis among state Republicans. Bob Dole had been a balanced-budget champion going back to the early days of the Reagan presidency, but out of deference to political reality and the Republican taxophobes elected to Newt Gingrich's Congress in 1994, he had held the balanced budget dream at arm's length until Governor Merrill, another budget hawk, endorsed him and came onboard the campaign. Energetic, articulate, charismatic, Merrill was neither unreasonable nor even particularly unseemly in assuming that Dole might be his ticket to a career in national politics, perhaps as chief of staff to the President if Dole made it to the White House, perhaps as a future contender himself if Dole didn't. This left the tax issue to Steve Forbes, in a state even more pathologically taxophobic than Newt Gingrich's Congress. State Republicans were thus being compelled to choose between two conservative, congenital tendencies. In the late weeks of December Forbes was catching on in New Hampshire even as there was much speculation Buchanan had peaked, and since Forbes wasn't accepting federal matching funds for his campaign, he was free to spend as much of his own money as he wanted. Forbes bumper stickers were everywhere, and like electronic locusts Forbes radio ads and TV ads filled the air, attacking Dole as though he had invented the Internal Revenue Service. Accused of trying to buy the election, Forbes offered the peculiar response that while he might not be above such a bribe himself, the public was: "The American people are not for sale" was the frosty riposte, though I don't remember anyone asking me my price, and you probably don't either.

Forbes' popularity was always curious, based as it was on the idea of imposing a flat national income tax of seventeen percent while leveling personal deductions like a thresher. It was the simplicity of this many found irresistible, because once you added up the math, the Forbes plan paid off big mainly for people such as Steve Forbes. That a state of financially modest people would embrace a rich man for a tax plan that benefited other rich men at their own expense could probably be deciphered only in that twisted part of the American soul that considers wealth righteous and modest means immoral. Asked what real-life experience he had that prepared him to understand let alone lead the nation, the best answer Forbes could come up with was that his children had given him "a few gray hairs at night," a citation millions of parents struggling without Forbes' resources may have found less than heart-wrenching. Still, as the campaign wore on Forbes made such a forceful argument—he was more impressive in person than on television—that one had to allow for the possibility he actually believed in it; he considered the present tax code corrosive to the soul of America, "complex and corrupt and incomprehensible," the seed of American despair in what should otherwise be a time of American hope.

The persuasive stump speech aside, though, Forbes was a constipated presence on the campaign trail. It was hard to know how much fun he was really having; he was obviously shy with people, and often left events as quickly as possible. As with Dole or Nixon, and unlike Clinton or Reagan, his whole manner raised the question of why such men go into politics when everything about their bearing and temperament suggests the experience for them is something to be endured. If one could learn a lot by the hand language of these candidates—the strained garrulousness of Dole's thumbs-up, for instance, or, as the *Rolling Stone* photographer pointed out to me, the way Buchanan clenched his hands together when he talked, like a fanatic priest locked in a particularly maniacal prayer—then what was interesting about the way Forbes slashed at the air when he spoke was that his slashing gestures were made beneath the podium, out of sight. I just happened to notice because I was standing off to the side for one of his lunchtime talks to a bunch of business lawyers in the atrium of a Manchester law building. It was as though the force of his conviction was something to be obscured and hidden, a secret passion, like renting pornographic videos.

Whether it was a secret from us or from himself, who knew? When I asked what his strategy was for winning the nomination should he win New Hampshire, the best answer he could give was that he would "take the campaign to Arizona," where a contest was scheduled for the week after New Hampshire. In short, he never really had a national strategy; moreover his situation was a potential conundrum, because his whole campaign was based on a single issue. Because he was hitting that single issue so effectively, he did well for a while, but then the better he did and the more seriously he became taken as a candidate, the more scrutiny the issue invited, until more people than not suspected it wasn't all that great an idea after all. And of course if the issue had survived the attention, and Forbes had won not only New Hampshire but Arizona, per his grand plan, he eventually would have had to speak to all the other issues—at which point his campaign would have lost its pure and highly focused appeal. This was exactly what happened to the antiwar candidacy of George McGovern twenty-five years before. So it was loony to think Forbes could ever win the Republican nomination, except for the fact that McGovern had won the Democratic nomination, although Republicans were never *that* loony, and if one wanted to pursue it seriously, the analogy probably applied more to Buchanan, whose candidacy had more of the same kind of visceral appeal of McGovern's. Thinking practically, the only scenario that came close to making sense for Forbes was a strong, scary second-place showing in New Hampshire that set him up for a place on Dole's ticket or cabinet. Of course, there was always the most confounding of speculations too: that Forbes was actually running just to make a point, expending far more money in the effort than even a new tax code, revised generously in his favor, could afford him.

40

I've made a mistake, I thought to myself a couple of nights before the New Hampshire vote. Driving twenty-five miles through a harrowing blizzard to cover a Buchanan appearance outside Manchester at a Christian Coalition rally, I was sure I would arrive to an empty banquet room, assuming I made it there at all. Instead the place was packed, lousy with more than forty cameras and media outnumbering three to one the Christians, who sat stonily awaiting the program's commencement while reporters stuck mikes in their faces and clicked pictures.

The next night three or four hundred reporters jammed together into a sweltering garage-turned-bunker to watch the last, lunatic debate of the New Hampshire campaign, during which snarling Republicans called each other liars, crooks, extremists, opportunists and socialists, and passed around baby pictures and photos of the family dog. Great attention was paid by the reporters at the outset, but within twenty minutes many were bored, and within thirty minutes, even though nine or ten television monitors blared overhead, the racket from all the idle chatter grew so loud the debate became impossible to hear. "Shut up!" someone would yell, at which point the talk subsided for about three minutes before growing again, when the process repeated itself. Afterward candidates and spinners descended on the pressroom, cameras blocking off each interviewee from everyone else; thwarted, the print press interviewed one another. Even I was interviewed, by a young woman from a New York paper. That was when I knew we were in trouble. Whisper an opinion in the ear of the reporter to your right and forty-five minutes later someone on your left was whispering it back in your ear—except it wasn't quite the same anymore, in the process having circled the room and gone through Robert Novak and Paul Gigot and Joe Klein and Al Hunt in his spiffy turquoise shirt *and* his spiffy purple ski jacket. "Dole held his own," I pronounced grandly, "and in these things, a tie goes to the front-runner."

Can you imagine actually saying such nonsense in public? "Dole held his own," a writer from San Francisco assured me not long after, this pearl of wisdom having made the rounds, "but in these things, a tie goes to the challenger," meaning Buchanan. By the time the larva of opinion had changed to a butterfly, it was the butterfly that took flight, even if the larva was a different insect altogether. You had to be an idiot to suggest, for instance, that when Buchanan defended one of his campaign chairmen against charges of being a white supremacist, even though no one else in the debate had brought it up, it might have been a shrewd move, since it was on everyone's mind anyway and reinforced Buchanan's image as a loyal straight-shooter; the ranks of opinion-makers quickly closed around the conclusion that it was a bad, baffling, perhaps fatal mistake. The day after the debate, however, the polls had Buchanan running even with or ahead of Dole, white supremacists or no. Even more interesting, a plurality of voters, not as privy to the press' bedlam of wisdom and not as determined in their indifference to those candidates with no chance of winning anything, thought wildman Alan Keyes had won, getting off the evening's most devastating indictment: "Does what they say," he asked witheringly of his fellow candidates, "represent their hearts, or their knowledge or experience? Who knows?"

Well, exactly. And if, as Keyes argued, the candidates could not know what was in their own hearts by reading the polls, the press could not know what was in the heart of New Hampshire, either. The only constant in the polls was that there were so many people who intended to vote but hadn't yet made up their minds that there wasn't much point to reading any of the other numbers. Given a void of Meaning, and a distinctly nonlinear storyline, the media couldn't take chances; and in the last hours before the final showdown, at both a Forbes event and then an Alexander event on Main Street in Nashua, I was struck by how the level of media panic was exactly the same at both, though one campaign was considered to be on the wane while the other was on the rise. The Forbes moment took place in Martha's Exchange, a local brewery and coffeehouse. The bus pulled up and unloaded the candidate and his daughter, who were immediately overwhelmed in the short six-foot walk from the bus to the restaurant by a frightening arsenal of cameras. The first time I had seen Forbes in December I had been one of exactly two reporters, the other a woman who worked for ABC and had been assigned to Forbes in what then seemed a thankless gig; now, standing inside Martha's, I looked over to see her next to me. In the seven weeks since, her man had lived an entire political lifetime. "I'm wondering if it's over," she said, and I wasn't sure if she said it regretfully or with relief.

At this moment it certainly didn't look over, as Forbes moved into Martha's. The press took over the restaurant as a base of operations, camping out at the tables and jostling the customers and every once in a while remembering the good manners to say, "Sorry," or "Excuse me." Given free-wielding, wildly swinging cameramen who yelled at civilians with signs for caring about politics as a conviction rather than a vocation, the encroaching pandemonium of Forbes' walk through the aisles of the restaurant was life-threatening; and I quickly decided I wasn't conscientious enough to die for *Rolling Stone*. I kept heading for whatever place everyone else wasn't. The problem was that Forbes, whose stricken smile told you everything you needed to know about how much less fun this had all become, had the same idea; he kept heading for daylight too, which is to say toward me. For a while Steve Forbes chased me around Martha's as the cameras chased him, until, cornered like a rat, I finally had an ABC camera in one ear and Forbes snarling in the other. "Constipated presence, huh?" I could have sworn I heard him whisper. Finally he moved on to the candy counter. "Is he buying something?" one reporter shouted. "He better be," muttered the woman behind the cash register.

The Alexander episode wasn't really any less insane, just not in as close quarters. In bitter morning cold Alexander disembarked his campaign bus at Library Hill, in the white winter shadow of a Civil War statue that rather pointedly called it not the Civil War but "the rebellion." From there he walked the length of Main Street to still another statue—actually, a bust—of John Kennedy outside the Nashua town hall, where Kennedy had begun his campaign for the presidency in 1960. An undeniably pleasant man, Alexander was politically like Dole while remaining the Undole, personally like Clinton while remaining the Unclinton, even as he came precariously close to being the Unlamar, or the Unlamar!, as his signs would have it. He had spent the week trying to fill in the details of something that might resemble a political identity, with the surprising help of staunch conservatives like William Bennett and Robert Novak, who were suddenly talking up Alexander and appeared this morning for the walk-along. Novak was a veteran columnist of nearly four decades, rabidly conservative over the last two, and the more notorious half of a team called Evans and Novak or, as they had long been referred to by other reporters, Errors and No Facts.

Follow a politician around for any length of time at all and you quickly notice the things he's good at. Alexander was good with children. He talked to all of them he met, asking if he or she had ever seen so many cameras. "I don't like them," one little five-year-old answered, wise enough beyond her years to intuitively understand that any one of the cameramen would have happily trampled her little body for a three-second shot. Alexander did like the cameras. No calculus presently known could possibly calculate the number of trampled children winning the New Hampshire Primary was worth, but it was likely to be at least a few; and over and over Alexander reminded us that six months before, when his poll numbers were disappearing into nothingness, he had walked this same street and not a single camera followed. Now coming on a strong third in the polls and widely identified by the press as the campaign "with momentum," though on exactly what basis no one could say, there were at least a dozen cameramen encircling him. The TV cameramen had a hard job. They didn't have as many opportunities as a writer to get what they needed, and if they missed a great shot that showed up on someone else's broadcast, they were going to have to answer for it. But as with the rampage through Martha's Exchange with Steve Forbes, they took this fact of life as a license for ruthlessness and perhaps decapitation by camera of whomever was standing next to them, though it might be nice if that person were not the next President of the United States.

Along the way up Main Street, passing the old churches and historical buildings and Dunkin' Donuts, the mob of cameras and townspeople and high school kids bused in with Alexander signs was ambushed by a man in a Bullwinkle suit, who was protesting the Republicans' positions on the environment. Another man followed with a boom box that played a little environmental jingle to which the moose danced. Soon things got tense. The high school kids began chanting "Lamar '96!" to drown out the moose, and signs, cameras and moose antlers became entangled in an altercation. "Get the moose!" the Lamar kids were soon shouting. For the rest of the walk everyone kept their distance from one another, except reporters who were now interviewing the moose, and cameramen getting the moose on film. Alexander ducked into a barbershop, a flower shop, a music shop where he played piano, and even looked longingly, though it might have been from the cold, through the window of Martha's Exchange. Inside a waitress shuddered visibly in relief when the candidate moved on. At the town hall Alexander dodged questions that had just begun to emerge over the previous few days about a stock deal in the early Eighties that netted him half a million dollars on a one dollar investment. ("When he says 'ABC, Alexander Beats Clinton,'" Forbes had cracked during the debate, "he means Hillary, not Bill.") Then he got back on board a bus heading for a rally at a junior high school. As he left, the moose danced one last dance.

Primary Eve I was hanging out in a hotel lobby having a drink when I got into a conversation with an older gentleman who looked like he had seen more than a couple of New Hampshire primaries. He turned out to be Murray Kempton, a legend among political columnists; I say I had a conversation with him when what I actually mean is that I provided an audience for a half-inspired, half-crackpot tour de force as he held forth on the last fifty years of American politics, including the dirtiest campaign he had ever seen (1952), the best candidate he had ever seen (Ronald Reagan), how Lamar Alexander had a complexion "imported from Madame Tussaud's," and how—like

Humphrey Bogart—Bob Dole looked better in black and white. He even got in an epitaph for Phil Gramm: "John Kennedy," he said, "could make charm look like an absolute virtue, while Gramm makes lack of charm look like an absolute vice." Though his politics had been unabashedly leftist his whole life, his hatred of Clinton was palpable and his admiration of Dole almost as much so: he now dreaded, from the standpoint of its political cost, what he called Dole's "lapse into common sense," remembering that in the 1988 New Hampshire Primary debate someone had asked the senator how to get the Russians out of Afghanistan and Dole had replied, "Send them a road map." It was an answer that had clearly endeared Dole to Kempton, and as one longed for the return of that Dole of yore, though it was now far too late, one also had to remember that, after all, Dole lost in 1988. This time, of course, at least in the case of New Hampshire, prefabricated political bankruptcy would serve him no better than common sense did then. I asked Kempton just exactly how many New Hampshire primaries he had covered, and I don't know if he didn't hear me or just avoided the question, but the answer was pretty obvious anyway: all of them. "This is my last," he said bluntly, and I could imagine that one didn't need to be seventy-eight years old to feel that way.

41

I like the man, Rob was telling me. An engineer who had voted for Buchanan against George Bush in the 1992 New Hampshire Primary, Rob had come to the Christian Coalition rally to check out Buchanan again. "I like almost everything he says, everything he stands for. I think he's obviously a man of integrity. But I look at him and I get the feeling, You're raw meat." What bothered him about the recent revelations concerning white supremacists in Buchanan's campaign wasn't the substance of the charges but that they made the candidate vulnerable to guys like me. "The media, no offense, will kill him." Now Rob wasn't sure who to vote for. He ruled out Dole: "Too willing to compromise." He seemed tepid about Alexander, but he certainly was looking for someone who could beat Clinton. "I'd vote for *you* against Clinton," he said, laughing.

"You'd be better off with Clinton," I warned him.

In the final hours before the vote the controlled, tightly wound campaign that took relaxed breathers in the afternoon finally popped a spring, and candidates were suddenly everywhere, around the clock. Like the others, Alexander made a show of going to church on Sunday in Bedford, then headed for Amoskeag Falls, Derry, where he appeared with Senator Fred Thompson from his own state of Tennessee, then Exeter, the seacoast town of Portsmouth, and Manchester. Buchanan was in Portsmouth before heading to Bedford to get good and skewered—most effectively by conservative columnist George Will—on *This Week with David Brinkley*, then to Manchester, then back to Bedford to appear live on *Good Morning, America*, then back to Manchester for a CNN appearance, then to greet workers at a lumber mill in Center Barnstead. Dole never did expose himself to the print media; by the weekend it was clear he had every intention of limiting his appearances to photo opportunities in snowplows and dogsled races, away from anyone who could ask him any pestering questions, like why he thought being President was a good idea, for instance. When, on the eve of the primary, he expressed shock that people were feeling the sort of economic desperation that Buchanan had spoken to so effectively, he demonstrated not only that he could never be a Candidate of Ramification, but that he wouldn't know a ramification if it came up and shook his hand. Now the best he could do was resurrect Phil Gramm, whose newest incarnation was as a paragon of Republican tolerance, appearing in the state briefly to denounce racism and endorse Dole in a last vengeful blast at Buchanan.

By the night of February 20, when the Ramification Candidate won over the Resignation Candidate and the Remaindered Candidate, even the wise men and women of the Wayfarer were not going to find much meaning in it, except the obvious, which was that in the Republican universe the forces of entropy were having their way with the forces of gravity. Degenerating into complete chaos and confusion, the New Hampshire Primary of 1996 had become the Pompidou Center of presidential campaigns, a monument to itself turned inside out, with all the inner gears and machinery transformed into their own artifice. Still, if in the early days of 1996 New Hampshire was a studio lot with facades for houses, no one told the voters; they were under the distinct impression this was a real election that involved the real concerns of a real America. When all was said and done, they did their job. After all, we wouldn't have wanted them to resolve things even if they could. Rather they cast the race for the Republican nomination in terms the rest of the country would have to sort out, between three distinctly different archetypes; and when you are the Candidate of Ramification who has set the terms of the debate, you must take responsibility for the rejection of your ramifications as well as the acceptance. In the shadow of the Oklahoma City bombing, three-quarters of New Hampshire voters may not have been as willing as the candidate to dismiss white supremacist confidantes as a trifle. "I voted for Dole," one woman told me, "because if Buchanan wins, I'm going to have to leave the state."

The night of the primary, the shadowy nature of my recent existence caught up with me. The Great Republican Freeze-Out that had begun in Washington and followed me to Orlando had now tracked me down in New Hampshire, one hotel room heater after another mysteriously going on the fritz; within the bleak claustrophobia of winter and my room's ever-closing walls, missing Viv whom I had not seen in weeks, and with the rest of the media already packing up for Arizona and South Carolina, I was bedbound with a fever of a hundred and three, and a throat so sore that at night it ripped my dreams down the middle. I plugged my laptop into the phone jack and zapped my report on the primary to the magazine in New York, and then in a blur of antibiotics plucked at the carrion of the now dead vote like a crow on garbage. Having flatly predicted in print in December that Patrick Buchanan would win the primary, over the course of the evening I received calls of congratulations from friends and colleagues far and wide. None, though, from *Rolling Stone*.

42

It had clearly become impossible by now. There were no pretenses anymore about what was the best way to cover the campaign or what the story called for, let alone what some conception of the truth called for; by now it was all about what would satisfy Jann, a distinctly inane consideration given that Jann himself didn't know what he thought from minute to minute. The day after the primary, still too sick to move from my hotel, I got a call from my editor telling me the piece I had filed was not what Wenner was expecting. He was expecting a piece about the media, and I needed to take out all that extraneous stuff about Phil Gramm and the actual election and include, I was advised, more gossip about the media and maybe some all-round ridicule for good measure.

There was no doubt in my mind that the media deserved all-round ridicule and worse. The problem was that however ridiculous the media was, most of the writers and reporters I had met in New Hampshire were pros who at least knew what they were doing, in sharp contrast to amateurs who had no idea whatsoever what they were doing—me, say. Reporters had been pleasant and helpful to me when, out of desperation, I had turned to those I was now being encouraged to trash. More than this, it seemed to me my piece might want to acknowledge that a *primary* had taken place, in which much energy and thought and passion and hope had been invested by ordinary people who cared about their country and their children and didn't give a damn who wrote *Primary Colors*. "After all," *Newsweek*'s Jonathan Alter told me, "you're the one who's here reporting the story, not your editors in New York," but that was the quandary in a nutshell: I was a novelist who had been hired to cover the campaign as a novelist and was then expected to cover it like a reporter, whereupon the editorial decisions it was my job to make as a reporter—or even, for that matter, as a novelist—were being made in New York not on the basis of the criteria by which reporters and editors usually try to make such decisions but rather by trying to second-guess a man so pathologically capricious as to be unsecond-guessable. Two days after the primary, in a toxic sweat, I finally got myself on an airplane to New York, where Viv was meeting with a local gallery to set up a one-woman show of her sculptures. I was flat on the bed in Viv's hotel room when my editor called with the news that Wenner had killed my New Hampshire piece, and I was flat on the same bed five days later when she called again with the news, untethered as usual to any stated reason—though it would be dishonest of me to pretend one was really necessary—that I had been fired.

43

So Viv and I ran for the hills. Returning to L.A. I sat staring out the window at the winding road that led up to our house in the canyon, guessing at the identity of headlights. The road twisted and circled back on itself so much that a man walking on it, destined to be hit by a car, could hear the sound of his own demise five minutes before it arrived. Viv continued creating her massive steel mandalas of stained-glass butterfly windows; if she felt a little badly chopping up the wings of butterflies, she kept trying to remind herself that it was not as though she had killed them, after all—they were already dead, and now she only hoped that just as beautiful butterflies metamorphose from something unbeautiful, she was providing a new metamorphosis, and a beautiful new incarnation. In complicity the butterflies and moths hurled themselves against the house through March and into April.

Soon, however, they stopped, either their homage or protest exhausted. When the butterflies stopped the flies and scorpions and mosquitoes came with the heat, filling the house as fast as we could kill them. From room to room we prowled, smashing mosquitoes until all the white walls of the house became speckled with blood. We hung one butterfly window after another over the carnage. Out walking one night I realized the small black forms fluttering around me were not birds but bats, and when Viv drove home from the city, owls swooped into the stream of her headlights and flew on ahead, so as to lead her down into the deep wild heart of the canyon. Coyotes howled all the way up the pass, the remains of half-devoured cats revealed in the following light of dawn. In the road snakes were crushed into the asphalt. Fleeing the city for the canyon we had traded one kind of savagery for another, as well as for whatever it said about the human species' self-disgust that the savagery of nature seemed more pure than the savagery of men.

From winter to spring I moved in a depression that alarmed friends and family, and which I pretentiously liked to believe approximated the mood of the presidential campaign. While I might have lucked into my Pat Buchanan prediction, I was wrong about Dole, having anticipated that his defeat in New Hampshire would be the end for him; because all the primaries were jammed together into one month, I had figured that just as Dole was the only one who could quickly cash in on a New Hampshire victory, by the same token he would fatally hemorrhage from such a deep and early cut, without time for the wound to cauterize. He would not have the chance to regain his footing as Walter Mondale had in 1984—another prohibitive, party-establishment front-runner derailed by guerrilla Gary Hart, and in such political peril after New Hampshire that when he went on to win a mere two primaries against an onslaught of Hart victories in that year's Super Tuesday, it was deemed by the press a resurrection. Similarly, the press would resurrect Bob Dole through its own bumbling. The night of the Arizona primary the networks all declared Dole finishing a poor third; when the final vote was in and Dole had run a middling second, trailing Forbes but beating Buchanan, the press anointed Dole's "comeback."

For Dole's part, as all around were losing their heads he was keeping his. In the disarray of his New Hampshire defeat, meeting Barry Goldwater at the Republican patriarch's desert home, Dole had enough humor to smile, albeit painfully, when the old coot laughed, "You know, Bob, we're the liberals now"—a pretty succinct summation of how far right the Republican Party had moved in the last thirty years, but about the last thing Dole needed said about him in Arizona. That Goddamned Goldwater, answered the wince on Dole's face, he never could keep his mouth from saying whatever true thing entered his head. In the meantime Steve Forbes was trying to eke out as much honor as thirty million bucks could buy, and Lamar Alexander's protestations that he was a winner while Dole was a loser couldn't help sounding a little preposterous when he kept losing to Dole in one race after another. Since we determine the seriousness of our presidential candidates not by what they say but what they win, Alan Keyes was never taken seriously by anyone but himself, except maybe one ex-*Rolling Stone* writer who couldn't keep his job. Keyes kept trying to storm various debates throughout the southern primaries where he was being excluded, actually getting himself arrested at one; he even went on a hunger strike. On TV Pat Buchanan grew inordinately fond of wearing a black cowboy hat and running around waving a rifle over his head, vaguely recalling old news footage of Vanessa Redgrave dancing with Arab terrorists twenty years earlier. If it was the campaign's most absurd bit of theater, it was also the most crucial, trivializing his candidacy of ramifications and coming at a moment when Buchanan had the momentum and people might have actually looked at him for a fleeting moment in terms of being a President. In this particular case the usually whacked-out Bay Buchanan was the more circumspect, advising Pat to calm down. But Pat was having too much fun, and you almost had to give him credit for it.

44

At the end of April I was invited to be part of an afternoon panel at UCLA called "Los Angeles: Dream City or Doom City," moderated by Mike Davis, who had written the acclaimed book on L.A., *City of Quartz*. The premise was presented as a contradiction, a choice; I offered the possibility that it was not a contradiction, that just as we have an instinct for survival, we have an impulse for self-obliteration, and Los Angeles is the urban American expression of that impulse. In the same way that self-obliteration is the other side of transcendence, it was not a matter so much of dream *or* doom as dream *of* doom: we believed the world was going to end in Los Angeles because we wanted it to. Our narcissism was such that we found it galling to think they might go end the world somewhere else. Given the pain and destruction of the 1992 riots, the businesses destroyed and the homes ravaged and the people hurt, it seemed perverse if not obscene to recall the giddiness of it, that exhilarating feeling that no one was in charge; even the presidential candidates obliged to traipse across the battleground that spring—Bush and Clinton and Jerry Brown—had this look on their faces of having stared into the void, since if there was one thing that freaked out a politician of almost any persuasion, it was sheer anarchy. If one was honest with himself for a single moment, he had to admit such a look was almost worth all of it.

Los Angeles has more a psychic identity than a civic one. It is a city where people share a common subconsciousness rather than a common consciousness, reflecting in the process America not as it is but would be. Seized by the same impulse that sends people from all over the world flocking to America, Americans from all over the country have flocked to Los Angeles, where nothing is rooted and therefore nothing is bound, the territory tending less to a cohesive landscape than to zones, patches and cul-de-sacs of the mind. In the disruption and upheaval of the Nineties, amid the fires and the verdicts and the fault lines, the city divided between those who fought to preserve it as a city, and those who knew it was over as a city, which didn't just beg the question of what was next but supplied its own answer, though one that couldn't be articulated. The name of this movie was *Death on the Nihil*.

No one was ever supposed to live in L.A. It's a desert. In John Fante's 1939 novel *Ask the Dust*, a young writer named Arturo Bandini, who lives in a downtown flophouse, describes the grit of the Mojave Desert in his furniture, his clothes, the sheets of his bed and the milk he steals; the red light that flashes on and off outside his hotel is blue through the silt of the air, and the area's largest natural reserve of water is a poisoned, undrinkable lake called the Pacific Ocean. If people have been drawn to Los Angeles by the bloody miasmic spectacle of the sun setting into that ocean, resembling as it does the end of the world, the fact is that no one ever really meant for there to be a city at the end of the world. And if the original dream of Los Angeles was Jeffersonian or even Marxian, if some of the original dreamers who settled the place were indeed political outcasts and religious heretics and prophetic cranks who might have actually given Jefferson or Marx a passing thought, those who made L.A. really alive had neither the patience nor the discipline to think of it in terms of any philosopher other than L. Frank Baum, who packed up his New York family in 1910 after writing more than a dozen Oz books and made a beeline for L.A., where he built and lived in a house called Ozcot.

Money was never the true dream of Los Angeles. Rather the dream was, and remains, that doomed, self-obliterating transcendence. The most pedestrian sort of transcendence, to be sure, and one that becomes more vulgar and self-obsessed as time passes, but to the earliest dreamers—the Spanish padres who took the terrain away from the Indians to establish a "village of angels"—Jesus was only L.A.'s first matinee idol, and every aspiring star who's come since has been looking for his or her own version of the afterlife. Understanding both the allure and chicanery of a transcendent city, because in Oz, after all, he had created one, Frank Baum was the first great L.A. novelist no less so because he never lived in L.A. at all, at least not until the end; he had to create an L.A. of the mind before he understood it was Los Angeles he had created, and that it was L.A. where he belonged, after an America of the senses had become too tarnished for anyone to believe anymore in an America of the mind—in Twain's America on the green boulevard of the Mississippi River, in Melville's America on the blue plains of the sea, in Poe's America in the red ravine of the family torture-chamber just down the hall. From Baum on down through the Twentieth Century stretches the lineage of L.A. novelists writing from the other side of the American Mirror, the immigrant Fante and the curmudgeon Chandler and the darkest of all, James M. Cain, whose name must have suited him just fine, to that child of Baum's vision at the other end, Philip K. Dick. That Dick despised L.A. and inhabited it sporadically only made him as ur-L.A. as Baum was for hardly ever having been here, but it also helped that the two great themes of his work were the two great themes of Los Angeles, the city at the end of the American Millennium. Those themes concerned the true nature of reality and the true nature of humanity, what it means to be real and what it means to be human, understanding that just on the other side of reality and just on the other side of humanity were eternity and God—in other words, the very transcendence pursued by prophets and crackpots alike, in a town full of people who would happily die in the next five minutes if it would only make them legends.

45

But then he was no less the quintessential Californian, and no less the quintessential American literary nomad of the last half of the Twentieth Century, for the ludicrous details of his life: committed to psychotherapy for agoraphobia as a teenager, married five times, suffering the real or imagined harassments of the Internal Revenue Service and the Federal Bureau of Investigation, experiencing various religious epiphanies, ingesting a wide array of drugs and treated for schizophrenia and paranoia, convinced the local Muzak radio station was conspiring to drive him crazy, attempting suicide on occasions both halfhearted and truly desperate, harboring longstanding and of course unfulfilled sexual obsessions with Linda Ronstadt and Victoria Principal, and writing more than forty novels between 1955 and his death in 1982. Most of these novels were paperbacks. Virtually all, on first publication, were commercial failures; at least eight weren't published until after he was dead. Virtually all, with rare exception, were critical failures as well, dismissed by the literary establishment—when it didn't ignore them altogether—as conceptually half-baked pulp, narratively sloppy, written with a haste to set teeth on edge. Not one can probably be called a Great Novel, assuming a Great Novel presents a complete, multileveled, self-contained worldview that sums up all its author's grand themes and concerns.

Philip Kindred Dick was a genuine visionary, however, his dozen or so best novels constituting as significant a body of work as that of any North American writer since World War II. In the Nineties, after years when most of his work was out of print, many of the novels were reissued, including some that had never been published in America in the first place. To say that with the Nineties his time as a novelist arrived begged a certain irony, apart from the matter of his already having been gone awhile; in Philip Dick's temporal universe he had not been gone at all, nor had he necessarily even been here yet. He might well be someone we remember who is yet to happen. In Dick's universe his books were published a long time ago, perhaps around the time of the printing press, which was invented before the wheel but after the telephone-answering machine. "Suppose . . . time is round," Dick wrote in 1977, "like the earth. You sail west to reach India. They laugh at you, but finally there's India in front, not behind. In time—maybe the Crucifixion lies ahead of us as we all sail along, thinking it's back east. The First and Second Coming of Christ [is] the same event . . . no wonder they were sure it'd happen, He'd be back." In the life he lived in his own universe, Dick was frantically rewriting books he had already written tomorrow, books we had already read—books we all remember and that serve, in turn, as memoirs of the Real Time we have dreamed together.

46

In Dick's *We Can Build You* (1972), a group of midwestern businessmen are constructing an Abraham Lincoln. It is a living, breathing, thinking Abraham Lincoln, different from the Lincoln of a hundred years before only by the wiring and transistors that take the place of veins and nervous system; in their audacity these businessmen suppose the second Lincoln will be the equal of the first. But when they finally turn on the Lincoln, he cries out in a wave of pain and torment, "a creature plopped into our time and our space, conscious of us and itself, its existence, here," and the businessmen realize their audacity has been modest, that this is not merely a Lincoln that's an equal of the first, it is the *same* Lincoln, awakened from the ether where an assassin's bullet sent him, and now returned in a moan of anguish to that cross-circuitry of memory and perception that defines humanity in Dick's work again and again.

Memory charts the time line that runs through that work. The recurring references to Proust are neither conceits nor pretensions; taken together—and taken together is about the only way they're really comprehensible—Dick's best novels form an American pop epic that might be called *Remembrance of Time Irreal*, to use a word Dick himself coined. Influenced in equal measure by Baum and Joyce, by Kafka and the magazines of his youth like *Amazing Stories* and *Unknown Worlds*, Dick was the great pulp irrealist of American fiction, whose imagination expressed itself in stories compassionate and blackly hilarious, sometimes quietly eccentric and other times wildly fabulous. Unlike most North American novelists of the last fifty years, that imagination wasn't rendered obsolete by the nuclear age but liberated by it, and liberated not just by its wonder but its abyss. Sometimes in Dick's work the abyss meets the wonder. In *Dr. Bloodmoney*, the abyss' residents snatch wonder from the sky when the survivors of a nuclear holocaust tune in every night, around the world, to the radio broadcast of an American astronaut who was launched on the morning the apocalypse began. Sometimes the wonder meets the abyss: in 1960's *The Man Whose Teeth Were All Exactly Alike*, a man carves a Neanderthal skull in his basement and buries it in the yard of the neighbor with whom he's been feuding. The resulting discovery, furor and exposure of fraud ripple across the interior topography of the neighborhood; in the novel's final scene the man sits watching his estranged pregnant wife and, irrationally terrified at the prospect of a deformed or retarded child, imagines carving his son's skull in the same way he made the Neanderthal—rendering destiny into artifact, subjecting past and future to the craft and talent of memory and desire.

As the American archaeologist of Twentieth-Century memory, Dick accepted that the past and present are a road always winding, like a figure 8, back to the same intersection of the present, over which memory hovers like a window in space. Only in the light of memory do the facts of history have meaning; in the shadows of amnesia they're worthless. The history of *The Man in the High Castle*

(1962) is one in which Germany and Japan have won the Second World War and carved up the United States accordingly: Chancellor Bormann (who succeeded Hitler) has just died in Berlin; Goebbels is the upset winner of a power struggle with Göring and Heydrich. Throughout the Pacific States of America, Japanese customs and values flourish: consultation of the *I Ching* is a familiar and daily ritual, and the literary rage is an underground novel about an alternate history in which America won the war. One day Tagomi, a Japanese businessman who lives in San Francisco, goes to the park to meditate upon something revolutionary—a small trinket that has no history or memory at all, which was made simply to exist and convey pleasure or peace by its own meaningless form. Holding the object between his fingers, profoundly unsettled by the very notion of an artifact shorn of meaning and existing only for its own sake, Tagomi literally commands it to reveal something. When it doesn't answer, he rises from the park bench and heads back to the city where he sees something that was never there before—the Embarcadero Freeway. When he goes into a diner, expecting a white patron to automatically give up his seat to him, and instead a man growls, "Watch it, Tojo," he knows everything has changed completely. Tagomi races back to the park and waits for the meaningless trinket to put things right. Space and time, he concludes, are creations of our own psyche.

In the most hallucinatory American movie of 1996, Jim Jarmusch's *Dead Man*, a Cleveland accountant named William Blake travels to a town called Machine, on a train crossing an America of an almost indeterminate era. Though it is, at first appearance, the America of the Wild West, as Blake continues his journey all the temporal fields that hold history together break down, and what is presumably some random year in the late 1800s might as well be 1999, when all the memories of America have collapsed into one another. It is as though the Millennium is the North Pole of history and, as we get closer and closer to it, the compasses of memory spin wildly, one incarnation of the country blurring into the next. As he descends into the vortex of the country, William Blake is mistaken by a nomadic Indian—if it is a mistake at all—to be William Blake the English poet, reincarnated as an American gunfighter who will "write his poetry in blood." By the time Blake has reached the far shores at America's end, time has slowed to a crawl, and the black-and-white landscape is, in truly Blakean fashion, part charnel house and part delirious paradise, bones and bodies piled against the lush trees beneath a sky the size of dreams. As Clint Eastwood's *Unforgiven* was the Western that William Faulkner might have written, *Dead Man* is the Western that Philip K. Dick might have written.

As such, it would only have been one of Dick's more serene conjectures. In his 1981 novel *Valis*, the conjoined twins of memory and history have become irrevocably severed, suggesting among other things that the last two thousand years never happened at all, and the aftermath of Jesus' execution was only a schism into which time tumbled; and that reality stopped in the middle of the Roman Empire and didn't start again until 1974, when America dumped Richard Nixon. It's become a lot harder, in the last few years of the Twentieth Century, to reinvent history in the fashion of a Philip K. Dick novel: the Twentieth Century keeps beating us to it, reinventing itself. The German and Japanese domination of America in *The Man in the High Castle* was more prophetic and ironic than even Dick anticipated, and behind the American era we have believed we're living in, another era now seems to have always lurked, waiting for that moment when it could slash the facade of our era down the middle, step through and show itself. Some of the most basic assumptions we were making about the Millennium as recently as the late Eighties—philosophical and political axioms of reality that had been true our whole lives, and which we expected to be true the rest of our lives—in fact have not survived the last ten years, let alone the next three.

Strung out and crazy at the end of the Seventies, soul-sick and suicidal, Dick began defining the havoc of time and memory in terms more inescapably personal, which meant coming to grips with the split in him that had haunted him since his twin sister died at the age of one month. Fred, the narrator of *A Scanner Darkly* (1977), Dick's most fully realized book, is a narc of the American near future. He wears what Dick calls a scramble-suit, a strange garb of refracted light that flashes out simultaneous images of hundreds of thousands of people—an opaque manifestation of Everyman. His identity is thus concealed from everyone: "Let's hear it for the vague blur!" is the way he's introduced at a Lions Club lunch. As Fred spies on Bob, a suspected drug dealer, his superiors believe his grasp on reality is becoming dangerously tenuous, his left brain separating from his right. Fred notes that for thousands of years a man's image of himself was based on the reflection he saw in a lake or glass—where, in fact, he saw himself exactly backwards from how everyone else saw him. The whole history of the human race is one of people dividing themselves into lefts and rights that are, to everyone else, rights and lefts. This is all particularly pertinent because Fred and Bob happen to be the same person, something Fred has forgotten. The detachment of memory from time reaches its most profound entropy in *A Scanner Darkly* and becomes the detachment of memory from self—a madness as familiarly American as it is fantastic. It is the madness of those who remember nothing of what they are, or remember too much: those who see their identities both forwards and backwards at once.

In defiance of the slapstick and disorder of Philip Dick's life was the great and moving fact that the last novel he ever wrote, *The Transmigration of Timothy Archer*, manages to rage passionately against the madness while not discounting its earlier insights. Angel Archer is a young woman in her early thirties who, in the twenty-four hours following America's murder of John Lennon, remembers those she has lost: her husband who committed suicide, her best friend who committed suicide, her father-in-law who died a particularly strange and unexplained death. In the course of these memories the pursuit of salvation is relived, and the truly human choice becomes empathy and sacrifice over epiphany and revelation. If Dick asked in his earlier novels whether the relationship between memory and time defined the nature of reality, the later work asks whether the relationship between memory and self defines the nature of the soul. In the face of the disenfranchisement of memory from time and self, and confronted by an increasingly insane world intent on one-upping any weird thing Philip K. Dick could have ever thought of, Angel Archer's stubborn hold on her identity, and her stubborn insistence on her sanity, represent a heroism that she would only contemptuously reject.

At the end of a life such as Dick's, the writing of *Timothy Archer*

on an outing—not retarded or mildly disturbed patients but people who howled in terror at passing cars and barking dogs. The butterflies of Brittany gravitated to Viv as they had in the canyons of Los Angeles, alighting on her finger or shoulder every time she turned around as though aware their existences were fleeting anyway and therefore they rushed to make themselves immortal in Viv's hands. While in Brittany Viv read a legend that every butterfly carries with it a human soul, wandering by wing in its nomadic search for salvation.

We drove all over Brittany from nine thousand American graves at Normandy to the granite gash of Pointe du Raz at the westernmost reaches of France, to the ancient city of Mont-Saint-Michel cut off from the rest of France by high tide, unified with the mainland only by quicksand when the tide recedes. At night a red fog drifted across the spires of Mont-Saint-Michel's Tenth-Century abbey, which had been converted by the government into a huge sculpture piece of chambers within rooms within chambers, wreathed with light and the music of John Cage, Sufi chants, forlorn cellos: the Second Millennium meeting the First, on the eve of the Third. In the village of Huelgoat where we spent Bastille Day night, old Bretons danced Celtic jigs in the town square to a strange music that linked the Middle East with Appalachia. The black sky exploded with red fireworks raining down like blood, celebrating the revolution that was the dark side of Paine's and Jefferson's. I became convinced that the hotel where Viv and I stayed for twenty-two dollars was in fact a cabal of Breton separatists, plotting the inevitable secession of Brittany from France in another Hundred Years' War; like in a movie, whenever we walked into the bar everyone would suddenly stop talking and look at us. The dog at the hotel was named Fidel. "Oh, don't worry," the concierge chirped merrily, "he won't hurt you. He's a very friendly dog." Fidel, snarling and lashing at the wire fence that barely held him back, gave a rather different impression. Fidel looked like he would as soon rip off your head as pee on your leg. Retiring for the evening we found a mysterious plastic liner between the top sheet of the bed and the mattress; all night it crunched beneath us, cold and brittle, until finally I leapt furiously out of bed ready to tear the plastic off the mattress when Viv said, "But what's *underneath* this plastic?" Just what was it we were sleeping with in Huelgoat, hotbed of insurrectionism—drugs, guns, secret plans? The embalmed body of an assassinated ambassador? We left the bed alone and checked out the next day.

One weekend Patti Smith performed in the medieval city of Concarneau, the next town over from ours. Once Lou Reed's successor as the poet laureate of punk rock, before becoming the American Rimbaud she always intended to be, Smith had dropped out of public sight for most of twenty years, living as a housewife, mother and finally widow in Detroit; she had just released her first new record in nearly a decade. Posters for the concert were everywhere. With great excitement I took a bus into Concarneau three days before the show to get tickets. I walked through the old outdoor amphitheater where she would sing, ocean waves just beyond the ancient walls; I chose my place on the ramparts where I would return to watch and listen. But three nights later, twelve kilometers away, my New Hampshire fever returned, and so I didn't get to see Patti Smith after all. Some of the students from the art school who went to the concert brought me back a poster. They told me she sang a song to the moon and spoke French badly. The night of the concert the first thing I ever heard her sing twenty years before drifted through my fever dreams—"Jesus died for somebody's sins, but not mine"—over and over, until I was begging her in my sleep to stop.

48

In the year 1996, at the junction of spring and summer, here was what was happening in America. Invaders from outer space were on the covers of the two leading newsmagazines in the same week. The worst drought of a lifetime razed the landscape of Texas, Oklahoma, Kansas, Nebraska, New Mexico, Arizona, Nevada, Utah and Colorado. First in the South, then in the Midwest, more than thirty African-American churches burned to the ground, only a half-dozen of which could even conceivably be explained as accidents. A popular economy airliner dropped like a stone into the swamps of Florida, a disaster that would come to seem only slightly more spectacular than the Federal Aviation Administration's subsequent litany of absurd justifications, unlikely reassurances and halfhearted mea culpas.

Nineteen young American soldiers returned home from Saudi Arabia in caskets, blown away by a bomb whose aftermath looked not a little like the federal building in Oklahoma City the year before. A security guard at an Olympics rock concert in Atlanta, who appeared to have saved many lives when he noticed a suspicious knapsack that later exploded, was then publicly suspected by the FBI of having planted the knapsack himself, before the FBI grudgingly allowed that, all things considered, maybe he didn't plant the bomb after all. In their coverage of the Olympic Games, if a Lithuanian placed first in an event and an Italian second and a Brazilian third and an American fourth, NBC's sportscasters interviewed the American. The life, habits and modus operandi of the man believed to be the Unabomber bore striking similarities to a character in Joseph Conrad's *The Secret Agent*; and Ernest Hemingway's beautiful granddaughter, a chic and successful model of the Seventies, was found decomposed in her apartment at the age of forty-one, after friends noticed they hadn't seen her in a while: in the weeks leading up to her suicide she had been reading her grandfather's work and letters obsessively. At a high school in a depressed area of Los Angeles where no one could afford to be chic in any other way *but* suicide, fourteen- and fifteen-year-old girls tumbled one after another off a local cliff into the sea. The First Lady of the United States was rumored to have communications with the dead, to which comedienne Rosie O'Donnell answered that Elizabeth Dole talked to dead people too, and sometimes Bob even answered.

In the Antarctic some fortuitously eagle-eyed explorer wandering Earth's icy rubble stumbled across a rock that scientists somehow determined, unique among all the other rocks, was from Mars. They announced that millions of years earlier the shard was knocked millions of miles clear of the red planet by a mischievous comet; investigating further, NASA found bacteria in the rock proving some form of life had once existed on Mars, if it did not still. The news was greeted with wonder and even glee, though the most profound ramifications remained largely uncontemplated. If, after all, over the eons Mars was nicked by a comet once, it was surely nicked often, with not just one piece of Mars but hundreds or even thousands cast Earth's way. And if these pieces of Mars were flung to Earth as much as thirteen million years ago, as scientists suspected, then in some mutated form their bacteria had become part of Earth's bacteria. We are all, in other words, literally part Martian. And if indeed we are created in God's image, then God is a Martian. In the way that every profound possibility defies ideology, the Mars news was greeted with a distinct silence from both Left and Right, the former annoyed that this would justify further budgeting of space exploration, the latter dismayed that Genesis had just been rewritten with the stroke of a germ.

There was no television to speak of in the little Breton village where I lived, and no radio that any of us who didn't speak French could understand. So the news of TWA Flight 800 arrived in that most ominous manner, by word of mouth. We actually heard it before a lot of Americans back in the States, particularly those on the East Coast who went to bed early just as the bulletin was coming in; while they slept the whispers invaded our lunch talk until there was nothing else to be talked about. Some of the students had taken the very same flight only a couple of weeks before. One distinctly remembered a pleasant conversation with a flight attendant whom she could now only assume was somewhere in oblivion. The whole experience of being blown up in a plane was not unimaginable but, to the contrary, too easy to imagine: "If you survived the initial blast," Viv wondered, "and were falling out of the sky, would there be just nothing but terror all the way down? Or somewhere before hitting bottom, would you make your peace with it?" Now we felt stranded in France by what we could imagine, by what terrified us. I had done a pretty good job, even with Patti Smith's songs in my head, of forgetting about America for a while—or so I assumed. It had been a relief not to think about America, to be in a place where America wasn't the focus of everything. To live for a while on old haunted land where history and memory were not arrogantly jettisoned but, if anything, molded together into a thousand legends and then perhaps clung to too tightly for far too many centuries, after which separating history from memory was practically a molecular impossibility. But in some way that one had to live to understand, the explosion of TWA 800 made returning to America not only more dreadful but also more irresistible, then inexorable. And all that remained was to look at the sky in one last expectation that, blown east across the Atlantic, two hundred and thirty butterflies would suddenly land all around us, wings defiantly fluttering.

I left Viv in Brittany, took a bullet train to Paris where I spent the night, and came home the next morning. It was a long flight, and seven miles up America met me halfway—not the America of geography, of course, not the America of airspace, but the America of imagination and terror. Sixteen hours after taking off from De Gaulle airport I was back in my canyon house alone, displaced, unsettled, and not feeling the slightest urge, and certainly not having a single reason, to pack my suitcase again seventy-two hours later, along with a now specious press pass, throw them in the car and head down the 405 freeway for San Diego, where the Republican Party was about to nominate Robert Dole for President of the United States. By Long Beach, then La Jolla, I still didn't know why I was going, and I certainly wasn't counting on the Republicans to give me an answer.

49

I really wasn't surprised that James Carville was the first person I saw in the lobby of the San Diego Marriott Hotel, even if it was in the middle of five thousand Republicans. It was the sort of symmetry I had always half believed in, even as common sense persistently tried to contradict it: Carville after all was the first person I had talked to a year earlier upon setting out to cover the presidential campaign; and now that, five months after having been fired by *Rolling Stone*, I had rashly and inexplicably thrust myself back into it, if only for the moment, it somehow made sense I would see him again. He was mobbed by reporters and fans and even Republicans for whom his Democratic politics were only a minor anomaly in the alchemy of his celebrity.

I caught his eye and he caught mine and some sort of recognition briefly flickered across his before vanishing, perhaps in the mutual embarrassment that together we had once expected so much of this election.

The summer before, when we thought this campaign was going to be so fascinating, it was because we assumed that what was happening in America would find its true political expression. The entropy of the nation would express itself in an appropriate if foreboding political entropy, exploding by the fall of 1996 in all the shrapnel marked Clinton, Dole, Powell, Perot, Buchanan, Bradley, Jackson, Nader. Now it was clear, in the summer of 1996, that the nation was so utterly disengaged from its own politics that in the course of this campaign America had become a secret unto itself. In the last election of the Millennium, in the same way that memory became more disengaged from history, all of America had gone underground, living out a subterranean psychic life of which the country's politics knew nothing. Politically the country was stupefied by the sound of its own monologue—not even a dialogue, really, no matter that the monologue was in two voices pretending to say something different from each other—while the sound was nearly swallowed up by a million whispers underneath it, brave, cowardly, idealistic, malevolent, desperate, disgusted, in the blasted aural mosaic that was the country's true portrait.

To rush down to San Diego to cover the 1996 National Republican Convention was to participate in an act not merely romantic, not merely antiquated, but so beside the point as to miss the point entirely. The last national political gathering by either party that had even been remotely like a classic convention was the 1984 Democratic affair in San Francisco that nominated Walter Mondale for President and Geraldine Ferraro for Vice President, because even though by then the political agenda of these things was wholly determined by the primary system, and the public relations agenda wholly determined by television, there were tensions in the party that still actually played themselves out on the convention floor. By 1996 it was long forgotten, for instance, that in 1984 the Latino caucus, committed to Mondale but angry with him at the time over some now-obscure issue, was seriously threatening to abstain on the first ballot, which would have actually denied Mondale the nomination, since his lead in the delegate count was that slim. Had that happened surely an unleashed convention would have instead nominated Mario Cuomo, who electrified the delegates with his speech the opening night and so alarmed the Mondale people running things that Cuomo was literally hustled out of San Francisco and back to New York in the following twenty-four hours. At the time not much of this was conveyed on television; to really get the feel of the dynamics at work in the convention you had to be there, awash in its buzz, which was all about Cuomo. By 1988 the two convention halls in Atlanta and New Orleans had been converted to mammoth soundstages for television extravaganzas, with little buzz worth buzzing about, and eight years later the Republicans were unabashedly boasting of the sleek MTV-style production they had designed for the San Diego convention, where even the buzz was completely scripted. In the days before the convention there may have been fantastic murmurs of dumping Dole, but had he collapsed on the first ballot as Mondale almost did, these delegates gave the impression they would not only have no idea what to do with such unfettered license, but would regard it as bordering on the hedonistic. On the one hand their passion for Dole was rather perfunctory, but on the other hand, for a lot of these delegates, perfunctory passion was the only acceptable sort.

As would the Democrats two weeks later, over the course of four days the Republican Party presented to the country an obsessively choreographed montage of imagistic hiccups: video clips and talk-show motifs and few speeches so interminable as to last more than twelve minutes. Attending the convention in person rather than watching it on television actually risked misunderstanding the story completely, and just so reporters covering the event in person could actually *see* the speeches, the print media had to negotiate with the Republicans to get TV monitors installed in the press gallery, which was located in a part of the hall where the speaker's podium was completely out of sight. Even before the convention began, the party's complete control of things down to the last detail had become a cliché. In order that there not be any unseemliness whatsoever, Dole had finessed a potential floor fight on abortion by caving in to the Religious Right on the matter of the party platform, which now included language that made abortion a criminal act even for a woman whose life was at stake. Because of their less conservative views on abortion, Governors Wilson of California and Weld of Massachusetts were diminished first to the status of nonspeakers and then nonpeople when the party predicated their convention appearances on conditions neither of them would accept, or just unilaterally edited them out of the proceedings altogether. Given the importance of their states in any election, and given how over recent years it was the country's Republican governors who had come to be the wave of the party's future, alienating such men seemed a little irrational, though it might have been a sign of how little the party really thought of its chances in those states anyway.

It was also a sign, of course, of just how spooked the party was by the ghosts of past disruptions, no goblin more terrifying than Patrick Buchanan's speech at the Houston convention of 1992. Needless to say, a party that found Pete Wilson inflammatory wasn't exactly clearing extra floor space and knocking out walls for Buchanan. Instead, quixotically heading down the 405 freeway in a haze of jet lag with Celtic French still rattling in my ears, I reached La Jolla only to catch Buchanan already in my rearview mirror, and barely in the Republican Party's sightlines at all, just as Ross Perot and ex-Colorado Governor Richard Lamm were already in my rearview mirror by Long Beach, where the Reform Party was holding its own revival meeting. So on the eve of the Republican Convention, two of the coming week's most important speeches had already been made—by Lamm ("Once political leaders were our compasses, now they're just weather vanes") and Buchanan defining more persuasively than ever his so-called conservatism of the heart, decrying the lobbyists "who hire themselves out to foreign corporations, buying and selling their own country. . . . We have forgotten that America is more than a gross national product." Any politician of any ideological stripe could have said that in 1996 at no risk of being upstaged by anything truer or more profound. Dismayingly but not surprisingly, none did.

Had the Republicans allowed Buchanan to give this speech at the convention, with some modification perhaps, it seems likely voters of all ideological stripes would have found themselves nodding to much of it. Funny and almost never especially scary (assuming we are still a country that can stand some intensity of expression), Pat choked up and broke down at the end, amid the bordello reds and golds of the little Escondido theater, before the dazed, wandering warriors he so affectionately called his "peasants with pitchforks." They had gathered to smolder in their humiliation and bolt a philosophically depraved Republican Party once and for all, and for half his speech it certainly sounded as though Pat might bolt with them, particularly when he told the story of the Revolutionary hero who fired a cannonball through his own house in order to repel the British, and subsequently died in poverty and ruin for his patriotic sacrifice. But that was only the half of the speech that needed to acknowledge the audience's passions; the rest was Buchanan pleading, as right-wing liar Oliver North had pleaded from the same stage moments before, that the humiliated not walk away from the Republican Party—though in fact not only the emotion of the speech's first half was more compelling but the logic. It was even possible that, midway through his speech, Buchanan still hadn't completely made up his own mind, wondering how much he could disappoint the peasants without altogether losing the allegiance of their pitchforks. At any rate, for all the gratitude the party might show, he was trying to bring them back to the Republicans, out of some loyalty to his own long history as a Republican, out of some foresight that his day might yet come in the year 2000, and out of some awareness that the Republican Party was now fully the Buchanan party he said it was.

"Wage stagnation and the decline of the two-parent family" was what Carville had told me nearly a year before was going to be the crux of the election. That, of course, was when I was trying to coax out of him the fancy abstract stuff about the Meaning of America, and he either didn't know what the hell I was talking about or just didn't have the patience for such lyricism. Now over the four days of the San Diego convention you heard it from Republicans high and low, exactly the same thing in exactly the same words: "wage stagnation," one after another intoned on television, "and the decline of the

160

two-parent family." John Buckley, the communications director for the Dole campaign, was gleeful. "It's a complete reversal," he exulted when I caught up with him. "Four years ago *we* were the ones trying to tell the country there was no economic insecurity—now that's what Bill Clinton is saying. Now *we're* the ones talking about the widening difference in incomes, which got worse under Clinton, after he consciously set out to punish the rich." Buckley's sense of irony was sharp enough to admit at least to himself what few other Republicans would, which was that any acknowledgment at all that wages were a legitimate political issue, to be addressed not only by the political system but government as well, and therefore not merely left to the free marketplace, was complete heresy in the Republican universe. In the meantime the Democrats were now talking, particularly in the wake of Dole's new plan to slash taxes across the board by fifteen percent, about . . . fiscal responsibility and the integrity of a balanced budget. In other words the two political parties had completely swapped economic identities, Democrats talking as Republicans had for most of the Twentieth Century while Republicans were championing the working class struggle, about to burst into a rousing chorus of the "Internationale" any moment. And at least in terms of the election at hand, more than anyone else the medium of this transference of souls was none other than Buchanan, addressing in New Hampshire the deepest economic terrors of the blue-collar family and providing in the process an array of villains from soulless corporate presidents to hungry frightened immigrant families living in cars. Thus again, as inescapably true as it was in September 1995 when I encountered him in the airport at New Orleans, Buchanan wrote the secret script for the election of 1996.

San Diego is among the first and most important of that wave of postnuclear American cities like Las Vegas and Orlando that actively pursues artificiality and celebrates it, and supposes that such artificiality will be the general order of things when the clock strikes 2000. By the time the glitter of its bay, perpetually speckled with sailboats, burns off the fog that shrouds every San Diegan morning—out of which Bob Dole sailed his ghost ship upon arriving in the city, skydivers swirling down around him in streams of artificial color—the whole city takes on the gleam that is part of the personality of wealth, so obviously suited for Republicans that it's startling they've never converged on San Diego before. In a city that triumphantly broadcasts its homogeneity even when that homogeneity is a complete illusion, the Convention Center is an architectural aberration, a jaggedly peculiar structure half moon-colony and half Big Top, its swooning peaks part lunarscape and part circus tents, perhaps in the spirit of the "big tent" that Republican bigwigs—as opposed to the fiercer delegates themselves—talked about ad nauseam this particular week in August. It is telling that the outside terraces of the center were constructed not to face the beautiful San Diego Bay but the skyline of the city, in case one is so besottedly romantic as to believe nature ever takes precedence over commerce. Inside the hall the ceilings are unusually low; when Bob Dole rose to the podium on the fourth day of the convention to accept the party's nomination, there was barely room—not much more than twenty feet—for the customary epic drop of balloons. So the convention hurried through the balloon drop to give Bob an epic drop of confetti instead. In person the convention was even more underwhelming than on television, where the baby-blue backdrops took on an icy sheen that conveyed Republican efficiency if not the warm ambers of human kindness.

For the second week of August in the summer of 1996, San Diego happily sold itself over to the Republican Party lock, stock and barrel, every hotel and motel large and small a headquarters of some political or media faction. Both the West Virginia delegation and part of CBS News were staying at the Best Western where I managed to ensconce myself, a twenty-minute walk from the convention. The week's true vortex, no matter who you were or what your intentions, was the Marriott Hotel next door to the center, where the contained, tightly wound life of the convention exploded into the closest facsimile of spontaneity the Republican managers would allow, not that they always had much choice. All week waves of energy and inertia ebbed and flowed according to the natural collisions of floor votes and TV schedules and newspaper deadlines, whatever feeble drama the convention might have once had severely beaten out of it the previous weekend when Dole startled the party and the country with his out-of-the-blue choice of one-time congressman and housing secretary Jack Kemp for the vice presidential nomination. From one end of the colossal Marriott to the other, from one floor to the next, the days were a mad rush between bars and computers and phone banks in which the wild bustle of a single hour sputtered forth Gerald and Betty Ford, Sam Donaldson, William Bennett (who had been Dole's real choice for vice president, before Bennett demurred too convincingly), David Broder, Cokie Roberts, Steve Forbes, William Kristol, Norman Mailer, Ed Rollins, Jeff Greenfield, Kevin Phillips, John McCain (whose speech nominating Dole would be the most eloquent of either party's convention in 1996), Mark Shields, David Gergen, Orrin Hatch, Michael Barone, Anna Deavere Smith, Henry Hyde, Robert Novak and Maria Shriver in the lobby and the hallways, amidst thousands of other nameless journalists and delegates, the most striking thing being that these surges never seemed to have anything to do with what was actually going on at the convention, since in fact nothing of any news value was actually going on at the convention.

There was a moment, just before the convention began, when a massive electrical power blackout swallowed up nine western states from Canada to Mexico, and it looked like serious chaos might win out after all. Tens of thousands of repressed journalists were newly and briefly exhilarated by the promise of a bumper-car ride into the Void. But in San Diego the lights barely flickered, and in the end order was always going to be the order of the day; so chaos was all the more conspicuous at a convention overrun with police. Apparently exuding the same sort of displacement I had months before in the Senate Press Gallery—except this time I really *was* out of place, since I wasn't actually covering the event for anyone—I was singled out for interrogation by cops before a hundred passing witnesses in the Marriott lobby. Jauntily I handed them my old *Rolling Stone* business card, sanguine that Jann Wenner had become so respectable I couldn't help being just a little respectable by association. I really didn't think I looked any stranger than anyone else, and I certainly couldn't have made an impression more bizarre than the scene I came upon moments earlier, when I caught sight of John Kasich, the Republicans' economic Robespierre, standing in the middle of the lobby peering

South. The bleak little runnels of reality that seep in through the invisible dome that covers Orlando are torrents in San Diego, so furious they run up-continent.

On the northern outskirts of the city, driving in from Los Angeles, one sees a strange traffic sign never to be sighted in Denver, St. Louis, Memphis, or even Canadian border cities like Seattle. It's the sort of sign you see on mountain roads in the wilderness, with the black silhouette of a deer or a bear, warning of animals that might suddenly lurch out of the trees before a coming car. But the black silhouettes on the caution signs outside San Diego are not of deer or bears, but of a fleeing family—a father, a mother and a child. Over the years hundreds of illegals, smuggled in trucks up from Mexico, have been killed on the San Diego freeways by cars smashing them at seventy miles an hour. Even in 1996 it would be harsh and unfair to suggest that the current sentiment against illegals, expressed in state propositions intended to squeeze such people out of California altogether and back to the dreams they came from, had become so intense that drivers might view the warnings as bloody invitations. Like a Mexican family dashing in panic across the freeway only moments after just entering America, the issue of immigration would rush across the consciousness of the Republican Convention before it became one more controversy to be suppressed, even as the Republicans nominated for vice president a man who not so long before couldn't help thinking, out loud, that his party's views on the matter verged on the bitter, if not the racist. Not a little ironically, it was Jack Kemp's difference with his party on this very issue that seemed, only a week before the convention, to have ended his political career forever.

Driving into San Diego, my headlights now flashed across a new sign I had never seen before. I think it was somewhere just south of the shimmering San Onofre nuclear plant: another sign of caution, except this time it was not the silhouette of a fear-crazed Mexican, but Bob Dole. There was no mistake about it, it was certainly Bob Dole on the sign I saw, the black outline of his form in a deeply hysterical sprint for political light. Having over the course of the previous three months run the worst shambles of a major presidential campaign in memory, as the most inept presidential candidate since George

McGovern if not Herbert Hoover, he was a man in search of a miracle, and his shadow was everywhere even as the rest of him was nowhere. Even in remote Breton villages one heard of Dole's shrewd insights on nicotine, to the effect that if a child was presented the choice between one measly, innocuous cigarette and an odiously white glass of milk so glowing in obvious unhealthfulness as to be practically radioactive, it was a decision to be carefully pondered. While the months of May and June had turned to shit for the President of the United States—what with former Arkansas cronies convicted for fraud, and an appalling episode concerning the White House's collection of FBI files on political opponents, which seemed separated from Nixonian extraconstitutional conspiracy only by the degree of botch involved—thus presenting Dole with one golden opportunity after another, Dole still could not buy a break, especially since he had no campaign money left. And if both the triumph of the Olympics and the tragedy of its bombing, on the heels of the TWA explosion, put the President squarely back in his element as both national celebrant and national griever, they also pointed up Dole's utter inability to connect with the public at all. So even the silly tax cut he heralded the week before the convention, and which his campaign insisted was turning the election around, was so transparently bogus it undercut the granitic integrity and no-nonsense maturity Dole was trying to convey in contrast to Bill Clinton. Now his campaign was reduced to a traffic sign, in which the shadow of Bob Dole silently begged the country not to flatten him with a mobile home careening down the highway.

In a contemporary political history characterized by obligatory nominations—Bush's in '92, Dukakis' in '88, Mondale's in '84—Dole's seemed particularly by rote. Perhaps never in modern political history had a convention delivered a presidential nominee who had less impact upon the proceedings and about whom the proceedings obviously cared so little. If Dole's connection with the American people was nonexistent, it was tenuous at best even with Republicans who were his delegates, and supposed to be more representative of who he was than who America was. Leave aside that men outnumbered women two to one, leave aside that fewer than one out of forty were black (though television coverage seemed determined to show otherwise): one out of three earned more than $100,000 a year, one out of five was a millionaire. More than eighty percent opposed any sort of abortion rights, sixty percent were Evangelical Christians, and at least a third were card-carrying members of Ralph Reed's Christian Coalition, their enthusiasm for Bob Dole somewhat less ecstatic than for the Jesus of their fantasies, in dark blue business suit with aviator glasses, CEO of Righteousness, Inc.

This Jesus certainly had his way with Dole on the altar of the party platform. By the measure of this rabid document alone the Republicans of 1996 were a Buchanan party, or perhaps more precisely and explosively a Buchanan-Forbes party, the populist social conservatism of the first wedded to the corporate economic conservatism of the second. But while Buchanan's social and cultural passions had been embraced almost in toto even by party delegates who were not Buchanan delegates, the convention was often a hilarious orgy of the party establishment protesting too much, from party chairman Haley Barbour to Newt Gingrich to Dole and Kemp themselves insisting they hadn't even read a platform that called for no less than half a dozen amendments to the United States Constitution. One defeated would-be president after another, from Lamar Alexander to Phil Gramm, scurried onto television to castigate Buchanan in snide and heated terms for not "joining the team," even though in fact he had done just that, endorsing the Dole-Kemp ticket the convention's first morning, however tepidly. Clearly these men despised Buchanan for accomplishing the superhuman feat of actually believing in something.

But if the Republican Party was a Buchanan-Forbes party, it was therefore a party of completely split personality, a party utterly at war with itself. As the true fragmentation of the nation had been hidden one last time in this century by the American political system at large, so the true fragmentation of the Republican Party would be hidden one last time in the nomination of Bob Dole for President. The GOP that had come so close over the last generation to making itself the country's majority party had been cruelly fast-forwarded to deal with all the inevitable dissensions of a majority party without reaping the decades of power and privilege in between; where it took sixty years for the majority-party Democrats to become irrevocably fractured, the headlong rush of history and technology pushed the Republicans to disintegration within months of its apotheosis, the seizure of Congress in 1994. The passions of Buchanan and the passions of Forbes had no use for each other. The corporate-friendly flat tax that Forbes loved was anathema to Buchanan's new economic radicalism, and one could almost hear the horror in Forbes' voice the first time he must have cried out loud, aghast, "Peasants with pitchforks?" assuming he could so mobilize his imagination as to conceive such an awful vision. Each side of the divided personality won its own victory in San Diego—Buchanan the platform, which might mean nothing in the present tense, as politicos insisted, but would yet be, as platforms always are, the map of the future; and Forbes the ticket itself, his influence most obviously manifested in the form of Kemp, who had committed the folly of endorsing Forbes for President in the spring, just a week before Forbes was completely finished. All this couldn't help but leave the party feeling rattled. And it couldn't help raising the question of whether the Buchanan soul of the party really understood even itself: it didn't come across on television, but inside the convention hall the most controversial moment of Colin Powell's opening night speech was not his declaration in favor of abortion rights but his line about how it wasn't right to cut welfare to poor people without first cutting welfare to corporations. Such scripture was right out of Buchanan's bible, a central tenet of the New Buchananism. But though the rest of the nation missed it, delegates booed.

It was Jack Kemp rather than Bob Dole who was the embodiment of the Republican Party's schizophrenia. He stood in the crossfire of Buchanan's and Forbes' passions; it was worth noting that it was out of deference to Kemp that Buchanan did not run for President in 1988. Kemp was his hero then, as Kemp was hero and heir apparent of the dominant Reagan wing of the party, "dominant" being something of a misnomer because, truthfully, there was no other wing. How Kemp came to be such a prodigal in the years since 1988 said more about the party than it did Kemp. If the Republicans, as Barry Goldwater noted, had moved so far right as to make Goldwater a liberal, they just kept right on going when they got to Kemp; and to a party now nearly as pure as Gary Bauer, Kemp had become suspect, what with brazenly humane positions on immigration, affirmative action, urban renewal and assault weapons, and withering characterizations of his own party as one of "small government and big prisons." It also said something about the party's desperation that these suspicions of Kemp were forgotten the moment his selection by Dole was announced, forgotten as quickly as Dole himself forgot all the reasons that Kemp was unthinkable to him as late as June. A new flurry of polls suddenly showed the Republicans within single-digit percentage points of the President, and gave Republicans heart, even if the more hard-hearted—and hardheaded—recalled the Gallup Poll of August 1984, when a post-convention Walter Mondale briefly ran ahead of Ronald Reagan.

For his part it was hard to say Dole embodied anything anymore. He was now famous for his stated willingness to be Ronald Reagan, "if that was what people wanted," and now he just as willingly acceded to the necessity of defining himself completely in terms of other men, whether it be Reagan, Powell or the new junior partner on his own ticket. It was a sad turn given that, not so many years before, Dole was one of the few authentic politicians in America, with his bravely stubborn refusal to sign on to phony tax-cut promises and his singular, highly developed sense of the politically absurd. One of the few other such politically authentic figures had been Kemp, and if there was anything sadder than Dole's new expediency, it was the former football star swallowing virtually all of his more courageous and independent principles by mid–convention week in a gulp so huge even Bill Clinton would have had to swallow twice, all for the sake of the team or the game, or the first down or the third down or the touchdown, whatever the unbearable football cliché of the moment was, the operative word apparently being down. In other words the things that had always made Kemp so appealing and attractive, and that had made him so valuable to Dole and the Republicans of 1996, which were his demonstrable integrity and compassion, became the first price paid for Dole and the Republicans to have him, and for Kemp to have them in return.

"It is not important that we win," Kemp said in his speech to the convention accepting the party's vice presidential nomination, "it is important that we be worthy of winning." Kemp was just smart enough to have wondered, even if he quickly pushed the thought from his mind, whether he had already made himself slightly less worthy. The speech both tried to rationalize his new capitulations—it understates the matter far too much to call them merely compromises—and hurry past them, arguing glibly, for instance, that "one must close the back door of illegal immigration in order to keep open the front door of legal immigration." There was certainly a case to be made for this; one simply wished that, coming from this particular man in this particular context, it didn't sound so baldly like horseshit. No doubt the Republicans found more significant Kemp's irrepressibility, a rush for both the convention and the party's coming campaign, though perhaps a little heavy on the political caffeine, since the campaign season was already occupied by one fully as irrepressible as Kemp, he being the President of the United States. In theory, if hope did not now spring eternal in the bosom of Bob Dole, simply because Dole's bosom was not naturally given to such geysers, it might have at least leaked a little; and that hope was that Dole's somber gravity could only contrast well with all this ebullience around him, in his opponent and his running mate and even his own wife.

Dole's own acceptance speech was curious, a Frankenstein monster of stitched parts that never seemed quite able to get up and walk on its own. If some of the pieces supplied by novelist Mark Helprin were pretty and even moving, they were also awkward, what with Dole waxing rhapsodic about city lights like "strings of sparkling diamonds." Bob Dole was not a sparkling-diamonds kind of guy. Of the speech's three most remarkable moments, two spoke to Dole's better angels and one to his demons: recalling his father traveling by train—and having to stand the whole way—from Kansas to Michigan to visit his shattered son in a military hospital after World War II, an emotional Dole nearly tumbled into one of his now patented losses of composure as the nation watched in both sympathy and horror. Then, pulling himself together and pounding the podium, he argued to those who thought he would savage Social Security or Medicare as President that he could never betray such "Americans in need . . . for to do so would be to betray those whom I love and honor most. And I will betray nothing." And to those who made the Republican Party theirs because they thought it would be some sort of restricted country club in which they would not have to consort with people of dubious color or gender, not even to mention convictions, Dole declared that the exits were "clearly marked," and that he would not back down before bigotry or small-mindedness.

This, of course, was the refutation of Houston 1992, and Pat Buchanan's malicious jihad. If the actual language was not Dole's own, it was certainly delivered with enough conviction that, listening to it, one didn't disbelieve it for a second. But unfortunately the single most persuasive moment of the speech was the gauntlet hurled at the feet of not just the Clinton White House but, by implication, a whole generation of spoiled children "who never grew up, never did anything real, never sacrificed, never suffered, and never learned." Almost certainly the truest expression of the Dole soul placed on display before the American people that evening, it illuminated what was really at stake in the contest to come in such a way as to make one shudder, if not recoil: "I think," Viv said to me later, "I took that personally," and I knew the moment she said it that I had too. The defensiveness about age, with one out of three Americans expressing concerns that he was too old to be President, had intermingled with Dole's bilious resentment about a life that had never cut him an inch of slack, and that now threw him into battle against some white-trash dreamboat who had fast-talked his way out of the shadows of the Ozarks to Georgetown into the White House, out of life's trials and tribulations and into the panties of a hundred dim, no doubt distressingly pneumatic bimbos along the way. Every time in the recent months that Dole had said, in one campaign stop or another, to one reporter or another, in one interview or another, that he had always had to do things "the hard way" and that was all right because the hard way was "better," not for a second did he really think it was better. Not for a second did he really think it was all right. Enough is enough already, was what Bob Dole really meant: I'm fucking *tired* of the hard way. And I despise those who have always gotten to take the easy way.

In the process, it was an open question whether Dole was canny enough to understand, if only on a level so subconscious he would as soon not acknowledge it at all, the paradox of American politics that Americans in all their self-satisfied notions of innocence resisted. In the year 1996 this paradox was harder to ignore: that one candidate might be the better man, but it did not mean he was the better leader. Only in 1980 had this distinction between commendable personal saintliness and compelling political leadership been as clear, when the country was faced with the choice between a Sunday school teacher and a divorced cut-rate movie star. Now perhaps, just perhaps, a newly sophisticated public was finally ready to confess this paradox to itself. According to the single most telling poll statistic in the first six months of 1996, given a choice between a man who better exemplified the virtues of honesty and integrity and a man who better understood the problems of ordinary Americans, Americans chose the empath over the paragon *three to one*. You could carve that statistic on the tombstone of Bob Dole's presidential hopes. The question now was whether, this late in the day, Dole had the imagination to recognize such a fact and address it, or whether he would just dismiss it as another of life's injustices and assume it was the hard way, the better way, to make America embrace him for virtues it didn't really care about.

To Dole's credit, one of the reasons his recent pandering somehow seemed so much more ludicrous and even tawdrier than Clinton's was that Dole just wasn't as good at it. He had too much residual honesty from years past to believe his own pandering. Clinton not only believed his own pandering, he believed it *joyously*, which was his genius; Clinton was completely cynical without *feeling* the least bit cynical, whereas when Dole was being cynical, he knew that you knew that he knew. If this election were between Clinton and the Dole of 1988 rather than the Dole of 1996, the Dole who once told hard truths and had not made himself, just a little too agreeably, the prisoner of the single most dangerous political force in the country, it might be a far more difficult choice for voters and campaign writers alike—or maybe it wouldn't even be difficult at all. But now the country was confronted by a Dole caught between the pandering even he didn't believe and his own perverse nature that cut him off, time and again, from his own best judgment, in the same way his life had tried so ruthlessly to cut him off from his own humanity. The result was a man who had spent a lifetime trying to cut himself off from everything that had hurt him, pushing people away while trying to connect with them at the same time, seething over those little overeducated snots in the White House who never had to do a real thing in their lives, against whom it was almost insulting, if you really wanted to get down to it, that a man like Bob Dole had to be measured. This only translated into a thousand such insults, large and trivial, against which Dole subtly or not so subtly lashed out: imagine, he must have fumed to himself, people trying to tell me that nicotine is worse than milk. As though I don't know that nicotine is worse than milk. Of course nicotine is worse than milk; do they really think I don't know that? Imagine. And the more he fumed, the more he implicitly insisted that milk could be as bad as nicotine.

When Bob Dole said to the convention, "To those who believe I'm too combative, I say that if I am combative, it's for love of country, it's to uphold a stand I was born and bred to defend," he was saying, in part, The cornerstone of my presidency will be this notably prodigious chip you see lodged on my shoulder. For days operatives like John Buckley had been confiding to writers and commentators that the primary objective of Dole's acceptance speech was "telling the nation who he is," revealing himself to a nation that he had, over the course of thirty-five years, managed to keep completely in the dark. Now the revelation of the convention's final night was: This is who I am, not my heart or my brain or my soul, but my spleen. The rage of Dole had not manifested itself so spectacularly—albeit this time with more of Helprin's literary flourishes—since the night he lost the New Hampshire campaign of 1988 and before millions identified George Bush as the sordid little rat he was. That it was Bush, liar, opportunist and promise-breaker extraordinaire, who rose before the 1996 convention to defend the "dignity" of the presidency, lost by him to someone who just aced him at his own game, was pretty funny if you could stomach it long enough to laugh. But what had clearly galled Dole was not Bush's defeat itself but defeat at the hands of a generation that never did anything "real," and so if there was anything impressive or significant about Dole's speech, which in political terms was the least effective thing about the convention, certainly less effective than the short Dole video that preceded it, in which Dole was witty, warm and insistent without being dogmatic, pious or resentful, certainly less effective than Jack Kemp's launching of his own presidential campaign for the year 2000 only moments before, or Elizabeth Dole's launching of her own campaign for the year 2000 the night before, if there was anything impressive or significant about what Bob Dole said this evening in the biggest speech of his life, it was the way he fused his personal rage with a larger rage about the country, and in the process stumbled onto the Great Elusive Question that hummed beneath the American earth like the vibration of an approaching stampede miles away, heard only by whatever Americans were pressing their ears to the ground like the Indians of a hundred years ago. And that was the question Buchanan had heard so clearly and answered in the negative, which was whether there was still a Meaning that America shared in common, the self-indulgent poetics of which Dole never had the time or tolerance for before, until a dearth of big, more comprehensible and less abstract issues, having to do with the economy or foreign crisis, left him no choice. At the zenith of his possibilities and in the pit of his resentment it was clear to him that America had failed itself by failing its own nostalgia, at the hands of a President and a generation nostalgic only for the future because it had been too coddled to have a proper nostalgia for the past. "Let me be the bridge," he said, "to an America that only the unknowing call myth. Let me be the bridge to a time of tranquillity, faith, and confidence in action. And to those who say it was never so . . . I say you're wrong, and I know, because I was there. I've seen it. I remember."

Thus Dole would be Rememberer-in-Chief, in a country and at a moment when the compasses of memory spun wildly and memory loosened itself from the very physics of history. What he would remember for all of us was not only the America he might truly believe once was, but the America of his own particular imagination and terror, the one that flashed across his consciousness in an Italian foxhole one last time before it was replaced by incandescence and then shadow. At that podium on the convention's final night he made no pretenses of remembering the future, only of bringing a shabby future full circle with a superior past; and he thereby assured that not only the convention but in some ways the election itself was substantively over, had ended three nights before not at the convention's close but its opening. Not only the meaning of the convention but of the election itself had collapsed into the twenty-four hours between the speech Pat Buchanan gave in Escondido and the one given twenty-four hours later by a man who survived his entire life by remembering the future, and by defying every conclusion Buchanan ever drew about the meaning of America, if not every conclusion Bob Dole had drawn as well, since Dole's life was its own meaning and he seemed as disinclined to draw larger meanings about his life as about the country. Colin Powell must have understood that his very appearance before the convention was his ultimate defiance of the past; the irony of his situation was that, presenting himself to his newly chosen political party, he at the same time presented himself to the only group in America not enthralled by him. Considering that that very day anti-abortion delegates on the convention floor had literally screamed at Pete Wilson and William Weld to get out of the party, Powell's reception had provided one of San Diego's few moments of suspense. So Powell rising to the podium in front of the most right-wing convention ever, compared to which the 1964 Republican Convention in San Francisco that nominated Goldwater was a Maoist block party, would almost seem audacity enough.

In truth it was more audacious than even Powell knew. The true political contest of 1996, the secret contest America could barely whisper to itself, had emerged for one moment in its brightest form—coasting in on the emotional coattails of a heart-wrenching valediction by Nancy Reagan to her husband—after vanishing twenty-four hours before in its darkest form. When Powell argued that "in America, justice will always triumph and the powerful searing promise of the Founding Fathers will come true," he surely understood that few others could make such a claim without it sounding entirely empty. The delegates responded with something between cordiality and real enthusiasm. A television camera briefly caught the look on Elizabeth

Dole's face, stricken with awful imaginings of everything suddenly getting out of hand and the convention embracing and nominating Powell by acclamation. But that was irrational. Powell wouldn't have gotten a hundred votes on this floor; choosing this political party as his own, he had doomed himself to political nowhere, which might have been his idea all along. Across the three thousand miles rolling northeast out of San Diego, an appalled nation was not just confronted but slapped in the face, not just with what might have been but with the failure of nerve that always seems to doom the country's best lurking possibilities. One could hardly blame an America that got up from its chair, turned off the TV, and retired in gloom.

51

So I had this idea, not necessarily an inspiration but a perverse impulse that became more and more irresistible, that I would just go right on covering the campaign. I would get in my car with my bogus press badge and my bogus business cards and I would start driving, a bogus correspondent without portfolio, and I would write the story of the campaign the way I had wanted to in the beginning, and the way I had foolishly supposed in the beginning that I was being hired to do, but now armed with moonshine credentials and a surreptitious itinerary of my own making. And I would keep on driving out past L.A. and back into America and into the last years of the Twentieth Century, on one last rampage through the national asylum just to make one last observation, one last comment, or even to tell just one last lie, just as long as no one expected from me one last answer.

52

It was in Brittany of all places that I heard this story, from one of the other teachers at Viv's art school, about this friend of his who went to Las Vegas not so long ago. He's sitting at a blackjack table in one of the casinos drinking, getting a little drunk, an attractive woman starts coming on to him, one thing leads to another and they go up to his hotel room. He didn't remember what happened next. All he knew was that, sometime later, he woke up and was lying naked in the bathtub filled with ice, and on the bathroom mirror written in lipstick was: "Call 911." How long was it—minutes? moments?—before he suddenly understood something was very wrong? Before he turned, ever so slightly, and with a gasp understood he was not altogether *right*? Sometime during the hours that he had passed out in his hotel room, someone had come in, sliced open his back and taken his kidney, and now he lay on ice with his back stapled, perhaps considering how far he might get, out of the tub and toward the phone, before the staples began to pop and he became undone, the rest of him spilling out on the hotel carpet.

Of course this was one of those stories that confounded assessments of credibility: too horrifying to be true, or too horrifying not to be true? A story that lurched beyond the bounds of apocrypha. All I knew, a couple of weeks after the Republican Convention, sitting at the blackjack table of the Rio Hotel in Las Vegas while the dealer kept dealing herself kings and queens and me fifteens and sixteens, as I grew slightly sodden on vodka tonics and began to suspect the blonde two seats down was winking at me, was that I had a slightly dull throb in the lower part of my back where I supposed my kidneys were, not that I've ever been entirely sure where my kidneys are. Outside the window of my room a silt fog from the dust twisters kicked up by the desert winds slid across town curling around the Vegascape of emerald Ozes and faux Manhattans and sand-bound riverboats and cursed black pyramids carved a little too freely with the hieroglyphs of Egyptian death gods. Having displaced Los Angeles as the ultimate city of vicarious experience, L.A.'s collective experience over the course of a generation having become rather too real, and unfazed by the limits of whatever passes for taste in San Diego, and visionary in audaciously perverse ways that Orlando cannot imagine, Vegas isn't just postnuclear, it is post-postnuclear: it has circled the clock of the nuclear heart so far as to come up on the dark side of whatever looking-glass the atomic blasts of fifty years ago froze into the Nevada sands. Now Vegas is caught in its own strange dynamic, expanding and contracting at the same time. Now fashioning itself a mecca not merely for sinful adults but rather for sinful adults with children, which is to say a city where sin and innocence can be compartmentalized as neatly as the imagination, the city has exploded with new casinos going up faster than people can fill them, a thousand people moving to Vegas every week not as visitors but residents in search of jobs, a thousand a week every week for the last six years. From the atomic bomb to Las Vegas, with guns and nuclear weapons and movies and pop music in between, history will record that at its zenith, in its greatest hour, the American Empire's two most important contributions to the human race were annihilation and *fun*.

But even as Vegas races to catch up with its own mad new vision, the vision begins unraveling back near the beginning. The Wizard of Oz display in the lobby of the MGM Grand is gone, a dud. The small amusement parks the new casinos built are dead: the children don't like them. The children, virtually abandoned by slot-crazed parents, run amok, to the consternation of the hotels. Cabbies don't just gripe, as cabbies everywhere are almost required to do by their job descriptions, they leave town altogether, in the wake of no business. On the casino sound systems they don't play Frank Sinatra anymore, they play the Beach Boys; and the unspoken glamour of the Mob, which ran Vegas once and who the insiders insist still runs it, the protests of Steve Wynn and the Chamber of Commerce notwithstanding, has been replaced by a new glamorous danger that middle-class America wants no part of: the weekend I was there, right outside the MGM Grand in the street following a Mike Tyson fight, a gangland hit went down killing rapper Tupac Shakur in what used to be called in the good old days "a hail of bullets." If the Mob *is* still in charge of Vegas, they will presumably attend to such business quick. Quiet murders out in the desert are one thing, flashy armed Negroes in big cars fighting it out on the Strip in plain view are another. Rather failing as the ideal family vacation spot, while the serious gamblers now head for downtown off the Strip, or Reno and Tahoe, or even the various

Indian reservations across the country where gambling is now legal, the city that has displaced Los Angeles as the capitol of vicariousness has gotten mired in its contradictions.

Without the serious gamblers the casinos fail. If the casinos fail the hotels die. Now, in my hotel room, I tried to imagine in its broadest scope America's utter failure of imagination, an imagination betrayed by the ways it would sell itself so cheaply, the failure compressed into the view outside my window of the desert sky, streaked by the vapor trails of American rockets on their way to Baghdad. Where once in Vegas the sins of the American imagination went wild without consequence, now there is a price to be paid, if not in blood in the streets then in what has become one of the world's biggest black markets in human organs: a kidney perhaps, or something even less expendable. Would the Republican nominee for President of the United States wake up in Vegas naked in a bathtub full of ice without his spleen, crying, like the Ronald Reagan he wanted to be, "Where's the rest of me?" Checking out of the Rio, on my way north toward Salt Lake City, walking down the long halls of my hotel in the early morning hours before dawn, I could hear behind every door the moans of people waking from the dull stupor of their imagination, stapled together and missing spleens, kidneys, livers, lungs, hearts, minds, dragging themselves across the carpet to the telephone. America—in red lipstick on the bathroom mirror—call 911.

53

North of Vegas, up I-15, America swooned into Indian summer, the land slashed in colors of rage and envy all the way to Montana. Past Mesquite and the Moapa Reservation, past Saint George and Zion and the Valley of Fire, this is where the memory of the past and the dream of the future collapses into the anarchic American moment. The earth bubbled with trees and cows and a huge billboard with the picture of a rattlesnake and a message beside it that read,

"PORNOGRAPHY . . . is just as deadly," so incongruous in its Mormon fury, so juxtaposed against the serenity and terror of the land, as to nearly be pornographic itself.

In my car I had loaded clothes, maps, bottled water, the novels of Charles Willeford and Cormac McCarthy, a biography of Orson Welles, and the American Soundtrack in a box of tapes: Sinatra, Dylan, Springsteen, Hendrix, Otis Redding, Patti Smith, Miles and Bird and Billie Holiday, Merle Haggard, Creedence Clearwater, Lou Reed, the Stooges, American Indian tribal music, Nirvana, Iris DeMent, Rosanne Cash, Ray Charles, the Doors, Eleventh Dream Day, Butch Hancock and Jimmie Dale Gilmore, Neil Young and Crazy Horse, and Dusty Springfield, actually British of course but an honorary American by virtue of the fact that black female rhythm-and-blues singers refused to believe she was white when they first heard her on the radio in the early Sixties. In the early weeks of September, in the twenty-five hundred miles from Los Angeles to Chicago, among the hundreds or even thousands of cars on the highways, I did not see *a single bumper sticker* for anyone running for anything; on the radio I never heard a whisper of politics. The airwaves were consumed instead by a baseball season winding down and a football season starting up, the only reference to politics concerning not any election but a United States senator's proposed legislation to ban job discrimination against gays, all the baseball and football interest apparently distracted only by the American male's unmollified obsession with the Homosexual Threat. I decided if I was going to make it across America in one piece I better start memorizing National League and American League standings, anticipating that crucial pop quiz I would inevitably encounter at the next truck stop.

Not a whisper of politics or history from the Rockies to the Badlands. Not a whisper across the seething Yves Tanguy landscape of Wyoming, the reds of rage and the greens of envy giving way to the fire golds of summer giving way to the dead golds of autumn, the black two-lane from Rawlins to Casper lined with dead animals each larger and more preposterously slaughtered than the last. In the gilded shimmer, beneath the sun at its zenith, people drove with their headlights on in order not to vanish into the glow completely. White dust genies swirled on the horizon. Small white crosses stood alone in the tall grass. My windshield become a glass charnel house to a thousand splattered butterflies from the Mojave to Minnesota. Then beyond the 104th latitude America dropped off into nothing, for almost a thousand miles to the banks of the Mississippi a flat vastness that couldn't even be called a landscape, couldn't even be called a plain, since it did not conjure the scheme of landscapes or inspire the contemplation of plains, it was only a huge *ground*, slamming the solitary driver with the reality that if something should happen to him on one of these roads, no one would ever know. I swerved north to the Black Hills, the mind-boggling dullness of Nebraska to be avoided *at all cost*, passing Sitting Bull's killing ground where, on the occasion of the country's first centennial, just like clockwork, Nineteenth-Century America met the consequences of its hubris, as American hubris seems destined to do in some cataclysmic fashion at least once a century: Vietnam was only the Twentieth-Century update of Custer's Last Stand. Beyond the Laramie Mountains the two-lanes were red, from either a strange red asphalt or the blood of the growing piles of animal cadavers, or blood's memory remembering itself before my windshield at seventy miles an hour. Alone, seen on a knoll as one approached the town of Gillette, a billboard by a national right-to-life group read, "If it is not a baby, you are not pregnant," reducing its argument to something like a Chinese epigram.

This part of the country lived in exile from politics and history. Not until 1929 did a single President come from west of the Mississippi, and then he arrived as either the last disaster of the old presidency or the first disaster of the modern presidency, depending on how you want to look at it; and in the tiny town of West Branch in eastern Iowa, somewhat to my surprise, I stumbled upon his birthplace, where I walked through the tiny house he lived in as a child. Quickly I came to realize I didn't know my history as well as I thought: I had it in my head that Herbert Hoover was a repressed New England type, not a repressed midwesterner, and that he came from money. In fact his beginnings were entirely humble; he was the second of three children by a Quaker blacksmith and a schoolteacher, both dead by the time Herbert was ten. Hoover was a self-made man in the classic sense, a geologist who earned his fortune in mining and went on to become something of an entrepreneurial adventurer, later translating his skills and resources into a humanitarianism that endeared him not only to his country but the world. Arguably no finer or more upright human being was ever elected to the American presidency, and it just makes one all the more uneasy that his shitty presidency was not at odds with his fine character but an outgrowth of it. Of course, the little Hoover Museum in West Branch doesn't see it this way. Its own historical verdict is: he was unlucky. The exhibit sidesteps the curious question of how a man who fed Europe twice could not bring himself to feed his own country once. But the answer, while curious, is not mysterious: the self-made American saw Europeans as children and Americans as a new breed of men. Americans were not beneath such charity but above it, and Hoover's sterling character, which he identified as the American character, and for which identification he was indeed elected in the first place, did not allow for an American need as desperate as that of European children. Beyond this, the museum gingerly concedes the man had trouble communicating with people, and while he was certainly not the last President to be elected with this deficiency, he may have been, in a new media age, the first to fail so utterly because of it.

Deeper into America, approaching the American event horizon of the Mississippi, militia clouds rose above cobalt hills, glittery barbed wire ran along fuliginous black roads. Silos stood like silver bullets against the wheat. I never assumed the peace of it all was any more or less real than the clouds of smoke; swirling down the drain of my rearview mirror, time was only mileage imposed on the wheel of the universe. Once America assimilated chaos into mythology, found a place for it, even a function, so as to then be able to deny it; fifty-one years ago, in the sands that stretched from Las Vegas to New Mexico, chaos consumed mythology and made assimilation a vain joke. Now the black clouds were the laughter of it all. Thus it was not only acceptable that we were unprepared for every particular mile of the wheel's turn, it was even sensible. We had not so much adjusted to the chaos of American presidential politics as come to accept chaos' own logic; this is not to say that sooner or later chaos won't undo us, or that the anarchy which has become the sound of the wheel won't be the last roar we hear. But it must say something about the country that we had fair warning and ignored it; or, more confusing and distressing, that we understood the warning clearly and made our choice anyway.

54

Quite unsettling is the possibility that history might have taken a turn even more fantastic: we might, for instance, have elected Ronald Reagan in 1980. After submitting the country to such an electoral crisis in that year, it was unthinkable at the time we could just go on doing it again and again and again; now, with no resolution in sight, it seems naive to presume that some subversive or self-destructive intent doesn't lie behind it all. If not intent, then futility. That's what most despairs the national soul, the prospect that should the current forty-four-month deadlock in the House of Representatives finally break in 1996, none of the three presidential candidates the House must presently choose from will be more prepared for the scope of what is happening in the world today than the current acting President, whose only preparation for the job was his many years in the Senate as a right-wing zealot from North Carolina.

Jimmy Carter's reelection by the House in January 1981, in the first such election thrown to that body in over a hundred and fifty years, may have been the expression of such futility. It may also have been an escape from a more dismal outcome, or—the darkest and yet in some ways most distinct consideration—it may have been the act of a country denying its truest impulses. If Carter's first election in 1976 was, as analyst Kevin Phillips has written, an artificial one, an aberration of the conservative dynamic that had already begun to take hold in the late Sixties and then was only briefly interrupted by Watergate, his second election was in many ways even more so, framed as it was by people's conflicting feelings about the man. Certainly a discontent with Carter existed at the beginning of 1980. The first signs of economic disaster were already evident by the close of the Seventies; and there was international trouble: the invasion of Afghanistan by the Soviets, and the seizure of American hostages by students in Iran, with the support of the Iranian regime. That Carter seemed at sea with all of this was a perception shared by many, expressed in the early months of 1980 by the political challenge in his own party of a liberal senator from Massachusetts. In the other party, a conservative former governor of California, while still running far behind Carter in the polls, was nonetheless consolidating his position and appeared on the verge of uniting Republicans behind a nomination many of them always considered dubious and ultimately doomed. The dazzling military rescue of the hostages in April 1980 changed all that, altering the psychology around Carter and thus the election; but it could just as easily have not. Had the American rescue mission been just one helicopter short, for instance, it could as easily have ended somewhere in the Iranian desert in disaster—in which case Edward Kennedy's challenge to the President might have continued all the way to the Democratic Convention that year, rather than collapsing so completely as it did. In which case Ronald Reagan might not have felt so desperate as to blunder at the Republican Convention in the fashion that he did.

The truth was that, to many people, choosing Gerald Ford to run as vice president or, more exactly, "Co-President" on the Republican ticket with Reagan never seemed a good idea. The year 1980 portended the almost cavalier confusion about the American presidency that later manifested itself in 1996's crisis; as well, the aberration in America's ideological shift that Kevin Phillips saw in Watergate continued to reveal itself in yet a new example of disregard by powerful men for the constitutional process. It's both indicative and unsurprising that the man who had the most ambivalence about redefining the American presidency at the 1980 Republican Convention was the man who had once been President (Ford) rather than the man who wanted so hungrily to be President (Reagan). At any rate, as the fall campaign of 1980 unwound, Americans were less and less impressed by a Republican presidential candidate who would so easily relinquish power and responsibility in order just to win votes; and by a

Republican vice presidential candidate who did not have it in his nature to defer to the top of the ticket, suggesting broadly in public that the top of the ticket might not be the top at all, and that the bottom certainly wasn't, in any real sense of the word, the bottom. When the bungling of disorganization and bad feelings between Reagan and Ford reached their nadir in October, and Ford withdrew from the ticket three weeks before the election to be hastily replaced by George Bush, the unpromising prospects of the Republicans were only somewhat rescued by a worsening economy and the quickly fading light of Carter's hero status, won for him by United States Marines in Teheran. It is still possible Jimmy Carter might have won reelection outright if not for the independent third candidacy that year of Illinois Representative John Anderson. It's also possible that, the fiasco of the fall campaign notwithstanding, Ronald Reagan might have won; whether Anderson's popular votes—and the electoral votes of the five small states he captured—were given to him by people more dismayed with the economy or with the Gerald Ford episode was never conclusively determined by pollsters. The point is that, but for one or two events, 1980 might have actually been the beginning of an entirely different history, and an entirely different America, than the one we know now.

Of course, it was the beginning of something anyway. The Electoral College deadlock was something the country hadn't seen since 1824, and the narrowly elected Republican Senate was something the country hadn't seen since the Fifties. And thus when the Republican Senate, per the dictates of the Constitution in such a situation, elected George Bush vice president while the Democratic House was reelecting Carter, the country saw something else it hadn't seen since the emergence of Republicans and Democrats as the country's two great political parties after the Civil War: an administration divided along partisan lines. It was fitting, then, that Jimmy Carter would preside over the political fragmentation of America, because it was a fragmentation twenty years in coming, since the assassination of John Kennedy in 1963, and because Carter's presidency *was* artificial, the product of and sustained by freak events, and as such a protest against what was really happening in the country. In retrospect the traumatic corrosion of the electoral process over the next four years

even briefer than William Henry Harrison's: "Well, at least I got to be President for three days."

55

Then, in the last years of the Millennium, copies of an anonymous, unpublished manuscript began to appear in New York and Los Angeles and Washington and Seattle. It circulated within whatever constitutes a cultural underground these days, then captivated the cocktail party conversations of the literary establishment during which someone would mention the book in passing only to learn that others had also heard the rumors or even, in some cases, actually seen the book in question. When several New York publishing houses wanted to publish it, no one could determine its author. The book was called *American Nomad*.

American Nomad is a work of fiction written as a history of the Eighties and Nineties, though a very different history than the one we actually lived through. In the process of reinventing history it presumes, for starters, the defeat of Jimmy Carter in 1980 and the election of Ronald Reagan. It's largely forgotten today that for several moments on Election Night in 1980 this outcome didn't seem so completely far-fetched. (This alternate history sidesteps the question of whether Gerald Ford remained on the Reagan ticket and thus became vice president.) In this alternate history Reagan's presidency is as much a disaster as Carter's or Koch's, though a disaster more banal than apocalyptic: four years of confrontation with the Soviets do not necessarily lead to nuclear conflict; and even the sort of Congress we've seen in the last fifteen years is not so inept and cowardly as to blithely accept Reagan's prescriptions of a massive defense buildup on the one hand and deep tax cuts for the wealthy on the other. Implicitly *American Nomad* argues that with a Reagan presidency, the country comes to exorcise some demon in itself; and with the collapse of a short-lived experiment in Reaganism comes the utter collapse of the American Right as well. Thus there is no American Primacy movement, thus Christian fascism does not grip the land.

Even should Reagan's presidency have been relatively benign, the book goes on, he obviously would not have run in 1984, since the country would never have accepted someone of his age (seventy-three) in the job. Rather 1984 sees the election of a charismatic Democrat such as New York Governor Koch or perhaps Gary Hart of Colorado, and with the replacement of a right-wing Republican by a moderate Democrat, and with the United States spared the traumatic confusion of electoral crises, the Soviet Union feels freer to choose a more reform-minded leader of its own and perhaps even to dally with China-styled experiments in an open economy. The result is that, rather than the current spectacle in Eastern Europe of brutal oppression by a massive Soviet invasion bent on crackdown, rather than the precipice on which the United States finds itself teetering today with the most reactionary commander-in-chief ever, the choke-hold of totalitarianism has actually loosened. Not that it would or could ever be broken—even a utopian fantasy like *American Nomad* accepts that in countries like East Germany, Czechoslovakia and Yugoslavia, Marxism-Leninism will never disappear—but there are instances, such as Poland, where the state feels secure enough to free dissidents from jail, ease the harassment of the secret police, and make other merciful if minor concessions to tolerance.

It's an interesting and imaginative scenario. It doesn't fully account, however, for why *American Nomad* became the cultural event of the Nineties. While its course of historical events cannot help but seem preferable to whatever outcome the world crashes toward today, the book is—perhaps with the author's intention, perhaps only in the collective response of those who have read it—disturbing for reasons that seem somehow inexplicable, as though this is a dream all of us have had but can't remember. In our sharing of it, however, lies the suggestion that it was something that really happened after all, in our common American night. If the implied argument of *American Nomad* is that such a history exorcised some demon in America, the hints of our common night are at deeper demons such an exorcism left unstirred. *American Nomad* robs of us a history when, for better or worse, Americans had to face the meaning of their country. It replaces such a history with a more oblivious one, ignoring not only the symptoms of a bankruptcy that's political, but human. The homeless. The plague-stricken. The economic affront to national self-reliance. The savaging of the planet, and of the ethereal atmospheric tissue that shelters it from space. The things that have made America soul-sick, that exploded in the firestorm of *our* Nineties, instead burrow deeper into the heart of *Nomad*'s Nineties; and a disturbed and decadent ennui is the result. A self-absorption that has all the narcissism of self-absorption, distracted by no insight and thus allowing self-deception. The history of *American Nomad* is a serpent swallowing its own being . . .

56

No, I realized somewhere on I-90, in the depths of Minnesota between La Crosse and Albert Lee, that isn't quite right. "Actually," I slowly said to myself out loud, in horror, "that's all wrong." The *sense* of history was right but the *details* were wrong, or the details were right but the sense was wrong: I was a little alarmed because the last time I had driven through America like this, three years before, I had gone a little crazy, and now I wondered if it was happening again. It was Rush Limbaugh who jarred me from my dream, talking the first politics I had heard since California, about somebody named Bill Clinton, a strange name that nonetheless sounded vaguely familiar, and Bob Dole—is he *still* running for President? I wondered with amazement. For a moment I thought that crossing the Mississippi I had crossed into a parallel America and into an alternate American history, but then amnesia broke and I wondered if it was the thousand miles between Denver and Madison that were the parallel country and alternate history, and that this was the "real" country, the "real" history, where the real fragmentation of America was being buried in an apparently benign presidential election that no one cared about in the least, unless one counted Rush Limbaugh.

And then it all came back to me, a flood of visions and memories, not as frightening as the dream I had, but somehow not as stirring either. In a way I felt relieved, but in another way I felt almost as dispirited as Limbaugh himself. Since his influence had finally begun to wane in the last couple of years, the turn of the political tide over the previous months had apparently chastened some of the nastiness out of him: no more jokes, as far as I could hear, about Chelsea's looks, no more bulletins about Hillary having Vince Foster's body moved from their secret Georgetown love nook out to the banks of the Potomac after she blew him away. Instead, what with the afterglow of Bob Dole's San Diego convention quickly giving way to new polls showing Bill Clinton ahead fifteen to twenty percentage points, Limbaugh was in a state somewhere between disgusted incredulity and homicidal hysteria—not incredulous at the polls, but at an American public that seemed so shrewd only two years before, seeing right through the Anti-Christ in the White House, and yet so duped now. In the meantime his dwindling flock were living in their own fool's paradise. "I don't know anyone," one caller after another assured themselves and each other, "who's voting for Bill Clinton," until finally Rush lost it. "Folks," he screamed at the flock, "take it from me, there are *lots and lots* of people out there who are going to vote for Bill Clinton!" If he could, he would have reached through his microphone and slapped the whole lot of them silly, to wake them up. They obviously did not understand that the end of the Republic was at hand, preferring to believe instead that the polls were just the usual liberal-media conspiracy.

It put Limbaugh in the uncomfortable position of defending, even by degrees, the media's credibility, in order to shake his army out of its self-delusion, or to prepare them for the awful shock that awaited them on the morning of November 6 and threatened to break their spirit altogether, not to mention perhaps Limbaugh's career. But while allowing that the media might well have inflated Clinton's lead, and in the midst of some pretty cogent if obvious political analysis by which Rush concluded quite correctly that Dole's only chance was to "go negative" (his words), Limbaugh missed Dole's more salient hope: "One week Clinton's ahead by twenty, the next week by two," he cried, "people can't be changing their minds *that* much," but in fact that was the point, people *were* changing their minds that much, their enthusiasm for Clinton as transient as that for Limbaugh himself; and therefore—on the dawn I drove into Chicago—the race was potentially far more fluid than Democrats wanted to admit or Republicans dared to dream.

57

"The convention was about denial," Tom Hayden would say after the election was over. "It was as though there had never been a Sixties, as though nothing at all had happened in Chicago in 1968." Of course, Hayden knew something had happened in Chicago in 1968, because he had most conspicuously been there, when his generation took its complaint about the Vietnam War specifically, and America generally, to the Democratic Convention of that year and to the rest of the country—even if much of the country recoiled. Afterward, as a leader of the so-called Chicago Seven, Hayden was tried for conspiracy and for crossing state lines to incite a riot; he was acquitted of the first charge and convicted of the second. Eventually he wound up in California as a state legislator. Over the years since, he kept himself in the public eye in a manner somewhat calmer than 1968, reconciling himself to the system if only up to a point, running for governor of California in 1994 when he won a special respect from the voters though not their votes.

Later, in his office in Los Angeles the week following the 1996 election, I would find him on the phone already urging Minnesota's Paul Wellstone, the most liberal member of the United States Senate, to run for President in the year 2000. He was also musing over whether he himself should run for mayor of Los Angeles, a race he didn't really expect he could win: "*Now*," he answered, without sounding unduly urgent about it, when I asked how soon he had to make the decision. I knew Hayden didn't think I was the Enemy, though I wasn't sure that made me all much more comfortable than Gary Bauer knowing I *was* the Enemy; I realized I was getting sort of used to being the Enemy, or at least an enemy of some kind. "This is a big deal to me, and not easy to answer," Hayden tried to explain when I asked him about his return to Chicago as a California delegate to the 1996 Democratic Convention, where he had gone not to make any peace with the past, since he had always felt at peace with his own past if not the country's, but to witness, perhaps, the country making *its* peace—though later he wasn't at all sure that that was what the country had done, or that it was even a valuable and honest thing to do. "Sure I felt enormous vindication and ratification from people on the streets of Chicago, and people on the floor of the convention, and the media. And you would have to be awfully bitter"—Hayden laughed—"to say, 'Well, here you are thanking me now, where were you back then, in '68?' But I was also watching the orchestration of some kind of television spectacle, obviously—the big money people inhabiting all the skyboxes in the convention center, like at a sporting event where the rich people have the box seats and the masses are wandering around on the floor, and if anyone gets out of line they're ordered to stop, the activists guarding each other, standing up and down and holding up their signs and acting like the robots they said they would never be. But then, a convention brings out everything, the good as well as the bad. I met children of Mississippi who had survived all these years and were friends of mine in '61, I met people from the streets of Newark who survived all the hell of Newark in the five years I was there . . . you know, in a situation like that, you see it all."

"It's possible," I argued, ever the sunny optimist, "that '96 wasn't a denial of '68. It's possible it was implicitly a recognition of what had happened in '68, even if the Democratic Party didn't feel that it could politically afford to be very up front about it."

"Well," answered Hayden, "I don't see what the difference is between an implicit recognition and a denial. It's all in the subconscious."

"But because it *is* all in the subconscious, there might be a *big* difference. Because we live in a television age where even the media has seeped down into the collective subconscious, an implicit ratification of '68 might be important."

"No doubt. One thing I remember this last time is that everywhere you went, bars, restaurants, whatever, there was always footage of '68 on. The whole city—"

"I don't think it was just the city, I think it was the whole country."

"But you could really feel it in the city. It was pretty incredible. And I guess it was generally, silently agreed that '68 was all a big mistake, but that it was in the past."

"A mistake on whose part?"

"Well, there were no apologies or accountability, of course, just a new consensus that it was a mistake, as if we were all somehow to blame, but now we're better off for it, and it's better not to discuss it."

"That may be as close as the power structure can get to apologizing."

"But there's no intention to get close to an apology," Hayden insisted. "It was just taken for granted in the questions of the reporters that I was a fine person now and had done a fine thing then, but that we can't say that, we can allow ourselves to reflect on the past only because what happened then has now entered the realm of an amazing American human interest story." He reflected on this. "So maybe there *is* an implicit vindication there."

"Do you have any regrets about '68?"

"No. What, 'I lost my temper'? Gee, I'm really sorry. My father hadn't talked to me for fifteen years, they were killing three hundred Americans a week in Vietnam—so I lost my temper."

"Why hadn't your father talked to you?"

"I see the Sixties as a failure of the elders. The elders committed the country to a despicable war and it resulted in the deaths of a million or two million people, including tens of thousands of Americans and tens of thousands more wounded. And for that to happen, our fathers had to concur, conform and participate in sending their sons to war, or disapproving of their sons if they didn't go. . . . So the war was fought out around the family table, not just the legislative table, and that's what I think they're afraid of apologizing for, because they have this grief and pain and guilt for having killed two million people. I would certainly have a hard time apologizing if I was responsible for that. I would construct my entire life to prevent accountability," Hayden said, quietly and without a trace of scorn. "My entire life. In my case, on a family level it meant that my father disowned me, remarried, had a daughter, never told her that she had a brother, and this went on for fifteen or sixteen years. I can talk about it now because we reconciled, again through family—when I had a child and my father became a grandfather, he could either take his stubborn Irish silence with him to his grave, or he could enjoy his family and enjoy being a grandfather, and I think that touched him. And, also, I had become more respectable, and more people had come to see the war was insane. But my father was someone who came out of that experience of World War II, who believed that what the government said was true, and believed that, you know, you probably *should* be drafted, and roughed up a bit to put some discipline in you, since your parents seemed unable to control you anymore. And those elders had also persuaded themselves—because they had assimilated so far into a middle-class American life, an established life, that they were now severed by amnesia from their own traumatic roots in exploitation, poverty, unemployment, immigration, upheaval from Ireland or wherever—that the problems in America were relatively minor, if any, and that our real problems were with Communists or revolutionary movements abroad. So they failed to see the urgency of civil rights, for instance, because that would be a blot on the American success story that they had accepted. The Sixties revolt was about that. It wasn't just about the war or segregation, it was about, Why is segregation still here and why are you, our parents, not doing anything about it? It was a youth movement because our parents had failed. If our parents hadn't failed, there wouldn't have been a youth movement. So everyone has come to kind of understand that now, I think, but it's taken all this time for it to rise to the surface. And, you know, there's still a problem in the unwillingness to apologize for the Vietnam War, which is amazing to me. It's amazing. It makes the power-dealers still dangerous to me, because I have memory. They haven't apologized, and that curse is still in them, and they'll do it all again, in some other way, in some other kind of Vietnam, and now that *we're* becoming the elders the question is whether we will repeat the mistake of not listening to our children. Clinton says"—Hayden quoted the Fleetwood Mac song that had been the Democratic campaign theme of 1992—"what, 'yesterday's gone, don't stop thinking about tomorrow'? So you look at Bill Clinton and you see the past and the forces that are shaping him—but we're not supposed to discuss any of that, we're supposed to move on, just as we did after the Civil War, just as we did after the Indian Wars, after all the Indians were dead. Move on."

"Well," I suggested, "America was born out of the idea that it could cut yesterday loose, that it could wipe the slate of history clean and write on it whatever it wanted to."

"A very powerful idea," Hayden nodded. "It can turn you into a very powerful, if misshapen, political figure or society, because then you can concentrate all your force on the future without the shadow of doubt cast by the past that drains you. I think Bill Clinton was open to the winds of change in the Sixties, but also wholly involved in the system, and trying to reform it, although I think in his darkest moments he may have once had doubts about it. But he remained on his career path, perhaps after some kind of spiritual crisis, and I guess the Left would call him an opportunist, the moderate coming to take advantage of the Movement and capitalize on it. I don't have that harsh a critique. I see it all as part of the inevitable pattern in which the movement builders get maligned and a new class emerges to capitalize on what the builders built, and that new class has mixed feelings. They've been touched by the Movement, but they're motivated by a desire for power and advancement. I'm sure the American Revolution was just like that. So Clinton is just like that. He's a transitional figure, from the establishment that went wrong in the Sixties, to an establishment that's based on the Sixties. I think he's more establishment than Sixties, myself. But," Hayden conceded, "he's not Bob Dole."

58

Finally, then, driving into Chicago where he was nominated once more by the Democratic Party for the presidency, it was time to consider at some length the matter of Bill Clinton. There was no avoiding it anymore, as much as one might have wanted to, for all the reasons embodied by Chicago itself, as the city of compromise and redemption for all of the Clinton Generation, which is to say Tom Hayden's generation and my own. Clinton, of course, had not been in Chicago in 1968 as a twenty-two-year-old, nor had I as an eighteen-year-old: he was in Arkansas packing for Oxford, England, plotting his way out of a war that America still can't quite bring itself to call misbegotten, let alone bad; and I was plotting to work for Richard Nixon for President, which I just barely brought myself to call bad, let alone misbegotten, by the time I voted uneasily for George McGovern in 1972. That Clinton's generation and mine had returned to Chicago to make him President represented a triumph of the Sixties counterculture that triumphed only by fundamentally betraying the very notion of counterculture. Maybe much of it warranted betrayal. If, at least for the moment, the Right had won most of the historical arguments of the last thirty years, certainly the Left won the two most profound arguments of the Sixties—Vietnam and civil rights. Now, thirty years later, Bill Clinton seemed truer to his convictions about the second than about the first, the most important and provocative questions about which he always dodged, of course, as adeptly as he dodged the same draft that many of us, from Bill Clinton to Dan Quayle and Newt Gingrich and Phil Gramm and Bill Bennett, tried to dodge, in one way or another.

Clinton had not come to Chicago in 1996 to talk about such things, however. Accepting renomination he did not talk about the war or 1968; giving him the largest possible benefit of the doubt, he may have concluded that just holding the convention in Chicago spoke for itself, though surely that's stretching it. Clinton had come to Chicago to ratify hope, even if the hopes he was ratifying were more his own than anyone else's. It was hard to hope for very much from

Clinton anymore, and I remembered the hopes of 1992 very well, because I was there, when hope was alive, as Jesse Jackson would have it, even amid the disarray of the days preceding Clinton's inauguration. Driving into Chicago on this particular morning in 1996 I couldn't help thinking of the Virginia road I drove in the early morning hours three and a half years before, when the temperature was well below freezing and the countryside flying by was void-black. Passing road signs said Bull Run, blithely casual in their historical explosiveness. I had been up twenty hours then and was literally nodding off at the wheel, on my way to the home of Thomas Jefferson because, more than any Democrat in a generation, William Jefferson Clinton understood political symbolism as well as Republicans did, which was why the choice of Chicago three and a half years later would not appear to be complete serendipity. And because he had understood political symbolism as well as the Reagan Republicans before him, he was going to be inaugurated President in three days, and that was why he was going to be at the home of Thomas Jefferson that cold Virginia morning in January of 1993.

I was covering that first inauguration for the weekly newspaper in Los Angeles, and the night I arrived in Washington I walked in the cold to the Mall that runs from the Capitol past the Washington Monument to the reflecting pools that lie before the Lincoln Memorial. The white tents had already gone up for the Reunion on the Mall, an arts-and-food fair celebrating national diversity and Clinton as that diversity's personification; a huge stage had been constructed at the memorial for an extravaganza that would mix movie stars, music and patriotic scripture. The growing inaugural hoopla was oblivious, perhaps appropriately so, to the fact that Clinton had just had the worst week of his presidency to date, not an inconsiderable accomplishment considering that his presidency hadn't even started yet. Even then there was confusion about his policy toward Iraq, as there would still be in the Indian summer of 1996 following the Chicago convention; his reversal on welcoming the exodus of Haitian refugees had dashed the hopes of thousands of people, which only an invasion in 1994 would partly revive. He had already reneged on his promise to cut taxes for the middle class, always the most dubious part of his budding economic program anyway and something that—though it was forgotten later—he began distancing himself from in the 1992 campaign. Also rattling around the transitional period was rhetorical bric-a-brac from the campaign about the size of the White House staff and the ethical standards of those in Clinton's new government; most damaging of all, the first woman he appointed attorney general conceded she knowingly broke the law, hiring illegal aliens to take care of her children when the demands of motherhood proved trying to her measly annual salary of half a mil. Finally, there were signs that the Congress—a Democratic Congress, one should remember—was taking the early measure of Clinton and concluding "wimp," as in "George Bush" or "Jimmy Carter."

The tents and concession stands and souvenir tables that night reminded me of an old 1951 Billy Wilder movie called *Ace in the Hole*, later renamed *The Big Carnival*. In *Ace in the Hole* a man is trapped in a deep hole and, as his plight becomes a national soap opera, broadcast across the country in one heart-stopping turn of events after another while workers try to rescue him, a cynical press descends on the location just ahead of a thrill-hungry public, along with tents and concession stands and souvenir tables. This particular weekend the big carnival was in Washington and Bill Clinton was the man in the hole. There was something unsettling about this analogy: in the movie, the man in the hole dies. As I always did when I was in Washington, I walked to the Lincoln Memorial to read, carved on its walls, the unvarnished words of an undaunted heart, words that blow away the cant of modern politics; and after standing in the light of the memorial and looking at the statue of Lincoln and reading the carved words I walked past the reflecting pools toward the Washington Monument and the tents beyond them. I kept well away from the water, not wanting to tumble in. Off to my left I saw, running alongside me, another pool glittering in the dark. After a moment I was startled to see people in the water, the silhouetted forms of their heads bobbing up and down in the lights off the pool's surface, and it was only after I got closer that I realized there weren't people in the water at all, because it wasn't a pool at all. It was the blank reflective slab of the Vietnam Memorial. It rose gradually from the earth one name at a time, to tower over my head holding back a bank of earth before dwindling back to nothing, muttering the last victim, Jesse C. Alba, into the ground.

For all the ways in which the Clinton presidency already seemed beset, Inaugural Week was shaping up as one huge party. Nobody was thinking about crises, and you could hardly blame them; a lot of people had been waiting for this particular celebration a long time, about a generation to be precise. "When was the last time *you* felt welcome in Washington?" Whoopi Goldberg asked the Lincoln Memorial Concert crowd, to which the crowd roared back: never. For all the ways that the talk about hope and change and generational transition turned so glibly into hype, there was no denying that the proceedings, from the Memorial Concert to the Mall Reunion to the Inauguration Eve Gala, kept coming as a shock. There was Bob Dylan's rollicking honky-tonk "Chimes of Freedom," and Aretha Franklin's displacement of Frank Sinatra as the country's singer-laureate, spell-binding the Mall with "Respect" in the same way that three years later she would spell-bind the Democratic Convention in Chicago with her version of the national anthem. By the afternoon of the Reunion on the Mall, as I made my way from tent to tent, from Al Green to Robert Cray to Loudon Wainwright and Buckwheat Zydeco, from Los Lobos to Salt-N-Pepa to the Texas Tornados and the Staples Singers, the arrival of the new political zeitgeist seemed so overwhelming and incontrovertible that one moment I was perfectly certain the song coming from the carousel was Dylan's debauched, surreal "Rainy Day Women #12 and 35" ("Well they'll stone you when you're trying to be so good . . . everybody must get stoned"), before I eventually realized it was "Three Blind Mice." And if the moment's show business seemed as ghastly one moment as it did great the next, it was partly because the new President had worked very hard and very deliberately at mixing the metaphor and mastering it, if only with mixed results: on the one hand it got him elected, the brainstorm of his bus tour from Monticello surpassed only by the theatrical genius of his walk down Broadway to Madison Square Garden on the night of his nomination the previous summer in New York.

On the other hand, such success may have encouraged him to play his first hand too heavily. The Monticello affair really wasn't such a brainstorm, but a bust of the first order. The idea had been a tour of the house in which Clinton would, in full view of the country, soak up the vibes of Jefferson himself, but there was too much press and too little house, so the reporters like myself wound up standing outside listening to the peculiarly disembodied observations of the tour guide inside, broadcast over speakers along with the banalities the Clintons and Gores giggled in response. The guide pointed out how narrow the stairs were and Al Gore burbled back, "I *like* narrow stairs!" This was followed by Bill and Al's conference with schoolkids outside about the meaning of Jefferson in the Nineties, which produced a pretty good sound bite for the night's news when a boy asked to what political position Clinton would appoint Jefferson if he were still alive and Clinton answered secretary of state, because then Clinton and Gore could resign so Jefferson would become president.

It was one of Clinton's better ad-libs; of course it was also complete horseshit, and not just because it got the line of succession wrong but because never under any circumstances would Clinton have resigned to let Jefferson, Lincoln, Washington, Andrew Jackson, Franklin Roosevelt, Theodore Roosevelt, Eleanor Roosevelt, John Kennedy, Martin Luther King, Mahatma Gandhi, Mother Theresa, Winston Churchill, Elvis Presley, F. Scott Fitzgerald, Albert Einstein, Sir Thomas More, Saint Francis of Assisi, Madame Curie, Isaac Newton, Geronimo, James Brown, Jesus Christ or anyone else become President of the United States. And on the day he rode victoriously into Washington, D.C., flag-waving crowds lining Virginia's Highway 29 cheering him on, Clinton's mix of ever-escalating metaphors reached both its apotheosis and nadir when he literally emerged for the Lincoln Memorial bash from among the towering pillars and the shadow of the Lincolngod staring down at him with trumpets blaring Aaron Copland's *Fanfare For the Common Man* and bomber jets screaming overhead. The whole thing was Woodstock Goes to Nuremberg. If Pat Buchanan had been standing in Clinton's place, those of us who supported Clinton would have been screaming about how fascist it all was, just as if Clinton were a Republican we would have been crucifying him for the Zoe Baird appointment before it ever got out of his mouth. Yet almost immediately the Leni Riefenstahl part of the show gave way to something else: the words of Lincoln fading into Ben E. King singing "Stand By Me"—and it was more than exhilarating, it was magic. It was also something you knew you would never have seen if George Bush had been reelected.

By the time Clinton's delight at L. L. Cool J's rap flashed across the huge video monitors to the multitudes on the Mall, it was clear the new President meant to try and validate cultural insurgency even while appropriating the trappings of conservative tradition that America adored. Clinton knew that American myth loves not only the bottom dog but the top dog that devours the bottom one; speaking to our confusion, Clinton always identified it as the contradiction that goes by the name of truth, which it often is. Of course it would be the nature of his new job to make decisions that always came down on one side of the contradiction or the other, and every time that happened it would test the faith that more people invested more intensely in Clinton than in any President of our political lifetimes, though it must be said that a whole other side of America placed similar faith in Ronald Reagan for not dissimilar reasons, having waited as long for him as many of us had for Clinton. The reasons that Clinton could mix his metaphors and, for the time being, get away with it, was that history kept mixing them for him, making mincemeat of ideology and leaving Clinton himself a cipher, despite all our efforts to acquaint ourselves with him. He was and, familiarity notwithstanding, four years later remained the chameleon who brilliantly lent himself to the shape of our imaginations, even though his own imagination was so prosaic. When asked what words of wisdom would adorn his Oval Office the way "The buck stops here" adorned Truman's, he could only quote Fleetwood Mac, after all, an early tip-off to how transparently ersatz he could be; and when he kept mouthing the words to Martin Luther King and John Kennedy speeches whenever someone insisted on reciting them, we knew even then, four years ago, that he was really going to get on our nerves, the contrivances of his persona sooner or later overcoming his sincerity and warmth. There were only so many words, songs and icons he could embrace with credibility and grace.

It was hard to separate Washington's response from the rest of the country's, but by the day of his inauguration Clintonmania was at hand, flawed transition or no. Around the country people prayed and lit candles for Bill Clinton; there was, deep in America, the conviction that this was the Last-Chance Presidency, the one that would deliver us or close the deal on America for good. At the various balls that night, such as the California shindig where I happened to be, the response to his appearance was a frenzy unlike anything since the rallies for Barry Goldwater and Robert Kennedy in the Sixties. The ecstasy was so profound and fervent it was frightening, a collective plea that he dare not let us down; and even four years later he would retain a rapport with people that didn't really withstand analysis, particularly with those who had always felt alienated by American politics, such as the young, women and particularly blacks, from whom he seemed to command more natural affection—removed from any consideration of policy—than any middle-aged white politician ever. After the California ball I headed for the MTV party at the Convention Center. The Mall carousel may not have been playing "Rainy Day Women #12 and 35," but the MTV Ball was still without question the hot ticket in town, the then-languishing music network having struck a startling symbiosis with Clinton, reviving with the 1992 election both its audience and its cachet, in large part through Clinton's accessibility and his willingness to take MTV seriously, just as he revived his campaign the previous summer with, among other things, a tour de force performance on the channel with a ninety-minute question-and-answer session. In the packed cab over to the Convention Center the three complete strangers in the back seat tried to bribe me out of my press pass. I arrived in time to be nearly crushed by a stampede of fans dashing madly after a departing Jack Nicholson.

Inside the ball, while waiting for R.E.M. to perform, I encountered a guy I knew who drove Clinton around New Hampshire during the desperate primary of 1992, and later went to work full-time for the campaign and transition. The last time I had talked to him, a few days after the election, he was flying high, naturally, and I expected him to be at similar altitude tonight. "The country is doomed," I was startled to hear him croak instead. "Are you sure?" I asked. "It's doomed, it's over," he just went on, and I asked him why: was it the deficit, I wanted to know, was it Clinton's appointment of too many slick, venal lawyers to positions of power? It was none of that. It was something my friend couldn't or wouldn't explain; and I was wondering if I had fast-forwarded into the illusion-ravaged future of the Last-Chance Presidency, when I was yanked back to the present by Don Henley. Yes, Don Henley. He was leading the audience in a version of Dylan's "The Times They Are a-Changin'" and the crowd was crying out the refrain, and one could think what one wanted to about it, but suddenly I saw the light. It was no time for cynicism, realistic as cynicism might be, and no matter how naive hope might be. "You're drunk," I turned back to my friend to say, "it's obvious he's going to be the best President in fifty years." But my friend was gone, weaving off into the singing crowd, and for all his cynicism I suspect he was singing too. That night cynicism wasn't smart, it was for cowards; and it was the naive, the hopeful, the innocent and the believers, those mid-air in the country's most reckless leap of faith yet, who were the Last-Chance Americans.

59

At the outset of the Nineties, with the clock running, the Twentieth Century still had to play itself out. The Eighties had ended with the century reduced to the cockeyed reverie of a historical nanosecond, in which walls that once seemed to have gone up forever came down in a day, in which countries that once invented themselves in an explosion of revolution and sustained themselves in a rage of nuclear power uninvented themselves. Those were the years, when the Eighties gave way to the Nineties, that the Twentieth Century nearly seduced us into believing it never happened at all. Nuclear imagination gave way to nuclear memory, to the temporal whisper of annihilation's possibilities that occasionally reminded us who we were and what we had learned about ourselves before the Twentieth Century vanished altogether. Those were the years in which those of us who called ourselves Americans became too alienated from the courage and audacity that created us to marvel at how we withstood the vagaries of the century—or to wonder if, given that alienation, we really had.

By 1992 we found ourselves having exhausted every impulse, the deeper ones as well as the shallower ones, and facing the question of whether we would shake off that exhaustion or succumb to it. Any contention that the 1992 presidential election was about the economy nearly to the exclusion of everything else was not wholly untrue; it might even be glib and insensitive to argue otherwise, in the face of all the social pain and anxiety that existed at the time. But the election of 1992, as would be the case again in 1996, was finally about ourselves. In 1992 we still had one more impulse to exhaust, after the others of idealism, realism, naiveté, confidence and heroism that had characterized the half-dozen previous elections; and that was the impulse of cynicism for which George Bush was a more perfect vehicle than we were ultimately willing to live with. By the waning days of that summer, the 1992 election was no longer a referendum on Bush. That referendum was over, and Bush had lost. By the early days of autumn the elections of 1992 became a referendum on whether Bill Clinton was a suitable alternative to the cynicism we would reject.

Cynicism is always the most bitter expression of broken faith. We are now at the end of a generation of broken faith in America that began in the Sixties with Presidents who lied to us and ended in the Nineties with us lying to ourselves. Ronald Reagan's pact with the American people was that leadership would henceforth define itself not by Presidents who told the people what they needed to know but what they wanted to hear: it took only slightly more self-delusion than sense to believe Reagan could increase military spending, cut taxes and balance the budget, as he promised in 1980 and for which we gave him a mandate. The real scandal of George Bush's pledge during the 1988 campaign never to raise taxes under any circumstances was our complicity in accepting it, when such a bankrupt promise clearly served self-interest rather than national interest. In 1992 the nadir of a political campaign during which the President of the United States virtually accused his opponent of once being a KGB dupe was tethered not just to Bush's cynicism but our own, after we rewarded similarly squalid libels made against Michael Dukakis in 1988. The great dirty secret of the 1992 election was our insistence that all we wanted from our politicians was the truth, when our history of punishing the tellers of hard truths, from Bob Dole to Bruce Babbitt to Paul Tsongas, insisted otherwise. "I wanted sunshine," a Midwest woman had explained her disenchantment with Bush, as though she were voting for a new wizard of Oz. "I wanted a rainbow."

If the American public found it difficult to take seriously the past and still support Clinton, it finally could not take seriously the future and still support Bush, or take seriously the present and support Ross Perot. Pervading every conversation and observation of the 1992 campaign was the prospect of waking up in November to a Bush re-election; the great collective mood of the country would not have been merely joyless, it would not have been simply depression, it would have verged on the nihilistic. Bush's cynicism, by which the shameless calculations of his "promises" lay not in their breaking but their making, by which "convictions" were characterized more by belligerence than belief, by which "commitment" was never more energized than when it was focused on the consolidation of power, had become so naked it could no longer be denied. We could never feign shocked hurt the next time faith was broken. In this light our electoral decision was more than simply political, let alone partisan; confronted with a similar prospect in 1980, we had no choice but to elect Ronald Reagan. It didn't matter whether he was going to be a better President than Jimmy Carter; the psychic consequences of ratifying Carter's failure were too dreadful. Similarly, to have chosen Bush again would have been to accept the inevitability of betrayal rather than dare one more time to have faith. To make a choice like that would have been a kind of spiritual death.

As 1992 was the last American presidential election of the Twentieth Century, 1996 would be the first of the Twenty-First, a century that will, by the definition and dictates of time and technology, devour itself faster than the century before it. And during the four years between 1992 and 1996, when the public consensus swung wildly and erratically from Bush to Clinton to Gingrich to Dole back to Clinton, the country grappled with the prospect that cynicism was the only national identity that remained possible. Let's get real: he was bound to let us down. Everything about Bill Clinton was always two-edged—blindingly smart to the point of glibness, immensely likeable to the point of obsequiousness, admirably politic to the point of expedience, unrestricted by the moral and intellectual limits of ideology and thus philosophically empty, youthful/callow, articulate/slick, confident/arrogant. He's always been him/us, which is to say you/me, which is to say we may have gone to high school with him but we never really hung out with him, we elected him class president and despised him as we did it, we were at the same parties with him but he was the one who insisted on playing the Fifth Dimension album when everyone else wanted to hear Sly and the Family Stone. He's lived up to everything expected of him in life while we have spent the last twenty years living everything down, and so one side of the slash was always bound to betray us, but what was really the mindblower was when it was not the him side but the us side, not the you side but the me side. Over and over after his first election we exclaimed in astonishment, "But that's us!" every time we saw him on TV; and the times he failed in his first term when we tried to say, "But that's not really us, it's only him," it never washed.

We elected ourselves a President of nuclear memory, having bypassed altogether a President of nuclear imagination, unless it was Richard Nixon. In Clinton we had the embodiment of an America that could now acknowledge remembering an abyss it never before quite admitted was there, and those of us in Clinton's generation dreaded from the first the ways he was bound to confirm what our parents always said about us in the decade we came of age—the Sixties, which we romanticized as soon as we stomped them into their grave: that we're a narcissistic generation indulged too much by the country that began inventing us back when we were through inventing it. Even three-and-a-half years later, having survived his initiation of the first two-and-a-half and shown some growth as a man in the process, Clinton still had yet to convey a wisdom that was placeless and ageless, which might be why his compensating intellect made us so giddy at first blush. Now our emotional investment in Clinton was frightening. For a while I found myself monitoring his every move, automatically defending every retreat on campaign commitments that were as cynical as George Bush's, reflexively justifying appointments that were as "brain-dead," to use Clinton's own term, as any Bush made, if not quite the low point hit by Reagan with Ed Meese, William Casey and James Watt.

On the other hand, on the other hand . . . Once we gave him the break of electing him President, as improbable as that was, we never really gave him another. He had the shortest "honeymoon" in presidential history, about seventy-two hours, before the press and the country started wondering aloud what was wrong. The press was always deeply schizophrenic about Clinton, hating the fact that it once loved him so much and so unabashedly, and therefore punishing him for it, until the electrifying Gingrich Congress of 1995 when the press found Clinton more pathetic than anything else, and the hapless Dole campaign of 1996 when the press decided Clinton was more than capable of taking care of himself. This schizophrenia was never more pronounced than in the weeks of late 1992 and early 1993 immediately following his first election. When he appointed his economic team, everyone said, "Oh, more white guys." When he appointed women and blacks and latinos, everyone said, "Oh, quotas." When he appointed old pols like Lloyd Bentsen, it was, "Oh, business as usual. What happened to the 'change' we kept hearing about?" When he appointed new faces like Donna Shalala it was, "Oh, left-wing radicals. What happened to the 'new kind of Democrat' we kept hearing about?" When he started talking about the deficit it was, "What about all those new programs?" and when he started talking about new programs it was, "What about the deficit?" When he made his first appointments slowly it was, "What's taking so long?" and when he made the last ones hastily, including some particularly ill-fated ones, it was, "What's the rush?" The Right, outraged by the sheer affront of having lost power, hated him as a new incarnation of Kennedy and Carter; and the Left, deeply suspicious of and thoroughly disoriented by the prospect of having actually won power, hated him as a new incarnation of Carter and Bush: "I did something today I never thought I'd do," a friend of mine snarled into my telephone on Election Day 1992, "I voted for a Republican. I voted for Bill Clinton." So the man was fucked at the outset, something underscored—in two-edged fashion—first by the mere forty-three percent of the popular vote he received (which the press, on the momentary upswing of its manic-depression about him, somehow characterized as "decisive"), and second by the Clintonmania that attended the closing weeks of his campaign and the first few weeks after, with near-riots in Southern California shopping malls. Thus he labored beneath the burden of no real confidence in him on the one hand and too much hope on the other, a mix by which the spirit of the country became weirdly combustible.

60

The margin of error in the Nineties had grown much narrower than before. There was no fooling anyone anymore like Reagan did, not simply because Clinton wasn't as good at it as Reagan, but because we weren't as good at it as we used to be, in those halcyon days when we could kid ourselves into oblivion, or at least a debt that dwarfed all previous national debts combined. And because Ross Perot, the phoniest "authentic" figure in American culture since Art Linkletter, was nonetheless more right about the deficit than either Clinton or Bush, Clinton's most specious 1992 campaign promise—the middle-class tax cut—gave way immediately to a tax hike on the wealthy and a fleeting moment of serious discussion about what could only accurately be called the impending calamity of entitlement spending. The unfolding of Bill Clinton's second term would tell the tale, but in the fall of 1996, with the President cruising toward reelection, it was daunting to consider that what had saved him politically were in fact the two worst and most irresponsible things he had done as President, for which we could only blame ourselves as harshly as history will certainly blame him.

One was a welfare bill, written by the Republican Congress and signed by the Democratic President, that brutally trampled the parameters of reasonable and necessary reform in order to level the single most draconian blow against the American people by its government since the Vietnam draft. As usual, the Left bore as much responsibility for this as anyone, having refused so long even to acknowledge the failure of the welfare system, let alone address that failure or, God forbid, suggest welfare might be predicated on work; it was a Democratic Congress, after all, that bluntly rebuffed their own President's more moderate proposals for reforming welfare in 1993 and 1994. Thus when the reckoning finally came, it was as sweeping as it was inevitable, with millions of children likeliest to pay the price. The second terrible moment of the Clinton presidency was how, in the 1995 battle of the budget and then later in the 1996 campaign, he knowingly poisoned the national debate on slowing the growth of Medicare and Social Security, by marshaling public sentiment against what he was too smart not to understand was economically necessary. There was, to be sure, much about the Republican budget that was awful, including the way it savaged both medical care for the needy and the Earned Income Tax Credit, which Clinton, in one of his best moments, had expanded, lifting hundreds of thousands of families out of poverty while at the same time encouraging them to work. Moreover, in a fashion too mind-boggling to be called merely stupid, the Republicans had tied these slashes to a colossal $245 billion tax cut for the wealthy, which Rush Limbaugh might find perfectly reasonable but the plain sheer unfairness of which an eight-year-old could comprehend apparently better than all of Gingrich's dimmer zealots combined. But it was in the matter of Medicare and Social Security, as well as an increasingly absurd defense budget that armed the country for not one but two independent and simultaneous hypothetical wars, that the country was going bankrupt; and Clinton's relentless characterization of slowing the growth of these programs as "deep cuts" by the Republicans might have saved his presidency but not the country. One would like to think he valued the second rather more than the first.

If saving the country meant undoing both the liberal and conservative dogmas of the nuclear era, as Clinton the Candidate often suggested in 1992, in 1996 Clinton the President often catered to both at exactly the wrong times in exactly the wrong ways. In fairness, such a dismantlement of orthodoxy was finally beyond the power of anyone but the people, who at the moment would as soon resist rethinking long-held assumptions from the bottom up even as instinctively they understood and even appreciated the limits of ideology. It was perhaps only coincidence that it would require Clinton to trash the legacies of the two figures with whom he really had most in common temperamentally. That he shared Lyndon Johnson's sheer southern effusiveness without Johnson's meanness, along with a relish for politics far more unseemly in 1996 than it was in 1966 when Johnson's presidency began to unravel, as well as political convictions that were always, shall we say, in flux, was obvious. That those convictions were molded as much by Oxford and rock and roll as by rural southern poverty might account for their added amorphousness, though four years later his presidency had yet to offer the definitive verdict of whether Clinton was just a complete political whore or his flexibility was rooted in a true intellectual adventurousness that vacillated on decisions of policy because it genuinely saw all sides of a question. Evidence supported each proposition. Like Johnson, Clinton figured just about anything could be fixed with the right application of power and charm. Unlike Johnson, he was not intimidated by intelligent and educated people, and because he was not intimidated, suppositions about power and charm were imbued with the self-confidence and sometimes rude self-appraisal that translated, time and again, into an almost unearthly tenacity in the face of insurmountable odds. He didn't appear to be driven by the deep sense of defensive inferiority that drove Johnson, Nixon and Carter. And it was this, in part, that produced the familiar cock of the head and shrug of the shoulders when he was about to finesse a question, the optimism that verged on either transcendence or self-delusion—it was hard to know which sometimes—and the inclination to transform any complication or difficulty into the perfect opportunity for making the case he had been trying to make all along. All of which reminded us of . . . well, to the alarm of conservatives and liberals alike, it was, of course, Ronald Reagan.

A version of Reagan at once better informed and less eloquent, to be sure, and an anti-ideologue where Reagan was the most ideological President of the Twentieth Century and perhaps since John Adams, another bad President we were lucky to survive. But Reagan nonetheless, eternally boyish in the same way and full of the same easy masculine swagger, utterly self-invented and so damned happy with the results, taking sheer disingenuousness to such dizzying convolutions that he became convinced of its overpowering truth. And so, translated into presidential terms, the two-edged truth of Clinton was that he seemed to possess both the worst and best of Roosevelt (connivance and a sense of the moment), Truman (bad temper and a sense of the people), Eisenhower (reticence and a sense of leadership), Kennedy (arrogance and a sense of vitality), Johnson (powerlust and a sense of politics), Nixon (expedience and a sense of surprise), Carter (inexperience and a sense of mission), Reagan (shallowness and a sense of drama), and Bush (amorality and a sense of proportion). (All right, I left out Ford; can you blame me?) What was nerve-racking about this litany was how the good things were so vague and the bad things were so specific, and how—with the exceptions of Roosevelt and maybe Eisenhower—the bad usually dominated the good.

As much as any presidency in memory, Bill Clinton's was the blind-faith melding of moment and persona. Since Eisenhower there had been only two Presidents—Nixon and Reagan—that we felt we really knew, and it was no accident that of all the recent Presidents they seemed to have the surest grasp of both public sentiment and the power into which it translated, and that they were the only ones, before Bill Clinton, to be reelected. We trusted them or, more precisely in the case of Nixon, trusted what we knew of them; only a scandal as seismic as Watergate, and more seismic than Iran-Contra, could breach that. Bush and Carter and Ford we never really knew at all, or even Johnson who was so utterly a creature of Congress' corridors, or Kennedy whose persona through the medium of television and incandescent martyrdom became ours to invent. At the same time, by the Nineties it seemed we had come to no longer tolerate in our presidential candidates the contradictions that routinely characterize the most complicated and unknowable of men, including our two most archetypal and mysterious Presidents—Jefferson, who lived like an aristocrat and thought like a revolutionary, calling for bloody upheaval every nineteen years, which was the amount of time he defined as a true generation, and something Clinton alluded to in his first inaugural speech (whitewashing it in the process); and Lincoln, who behaved like a schemer and believed like a mystic, racked with dreams of his own doom and, for periods of his life, seemingly unhinged, on more than one occasion having to be protected by friends from doing himself physical harm. By the end of the Eighties, following a national election in which the most salient issue of the campaign was whether one had the right to burn a flag (the Constitution says yes, the country said no), even as the iconography of Jefferson and Lincoln continued to be ransacked in the time-honored tradition of American politics, neither man would have been considered American enough to be American, let alone President. And as recently as 1988 a known womanizer would not have been elected President either, nor a draft dodger.

Of course, we elected both in one man in 1992. (Actually, we had already done the same exactly a hundred years before, with a candidate well known not only to have fathered an illegitimate child but to have paid someone to take his place in the Civil War draft of three decades earlier. In the end Grover Cleveland may have been one of the better late-Nineteenth-Century presidents, though that certainly isn't saying much.) While Bill Clinton's election was a strange moment in which we swallowed all of our earlier suspicions and hesitations, it was also the culmination of what had become the great prevailing eccentricity of recent American presidential elections: the perverse choice that had no historical likelihood about it at all. It may be the last time we had a truly *likely* President was Martin Van Buren, which was also the last time before George Bush that a sitting vice president was promoted directly by election rather than pneumonia, stroke, gunshot or the prospect of impeachment, and without an interim of political exile. Since the Second World War we've had only two presidencies that, from the vantage point of history, had any likeliness about them at all, Eisenhower's and Bush's, both crescendos of power that seemed clearly dictated by the trajectories that preceded them, in one case the greatest military triumph since Alexander the Great's, and in the other the most majestic display of groveling ass-kissing careerism ever witnessed outside a major Hollywood studio. All other modern presidencies have been shots out of the blue (Truman, Johnson and Ford), screwball leaps of faith (Carter and Reagan), or seriously deranged defiances of common sense (Kennedy and Nixon), with Clinton all of the above, and least likely of all. When all the big guns of the Democratic Party ran for cover in 1991, in the face of George Bush's ninety percent popularity in the polls, Clinton passed the test they failed—that of political courage; and so as the moment of his presidency melded with the persona of the President, the sheer *phenomenon* of Clinton became the bridge between his idealism, which was the vague, self-congratulatory idealism of his generation, and the rawness of his ambition, which was at once the most awesome and frightening thing about him. In the depths of his '92 campaign, the days just before the New Hampshire Primary when the Gennifer Flowers and draft-evasion stories broke in a lethal double-whammy, his poll numbers plummeting seventeen points in hours and his political career stone dead, I watched him talking to a small rally of the sort of people who probably attended car wrecks and funerals as spectator sports. Impassioned, fiery and mesmerizing, he wasn't simply the most impressive I've ever seen him but the most impressive I've ever seen an American politician. As an act of sheer will, it was primal and unprecedented.

To anyone who remembered this, the recurring questions by the media and the public early on as to his "toughness" were laughable, and finally faded in the last months of 1995. Now the question in 1996, before a country reconsidering the prospect of Bill Clinton as President, was not whether he was tough, not whether he was effective, certainly not whether he was politic, but whether he was good. At the outset of his presidency it was clear that if Clinton's mastery of political and cultural symbolism, whether it was MTV or Monticello, was to prove anything more than empty, it would have to be informed by conscience and judgment, the second more dubious than the first. Four years later, both the most reassuring and dismaying thing about his presidency was that the first was more dubious than the second.

The most skeptical of Americans had decided Bill Clinton was not good, while the most generous dismissed the question as somehow irrelevant.

Everyone else in between just deferred it, until having resolved something more basic, which was not whether Clinton was necessarily a successful President or a failed one, but whether he was any kind of a President at all. Until relatively recently Americans hadn't been sure. At the low point of his first term, the 1994 congressional election, Americans in fact seemed quite certain of the contrary, that he was out of his depth. Then something happened in the period between the summer of 1995 and the summer of 1996 that had nothing to do with political positioning or rogue advisers destined to be disgraced by aging prostitutes; it had nothing to do with the clumsy heavy-handedness of political foes. Or it had to do with all of them, and then something else. To conclude that Bill Clinton was simply following poll results was only half the story, which is to say it missed the real story completely: Bill Clinton was following his instincts, which meant knowing when to listen to polls and when to defy them. For all the weight given to the advice of adviser Dick Morris by the press and Morris himself, the President's political corpse began twitching with unseemly simulations of life when he disdained Morris' advice not once but twice, not on trivial policy considerations but on the two biggest matters facing him: going to battle with the Republicans on the budget, rather than cutting the deal that Morris heatedly recommended; and sending American troops to Bosnia, rather than leaving the matter to feckless Europeans congenitally predisposed against learning anything from history whatsoever.

In November of 1995, a year before the election, what the country saw on the front page of its newspapers was a President not only daring to isolate himself politically on all fronts, but striding at the head of American troops in Germany on their way to Bosnia, wearing a Churchillian overcoat and actually looking determined in his course of action. Something seemed wrong with the picture—and then it sank in what it was: what seemed wrong with the picture was that *nothing* seemed wrong with it. What seemed wrong was that for the first time since taking his oath as commander-in-chief, Bill Clinton did not look completely out of place walking at the head of troops in a Churchillian overcoat. Back in Washington, locked in combat with Bob Dole and Newt Gingrich, what only months before had been Clinton's greatest personality deficiency—a weasely vacillation and overeagerness to compromise—now became a virtue: he was the Last-Chance President after all, the Last Reasonable Man in Washington holding the line against manifestly unreasonable men. Somewhat to its amazement, America found itself relieved he was there. Then he went to Ireland, where crowds in the thousands went berserk for him, and Clintonmania was back, on foreign shores at least, on American televisions certainly, and if not in the hearts of wary countrymen, then at least in their hopes.

Thus, having resolved the question of whether he was tough, having resolved the question of whether he could be President, having crossed a threshold of credibility in the job that Jimmy Carter, say, never did, there remained, by September of 1996 as I crossed the black waters of Lake Michigan by ferry, from Milwaukee to just north of Grand Rapids, only the question of whether he was good. It wasn't that the question had never mattered before; it always mattered. The question was only how much it mattered. To an extent, as a people no longer as good at kidding ourselves as we used to be, we had accepted a certain image of Clinton that was simpler and more cynical than the one we really believed. In one poll after another throughout 1996 we admitted we didn't much trust him, that, for that matter, we even trusted his opponent more. But if that were really true the country would never have elected Clinton in the first place, or re-elected him in the second. We told the pollsters we didn't trust him because we knew it was expected of us; we had heard for so long that Bill Clinton was not to be trusted that to suggest anything different would have looked foolish. But our feelings about Clinton had always been more complicated, because the one thing about him we *did* trust was the empathy that so often verged on the lubricious; lubricious or not, we valued that empathy. It might be the only thing about Clinton that seemed real but it was of more value to us than the things about Bob Dole that we found more honest. When in his Chicago speech accepting renomination Clinton spoke of swastikas painted on the doors of black Special Forces soldiers ready to lay down their lives for their country at a moment's command from their President, his voice took on an indignation that was the sort of thing we in fact immediately trusted about him. Clinton struck just enough sparks of sincerity on just enough of the things that mattered, things that had less to do with issues than with people, that it overcame everything else we distrusted: the one and only thing about the President that people firmly believed was that he cared about them, which meant that there was after all, in the final analysis, something he cared about besides himself. And this was what, albeit by the narrowest of considerations, justified the flimsiest expression of faith in Bill Clinton; and a flimsy faith from us was the best he could ever hope for.

It was from the Zone of Perceived Faith, and from the heart of all the contradictions the public felt about Clinton, that he made his shrewdest political move in the election year of 1996. This was a secularization of the very spiritual crisis that the Religious Right meant to address. First lopping off the issue of abortion and allowing it to float out into moral space, Clinton transformed the national spiritual crisis that Bill Bennett and Gary Bauer spoke of into the sort of nuts-and-bolts policy matters that Clinton not only had just enough credibility to get away with co-opting, but that America found him particularly suited for solving. The press might sneer at a campaign based on such banalities, but it was possible that in a profoundly televisionized culture, for instance, nothing would or could calm the deep alarm of the national psyche more than an installed computer chip giving America more control over its television sets. As sex had become technologized in the last years of the Millennium, so spirituality, resist as it might, seemed to become technologized; and to the extent that technology could be negotiated in all of these new metaphysical exchanges, who was a better negotiator than Bill Clinton, so transparently a fallen man, yet touched not only by technological intelligence but just enough old-time religion to manage the synthesis? "If you were just a little bit better boy," Clinton liked to quote his mother as telling him when he was young, "you could be a preacher," and though one might respond, Well, actually, perhaps a *much* better boy, the point was neither lost nor so suspect.

And yet while in 1992 the country had decided the question of his goodness didn't matter so much if he could just do the job, now that he was doing the job, if not superbly then adequately, the question of his goodness seemed more inescapable, and the country was confounded by it again. "Presidents," George Stephanopoulos had assured me in January, "are reelected between April and August," but in fact Clinton had not had such a great May and June and July, what with indictments pending and the White House's highly suspicious collection of FBI files on nearly a thousand Republicans, including a former secretary of state or two, and the general feeling one always seemed to have about Bill Clinton, that everything might come apart any moment, that Clinton wasn't just always sitting on dynamite but had taken up residence on top of Three Mile Island. The historical phenomenon of Clinton that bridged his vague idealism and his raw ambition was a minefield; and whereas in 1992 I had voted for him with more sheer hope than I had ever voted for a President, I couldn't imagine voting for him again with anything but misgivings. America hadn't done very well with landslide Presidents in my conscious lifetime—the three before Clinton, in 1964, 1972 and 1984, had seen their presidencies totter and in two cases collapse—in part because America in the process of reelecting these men had not been willing to read the ominous signals that were already there. I certainly didn't want to have it on my political conscience that I had voted into office a constitutional crisis on the order of 1973 and 1974 simply because my biases made me unwilling to recognize what my biases made me perfectly happy to recognize when it was Richard Nixon's reelection at stake.

"I suppose Clinton's going to get in again," a woman mused on the Lake Michigan ferry, "which is kind of a shame, since we need someone to run the country, not spend all his time putting out fires." There was only so much I was willing to stick with Bill Clinton through. A lot of excuses had been made for him over the years, and at the outset some of them seemed reasonable: the Whitewater real estate scandal had been investigated from one end of the first term to the other by glory-hungry reporters, Republican committees and special prosecutors, with no conclusive evidence of illegal conduct by either the

President or the First Lady, and like most of America I was ready to withhold judgment until such evidence existed. But seven weeks before Election Day 1996 the President's closest adviser was confiding matters of state to a hooker, reportedly suggesting to her that, now that you mention it, Hillary found those FBI files pretty darned interesting reading after all; and a former business partner in Arkansas was going to jail for eighteen months on top of a two-year sentence she had already received for fraud, for refusing to answer questions concerning Clinton before a grand jury, when two or three simple responses absolving the President would have closed the matter. And about then only the most formidable of biases could have pretended it was all just a Republican plot, or prevented one from asking himself: *What* is going on here?

But in the seven weeks before the election, Bill Clinton's greatest symbiosis of genius and luck lay in his having exhausted all biases for and against him, mowing them down with his very relentlessness. Of course, it was now clear that the disastrous 1994 election was the best thing that ever happened to him, providing not only a huge hole in the American political center that Clinton could fill but also a political presence more odious than Clinton by half, in the undulating form of a Republican Speaker of the House who in his own amoral brilliance was basically a Clinton of the Right, except without the looks or warmth or charm. Moreover the '94 election had lanced the boil of Clinton hatred, not eliminating for good the Clinton-haters, in the same way even Watergate never eliminated for good the Nixon-haters of twenty years before, but drying up the ferocious ooze of it; most people just got tired of hating him so much. Not unlike Nixon, in his own notorious fashion Bill Clinton had won them over by outlasting them: "Oh, admit it," he seemed to smile to the country, "deep down you really don't mind me so much." When Dole, ever frantic as his May and June and July proved even worse than the President's, asked Americans who they would rather have raise their children, Clinton just laughed and asked in return who they would rather have order the pizza for the party. Even the haters secretly had to hope they never wound up in the same room with him, because they knew he'd seduce them the way he seduced everyone; Newt Gingrich actually admitted to his wife and confederates during the battle of the '95 budget that it was dangerous for him to be left alone with Clinton. "I melt," the Speaker had sighed, like a sixteen-year-old staring at her Brad Pitt poster on the bedroom wall. If Dole had his own sort of charm, it was a sardonic curmudgeonliness that, amusing in the more selective company of, say, two, was lost on a country of two hundred million. By the outset of autumn Dole's chances of winning election were reduced to some freak revelation of such finally intolerable tawdriness that by such squalid lights the Clinton charm would appear as fully evil as Gary Bauer truly believed but was unwilling to admit for publication.

It was in the first presidential debate, in early October, that I was struck by something I think had been there in the back of my mind all along, to be avoided. It was there in the way the elder Dole scolded the younger Clinton for not having addressed George Bush in the 1992 debate as "Mr. President"—how long had Dole been fuming over this, nursing a grudge about something no one else had even noticed, except undoubtedly a still enraged Bush himself, who just happened to meet with Dole that very afternoon a few hours before, offering counsel?—and it was there in the way that Bill Clinton was the candidate of dreams while Bob Dole was the candidate of memory, even if Clinton represented dreams at their most stunted and Dole memory deflated of wisdom. What I was struck by were the ways in which Dole reminded me of my father. Reserved, proud, self-possessed, with a similar deadpan humor, he was, to be sure, my father pushed to extremes, buttoned-down but to the point of complete self-repression, capable of surprising emotion but to the point of the mortifying breakdown. And as every son knows immediately, given a choice of voting either for oneself or one's father, on an emotional and psychological level the decision is simple: of course one votes for one's father, hating oneself and the father in the process; one votes for one's father not only to go on evading the responsibility that the father has always taken upon his shoulders, not only because in some inexplicable fashion it also has the potential of getting the father out of the way by putting him at risk once more, but because down deep a son finally trusts the father more than himself to know what is really right.

But as the son also knows, eventually he has to choose himself, and it only confirmed everything said about this generation that at the age of fifty, or close to it, it was still convincing itself it could grow up or even wanted to. Bob Dole's generation, and my father's, was the last to have something that once came naturally to generations of American men, which was a crucible, a national and historic test, something to be overcome whether it was the war that mauled Dole or the hungry frightening years of the Depression, or World War I or the taming of the West or the Civil War, or the building of a country, or the making of a country in the first place. Avoiding a bad war, as Bill Clinton did and as did I, didn't have quite the same weight or resonance of meaning, and didn't sharply and unmistakably define one's manhood in the same way. Rather it procrastinated the definitions of manhood. And so the crucible of our generation has become its own self-loathing, which made the choice of Bob Dole fleetingly attractive, even if it was ultimately as impossible as moving back in with Mom and Dad long after childhood ends, not long before it is time for Mom and Dad, in their last years, to move in with us.

61

Here was what was happening in America in the fall of 1996. In a year when for the first time in the Twentieth Century cancer deaths dropped rather than rose, medical researchers discovered that while there might never be a cure for the common cold, the common cold virus might in fact prove to be a cure for cancer. Scientists isolated the gene that causes prostate cancer, and discovered that estrogen was effective in the treatment of Alzheimer's disease. A new drug appeared to significantly improve memory, particularly in elderly patients, and American women were fascinated by yet another drug that promised to make them thinner. American men were as fascinated by a hormone that promised to make them younger. In one modest but crucial breakthrough after another science promised men and women afflicted with an array of medical problems, including Parkinson's disease, stroke, multiple sclerosis and rheumatoid arthritis, not necessarily cures but at least lives of managing their diseases reasonably. Still without a cure, but facing longer lives of managing their disease reasonably, AIDS victims were braking at the brink of death, the psychological whiplash producing a confused, even conflicted jubilation.

Newly discovered journals written by the man suspected of being the brilliant, cracked Unabomber confessed to not one, or some, but all of the sixteen crimes with which he was charged. The man openly and publicly suspected of having set off a bomb at the summer Olympics was finally cleared, after three months, and with a notable minimum of regrets by the Federal Bureau of Investigation. Slowly and with diminishing confidence, investigators caromed between conclusions that TWA 800 was blown out of the sky by terrorists and by a disastrous mechanical mishap of the Boeing plane; this followed a flood of rumors, advanced by no less than a former White House press secretary, that an American missile had accidentally shot it down. In Denver a young veteran of the Gulf War prepared to go on trial for killing a hundred and sixty-nine people in the single worst act of terrorism ever committed by an American on American soil. The acquitted African-American defendant in the most sensational murder trial of his time found himself on trial again, this time in a civil suit filed by the families of the murder victims; in contrast to the first trial, which was heard by an almost entirely black jury, the selected jury of the new trial was almost entirely white. When the judge in the new trial banned television cameras from the courtroom, a cable station hired actors to portray all the different characters involved, each night broadcasting reenactments of that day's proceedings in a new ongoing TV series.

In the final days of the baseball season, two episodes somehow became emblematic of social chaos, cultural disorder and the breakdown of American life. In the first case the star second-baseman for the Baltimore Orioles hawked a big one in the face of an umpire who made a bad call; the player was given what by all accounts was an inordinately light punishment, and en masse the umpires of baseball threatened to go on strike, until a court order dissuaded them. Not long afterward the Orioles were leading the New York Yankees in the ninth inning of their first American League playoff game when a Yankee fly ball, just skirting the bleachers in its descent, was deflected into the seats by the ambitiously wayward hand of a twelve-year-old boy, leading an umpire in yet another bad call to award the Yankees a home run and thereby the game and, eventually, the American League Championship. Few if any suggested the obvious tit for tat between the umpires and the Orioles, or, as the case might be, hit for spat. Given the zeitgeist it was probably not surprising that the affairs of both Roberto Alomar and young Jeffrey Maier became political parables; George Will used the occasion to comment on the silliness of liberals who feel, in a universe so cosmically and manifestly unfair, that they could or should try to address life's myriad and more banal unfairnesses, such as the Orioles being robbed, for instance. In a manner less Darwinian than mythic the Yankees went on to win the World Series. For all the good it would have done, the campaign of Robert Dole for President might have drawn momentary hope from not only the Yankees' rousing come-from-behind triumph but the fact that every time a presidential election had ever coincided with a Yankees victory in the World Series, the Republicans won.

A fifty-three-year-old woman set an American record for living in outer space, floating gravity-free for six months. It was naturally assumed that once her shuttle returned to earth she would have to be carried from it; upon landing, she walked off. The new Miss America was Miss Kansas. The Dole connection notwithstanding, she was quickly revealed to be the Bill Clinton of beauty queens, ruthlessly dreaming of a Miss America crown since childhood, obsessively studying over five hundred videos of beauty pageants. In a court case involving a gay man who claimed to have been sexually harassed by his male boss, the judge ruled that sexual harassment was not possible in this particular instance because it involved homosexuals. In North Carolina a six-year-old boy was suspended from school on sexual harassment charges, for kissing an apparently nonplussed six-year-old girl; in the meantime a sixteen-year-old honor student was suspended from high school on drug charges, for taking a Midol pill for her menstrual cramps and giving one to a girlfriend. Any more evidence that America was losing its mind would almost be superfluous. Nonetheless there were also the two American girls of Korean descent from Orange County, California, twin sisters and co-valedictorians in their high school class, whose bond presumably changed forever when one twin not only conspired to kill the other but to take over her identity. There were the two Jersey teenagers, boyfriend and girlfriend, privileged and popular and promising, who had a baby in secret from friends and family and then allegedly crushed the newborn's skull and left him in a dumpster. There were the two Texas honor students in the United States Naval Academy, also boyfriend and girlfriend, who concluded that the only way he might redeem a sexual indiscretion with another girl was for the couple to kill the jezebel together, which they did by bashing in her brains with a barbell weight after trying to break her neck in the way they had seen done so smoothly in the movies. It was not as easy in real life.

In the hundredth year of motion pictures, the great subject of the American cinema, excluding invaders from outer space, had to do with sex and the various ways it dismayed the nation. As a cultural rite of passage women flocked to a revenge comedy about middle-aged wives deserted by their husbands for younger ones; men resisted in terrified droves. An old Alfred Hitchcock masterpiece that had been dismissed on first release forty years before was restored and rereleased to the theaters, where younger audiences laughed at James Stewart in the single most uncompromising portrayal of erotic obsession ever committed to the screen by an American actor. A forty-year-old play about the Salem witch trials, originally an allegory of McCarthyism, now seemed relevant more for its libidinal hysteria than its cautionary leftism. In the season's most provocative American movie, *The People vs. Larry Flint*, the country's most implacable sexual obsessions became hopelessly entangled with its most profound principle of freedom; at the crossroads of the two, the film's central figure built a pornographic empire on the obsessions before becoming the principle's most scabrous martyr, wearing an American flag as a diaper and broadcasting on his T-shirts an array of bulletins ranging from the pithier "Jesus Is an Anarchist" to the rather less insightful "Fuck the Court." Co-produced by Oliver Stone, directed by the Czech Milos Forman, whose parents were murdered by Nazis and whose early work was repressed by Stalinists, and with a cast nearly as perverse as Larry Flynt himself, including James Carville as a prosecuting attorney and Rudolph Giuliani's wife as Jimmy Carter's evangelical sister, the movie was the decade's Anti-*Forrest Gump*, purposely deteriorating from broad vaudeville not into saintly stupidity but rather stoned decadence and then a degeneracy that put the meaning of America to its severest, which is to say its truest, test. If one might not so blithely and breezily assume that a hundred years ago everyone knew Walt Whitman was art, as Peggy Noonan would have it, one might still assume a hundred years from now no one will confuse Larry Flynt with art; but perhaps by then no one will so conveniently miss the point that it doesn't matter. *The People vs. Larry Flynt* might have been the *Forrest Gump* of a dark, alternate looking-glass America, but on either side of the looking-glass it was still evident, to anyone who wanted to think about it, which of the two films was truly the cynical one, and which the truly idealistic.

The thirty-five-year-old son of the thirty-fifth President of the United States married. It was pointless to ask who cared; for whatever reason, many did. The would-be Marilyn Monroe of her era, a popular singer of passing talent who shrewdly used sex in the bold manner of a thousand male singers before her, had a daughter by her personal trainer or body builder, or bodyguard, or something; it was unclear whether an electrified nation received this news with relief or horror. Coinciding with the centennial of the movies, the centennial of F. Scott Fitzgerald's birth was celebrated in St. Paul, the place he was born and a city he always hated; as arranged by Garrison Keillor the occasion included the unveiling of a statue, readings from *The Great Gatsby* and *Tender Is the Night* by prominent authors, and a Gatsby Ball with Keillor crooning Gatsby-era songs as four thousand people danced into a moonlit autumn haze. Though no one quite said so, it could only commemorate a lost America of the imagination. Spiro Agnew, the worst vice president since Aaron Burr, died. McGeorge Bundy, perfectly representative of liberal intellectualism at its most arrogant and disastrous, died. Rufus Youngblood, the Secret Service man who protected Lyndon Johnson in the same motorcade in which John Kennedy was murdered, died. Mario Savio, who single-handedly galvanized the Berkeley Free Speech Movement of the Sixties, died. Cardinal Joseph Bernardin of Chicago, who inspired admiration even among those deeply skeptical of the Church he served, died. Bill Monroe, the father of American bluegrass music, died; Tiny Tim, at once the most laughable and creepiest incarnation of the Sixties flower child, died. Joanne Dru, so tough and sexy in Howard Hawk's *Red River*, and one of the few actresses to hold her own in a John Wayne movie, died. Having once agitated—ostensibly in different ways, but not really—the likes of both Nikita Khrushchev and Frank Sinatra, and presumably many men in between, dancer and actress Juliet Prowse died. Hospitalized reportedly for a pinched nerve until doctors finally conceded pneumonia, among a rash of more alarming rumors that in fact his heart had failed, and though there was the unshakable sense that he had finally passed from the American scene once and for all, Frank Sinatra did not die.

All year I had it in my gut he would. The awful premonition stayed with me through the American Midwest into the green hills of Illinois, Indiana and Michigan; in my head I had written his obituary. I had him on the cassette player constantly as I drove, a tape I compiled called *Sinatra Remembers*, obscure songs mostly from the Sixties when he was past his prime. While perhaps the most conspicuous exception to Fitzgerald's dictum about American lives having no second acts, Sinatra was also the Gatsby of American music, having left his heart and dreams behind in the Fifties to find fortune (however bloody) and glory (however tainted), and having returned in the Sixties to find that everything had so changed neither money nor notoriety could make him again what he once was or give back to him what he had once lost. For even the greatest of American artists the peak never lasts long, and despite the duration of his career the peak for Sinatra was the six years from 1955 to 1960 when, squarely in the face of musical upheaval, he became the great male torch singer of the century, bearing witness to the firestorm and ashen aftermath of American romance in the way female singers had for years. If the Joe Christmas of

American music, Elvis Presley, made America accept the idea of a white man singing like a black man without really sounding like one, the Jay Gatsby of American music made America accept the idea of a man singing like a woman without sounding like one.

That was about as much revolution as America could handle in one decade, and probably more than it knew it was getting. Unlike the emerging rock and roll singers of the time whose emotional range was liberated by black music, Sinatra's emotionalism remained yoked to notions of masculine dignity that may have been quaint but within the confines of which melancholy and sorrow took the form of existential heroism; by the mid-Fifties, as he entered middle age, the slightly frayed world-weariness of his singing tempted you to believe that on "I Can't Get Started" or "She's Funny That Way" the voice might abandon him at any moment, as had his dream, or at least break, as had his heart. Like the legend of Robert Johnson's crossroads pact with the Devil, it may be that the one about Sinatra's love affair with Ava Gardner in the late Forties and early Fifties is apocryphal—that it was only after losing her that he became a great singer. But the fact of the affair itself and its excoriating effect on both Sinatra's emotional life and career were indisputable, and whether or not the apparent beginning of the end of his career in 1947 just happened to coincide with the affair, the two certainly spiraled downward together over the five years that followed. Married at the time to his first wife, the father of three children and still enough of an Italian-American Catholic kid from New Jersey to feel damnation lurking over his shoulder, Sinatra's Gatsby nonetheless pursued and eventually wed Gardner's irresistibly sluttish Daisy with an obsession that exceeded even his merciless pursuit of fame and success.

In the meantime his records, which sold ten million copies in 1946 alone, fell off the charts, his name vanished from the year-end *Downbeat* magazine polls, and he was reduced to recording novelty songs with barking dogs when he wasn't trailing after Ava to one film location or another, carrying her bags and fighting off smitten matadors. As Gardner's star ascended, Sinatra's dimmed and then, one April night in 1950, went out: walking onstage at New York's Copacabana in a make-or-break engagement, he opened his mouth and heard only the death rattle of his artistic demise. To an equally silent and stunned audience he croaked good night and rushed off, finished. Amid the ruins, of course, Sinatra begged for a role in the 1953 film *From Here to Eternity*, accepted the part for an embarrassing pittance, and subsequently won an Academy Award; but the price of American romanticism is steep enough that not even a defiant and startling comeback, or an increasingly public and appalling love affair annotated by his incessant pummeling of reporters and photographers, could portend the singer who emerged afterward. On his 1957 performance of "Autumn Leaves," for instance—a song so familiar it would seem no one could make it distinctive, let alone original—Sinatra foreclosed forever any other interpretation, with a vocal of such bleak desolation one still doesn't know whether to find it mesmerizing or unbearable. And the way he sang "To share a kiss the devil has known" in "I'm a Fool to Want You," it was hard to believe something searing and irrevocable hadn't happened to him, given how no one else could have gotten away with the melodrama of it. Given that Ava Gardner was already ancient history. Given that Frank Sinatra wrote the lyric.

A revolutionary and romantic country like America appreciates the spectacle of neither its revolutions nor its romanticism, which is to say it would rather ignore its true nature by entertaining a more diversionary one. Sinatra's diversion from his American romanticism was to become the hedonistic American swinger, singing sometimes as the man whose love for Ava Gardner overwhelmed both his career and guilt over leaving his wife and children, but other times as the bachelor who underscored his masculinity, for both himself and us, by fucking Juliet Prowse, Marilyn Monroe, Marlene Dietrich, Lana Turner, Lauren Bacall, Anita Ekberg, Kim Novak, Shirley MacLaine, Jill St. John, Angie Dickinson and Mia Farrow—a list even John Kennedy would have envied, not to mention a poor star-struck sex-crazed southern boy like Bill Clinton. How a man could have been as boorish and hostile as Sinatra often was and still capable of his most starkly sublime confessions is one of those questions about Sinatra in particular and artists in general that even artists are at a loss to answer; the uneasy truth is that it may have been the hedonistic swinging Sinatra that kept the tortured romantic Sinatra from going off the

62

There is a sort of blow to one's soul, Scott Fitzgerald once wrote, "that comes from within—that you don't feel until it's too late to do anything about it, until you realize with finality that in some regard you will never be as good a man again." A few sentences later he wrote the line about how, during a dark night of the soul, it is always three o'clock in the morning; and one night a few years ago, outside Coeur d'Alene in Idaho when it really *was* three in the morning, I began to understand that just as it is required of Americans to dream ridiculously, it is subsequently required that they succeed or fail ridiculously too, the success almost too grandiose or the failure almost too catastrophic to take seriously. Writing *The Crack-Up* at the age of thirty-nine, Fitzgerald had already begun his suicide of a sort, though perhaps that's unfair given the grace and heroism with which he struggled against it. Nonetheless, by then the distant beckoning green light at the end of *Gatsby* had pulled far out of Fitzgerald's view, along with the harbor where his dreams were docked; he was just beginning to see American failure for the nightmare it was, having already seen its success for the paradise it promised a young man, before that paradise was lost. Fitzgerald's crack-up was in L.A. It was probably just as well he wasn't staying in a motel outside Coeur d'Alene. L.A. either bought him a few years, if you want to look at it that way, or robbed him of another forty, if you want to look at it that way. At any rate it was a pretty good place to find out that there is no place worse than America to be prematurely on the downward slide of whatever your particular trajectory is.

That last time I was on the road three years ago, I went a little bit insane. Once I was a traveler by nature, rootless by nature, but three years ago, the last time I descended rootlessly into America, I lost myself somewhere east of Montana, for reasons not worth going into now. If you want to know how crazy I was, I was this crazy: after cracking up, I fled as quickly as possible *to Las Vegas*. Anytime you go to Vegas to get *less* crazy, well, that's crazy. The psychosis of the

American landscape accommodated just a little too easily the way in which all my dreams had come to seem lost or trivial, and the way that I had systematically cut myself off from everything and everyone so as to punish myself for having failed the life I had aspired to for so long. Now back on the road three years later, closing in on three thousand miles, I kept telling myself I wouldn't go crazy this time because, after all, this time I had a purpose to my journey, though every time anyone asked me what it was—"Yes, but: if you're not actually writing about the election, then what *are* you writing about?"—I babbled like an idiot. And I could feel the craziness lurking just down the highway, and I kept swerving to avoid it, taking obscure detours, hiding out in motels until I convinced myself the danger had passed. Soon I wasn't playing Frank Sinatra's memory songs anymore, I had moved on to somewhat harder stuff, a lot of Dylan for a while, then a new live record of Kurt Cobain singing from beyond the white blast of the shotgun with which he took his life, and Patti Smith's new record, an American Songbook of the Dead, elegizing every mortal thing around us that has passed away, including Kurt Cobain. Somewhere just south of the Great Lakes there was a left turn on the map for Cahokia, the last great American city before the Old World found the New and presumed to call it new, now buried in the plains of southern Illinois.

In a perverse way I was covering the presidential campaign perfectly, since it had slipped the moorings of logic as easily as I had. At the outset the strategy had seemed as clear-cut to my mind as it must have to Bob Dole's, which was to plant myself in the bull's-eyes of Michigan and Ohio and wait for the campaign to come to me. "Well," John Buckley, the Dole communications director, had told me in late August, "if you're in Michigan and Ohio, you'll be seeing a lot of us." At that time Buckley was feeling as good as he ever would about the Republican chances: "The campaign is exceeding our wildest expectations," he had assured me. "You know that we had some rough months there in May and June and July, but since late July everything's been clicking—a single-digit race, an exciting vice presidential choice, a good convention, a bold economic plan. You have ten weeks in the campaign. With two candidates, the presidential nominee and the vice presidential nominee, that's the equivalent of twenty weeks. At least half of them will be devoted to the economic plan." At the time I noted to myself that Buckley was already referring to the "economic plan" rather than the "tax cut," which seemed to me an early sign that the tax cut per se wasn't taking with the voters, that it seemed narrow and opportunistic and far too bald an effort to bribe the electorate. And though I had not kept count, breaking up the calendar as systematically as Buckley had, it seemed to me the campaign was spending rather less than half the time talking about either the tax cut or the economic plan, however you wanted to call it; and one could only assume that was because Bob Dole never truly believed it himself, too smart and too honest to truly believe it.

In yet one more example of my own naiveté, I had hoped John Buckley was my ace in the hole in terms of following the campaign. I had met him briefly seven years before at an *Esquire* party in New York; at the time he had just written a generous review of one of my novels for the *Wall Street Journal*. The slightly eccentric and iconoclastic nephew of William Buckley, he was a novelist himself and former rock critic. Around that time he was quoted as saying, "I don't see any contradiction between being a conservative interested in economic growth and a strong national defense, and going to see the Pixies on a given weekend night," and my reaction at the time had been twofold: first, that he was absolutely right, that it was small-minded and bigoted to assume such a contradiction; and second, that of course it was a complete contradiction, given the Right's clear, documentable predisposition to judge experience rather than understand it. I don't think even Buckley would argue that the Pixies, whose most memorable song was called "Debaser," were what Bob Dole or Bill Bennett or Pat Buchanan or Ralph Reed had in mind when making the case for a more wholesome popular culture.

Nonetheless, seven years later Buckley seemed open to my entreaties concerning the campaign. By the middle of September, having reached Grand Rapids, I was calling his office on a regular basis; I didn't take it personally when, sooner instead of later, he started not calling back. By now campaign reporters were openly complaining in print and on the air about phone calls routinely unreturned by the Dole campaign and an unprecedented level of restriction the campaign had imposed upon the press. Not really in the business of reporting anymore, I could afford to be understanding about it: the Dole candidacy was either collapsing altogether or coming apart at all the hinges and joints, whichever metaphors of gravity or entropy or centrifugal force you wanted to apply to the situation. The problem with my plan of focusing on Michigan and Ohio was that Dole was focusing on them with something less than the single-mindedness I had expected; all you had to know about how this campaign was going was that while Clinton was holding wildly enthusiastic outdoor rallies on Lake Shore Drive in Chicago, Dole was frantically touring prisons in Arizona, the most congenitally Republican state in the union except for Utah, trying to reinforce his credentials there as a good law-and-order Republican. In breezy response the President not only picked up the endorsement of the largest police union in the country—the first time ever for a Democratic nominee—but had the chutzpah to visit Arizona himself, personally dropping in to pay his respects to Barry Goldwater, who was in the hospital recovering from a small stroke and was quoted in a major newsweekly as saying that while he supported Dole, he had to allow as how, all in all, Clinton had really been a pretty good President. Conservative Republicans whose first political hero had been Goldwater now fumed privately that he had gone senile. Perhaps so, but it was a plague of senility that had descended on not only Goldwater, not only the police, not only the country's leading CEOs, who as a group also endorsed Clinton as "good for business and good for America," but Arizona as a whole, which in fact would vote for a Democrat on Election Day for the first time since Harry Truman.

So it was not so easy catching up with the Dole campaign in Michigan and Ohio, because the campaign was just as often in Arizona and New Hampshire and South Carolina and Alabama and Texas *and Kansas*, a slew of Republican strongholds neither strong nor necessarily holding for the Republican nominee. Along with Arizona, New Hampshire would ultimately go for Clinton. Though in the end Dole would do better than his shambles of a campaign had the right to expect, losing by only half the margin predicted in the polls—decisive to be sure, but not abject humiliation—and taking nineteen states, virtually all of them in the South and the midwestern plains that I had crossed between California and Illinois, in late October Dole had only seven states he could comfortably consider in his pocket. These were led by Mississippi, the thirty-first largest in the union, followed by such teeming powerhouses as Utah (thirty-fourth), Nebraska (thirty-seventh), Idaho (forty-second), Alaska (forty-eighth), Wyoming (fiftieth), and, yes, probably Kansas (thirty-second), all with thirty electoral votes between them. The only large states where he appeared to have any realistic chance were Texas and Florida, and it was only the most spectacular measure of how hopeless Dole's cause was that either was in question at all. In fact he would lose Florida.

"My wife Elizabeth and I have traveled to the scenes of many natural disasters over the years," Dole joked with crowds in early September. "That doesn't include my campaign, of course." By late October it didn't seem so funny. Organizationally the campaign certainly had the appearance of complete disarray, if the sudden upheavals of the schedule could be taken into account: the night Peter Jennings was announcing on his ABC evening newscast that Dole would be in Grand Rapids the next day, campaign headquarters in Washington was announcing that it was Jack Kemp who was going to be in Grand Rapids; Bob Dole would be in Lansing. Actually the next day it was Jack Kemp who was in Lansing and Bob Dole was in Detroit; and by the time one shifted gears in time to reach Detroit, Bob Dole was in Ohio. Then as America shuddered into the prematurely frigid autumn, and I hurtled ever more quixotically down the shores of Lake Michigan past the huge mansions of Nineteenth-Century lumber barons, and beaches of long-sunk shipwrecks and the bare branches of autumnal trees filled with huge glistening spider webs, the Dole campaign made the truly desperate and audacious decision to relocate itself for the duration to California, where no sane person could really believe the Kansan had a chance, one or two modestly—and fleetingly—encouraging state polls notwithstanding.

By now Dole's speeches about the economy and tax cuts gave way to harangues about drugs and even the old George Bush favorite, constitutional amendments to ban burning the flag. (Republicans never propose amendments to ban burning the Bill of Rights.) On only a barely subterranean level these speeches were really about the Sixties, for which Clinton offered such gossamer representation, what with Dole commercials showing the President on MTV some years earlier at his shit-eating worst, grinning that if he had the chance again he would take a good puff of the old devil weed just to let the kids know he was cool, and then the usual ridiculous retraction a few nights later to Barbara Walters. With a frenzy that belied the aura of calm decency he was trying to sell the country, Dole was still trying to take America back to where it had all really gone wrong, thirty years before: he was Dole the Rememberer again, keeper of the past's Better Days. Amazingly, before he switched back to talking about the tax cut, almost no one in the Republican camp seemed to notice that the drug issue showed signs of working for Dole, with the President's lead shrinking to below ten for the first time since the San Diego convention. There was a part of the collective American spirit that believed Dole was right, that something about the country *was* better back when all of us could feign a child's innocence together, beyond the reach of consequential choices, even if the country never seemed to believe that Dole was the one who could make it so again, or indeed that anyone could make it so again. The green light in Gatsby's harbor had disappeared altogether from view and, for better or worse, it was Bill Clinton, not Bob Dole, who was going to sail us to whatever port could still be reached.

That Bob Dole might be right, that Clinton might be, as the Republican nominee put it following the second presidential debate, a man who just talked in his slippery silver-tongued fashion of "promises he hasn't kept, votes he hasn't earned, goals he hasn't accomplished and virtues he hasn't displayed," was irrelevant. The American public was being notably hardheaded about the whole thing: not a single bumper sticker, in twenty-five hundred miles from Los Angeles to Grand Rapids, for Clinton or Dole or Perot or Nader or Jesus or Elvis; not until I got into downtown Chicago did I finally see one for the President. And it might well have been that America not sad. If he did not necessarily deserve to be President, he certainly did not deserve these final weeks: the Republican Party he had served loyally to the point of near self-sacrifice in his 1974 reelection to the Senate, only three months after the resignation of his hero Nixon, who he had continued to passionately defend when everyone else stopped, was now cruelly cutting him loose in an ultimately successful bid to hold Congress. Rather like Robert Lee after Pickett's Charge, watching his troops cut down and muttering, "It's my fault, all my fault," as the wounded and bleeding staggered back to camp, Robert Dole assumed responsibility accordingly, no matter that it wasn't Dole who might be losing the Gingrich Congress but that in fact it was the Gingrich Congress that had lost the Dole presidency. And for its part, the national press, now starved for carnage after years of piously bemoaning negative elections, splendidly outdid itself in its hypocrisy, sneering at a campaign so bland and polite, wondering aloud when Dole was going to "take the gloves off" and give the people the show they wanted, though in fact the people wanted nothing of the sort. The spectacle of a media that had written Bill Clinton off for dead after the debacle of November 1994—suggesting, as one had at the time, that Clinton should just spend the next two years of his presidency flying around in *Air Force One* and "enjoying life," like a man with a terminal illness who had a few moments left to smell the roses and put his affairs in order—now writing off Bob Dole, was a little outrageous even to those who stopped being flabbergasted by the press's arrogance long ago. Dole clung to his dignity as long as he could. When he finally took the bait in the second debate he did it rather awkwardly, reducing the attack on the President's character to the usual non sequiturs that always bespoke Dole's healthy sense of the surreal in modern politics, even when nobody else could ever quite figure out what he was saying. While the charges were well within the bounds of proper political discussion, concerning not sexual misadventures but lapses within the Clinton White House that the public would do well to consider, such as the business of the FBI files, Dole was so uncomfortable that even if he could intellectually make the distinction between public character and private, emotionally he could not and would not. And so, though he stepped up the assault, what it gained in volume and even feigned ferocity it never quite matched in conviction.

In utter frustration, the bomb of Dole rage finally detonated, and the most consummate of contemporary American politicians did what even the least consummate of politicians knows is fatal. Like Jimmy Carter openly bemoaning the public's malaise, Bob Dole openly bemoaned the public's stupidity. The hell with all this raggedy-ass dogshit about drugs, flag-burning, tax cuts and whatever else, none of that mattered, what mattered was that, even as the Democratic Party was awash in ever-seedier scandals concerning illegal political contributions and shadowy Indonesian power brokers and fund-raisers in Buddhist temples trafficking in laundered money and brazen drug lords dining at the White House, all of which the President's reelection campaign simply dismissed with a breathtaking disdain not dissimilar to Richard Nixon's 1972 reelection campaign, Bob Dole was about to get creamed by the likes of Bill Clinton, a man who ran for attorney general of Arkansas the year that Dole was the Republican nominee for Vice President of the United States. Plainly the very idea was inconceivable to Dole, too absurd and surreal even to a man whom an unapologetically absurd and surreal universe had taught one lesson after another about the cruel vagaries of life going back half a century. And so after first reducing himself to a litany of James Watt bleatings that were beneath him—"He's a liberal! liberal! liberal!" in Georgia, and then, "Defeat liberals and send conservatives to Congress, that's the American way!"—Dole could finally only sputter in disgust to a throng in Florida, "I wonder what the American people are thinking, or if they're thinking at all," moments after it was revealed that he had gone chasing after Ross Perot in Texas, figuratively if not literally, trying to talk Perot out of the race. It was a pitiful display that vaguely recalled George McGovern in 1972 running around futilely begging various Democratic bigshots to be his vice president. Perot characterized Dole's overture as "weird" and momentarily shot up in the polls from four percent to twelve, before finally splitting the difference at eight.

Given what he must have viewed as the sheer, almost intolerable injustice of losing to a President so transparently unworthy, Dole would only have found it all the more difficult to understand the limits of what even a conservative America could accept. "They're going to have to work out all this Religious Right crap," a retired food caterer told me in Grand Rapids; he had always voted Republican and would vote for Dole, with neither enthusiasm nor expectations. More remarkable were the women I talked to. Young conservative women in their thirties or early forties, Republicans who by almost any definition would be considered pro-life, mothers who were unlikely to ever personally consider having an abortion, who even spoke vaguely of abortion as "death" if not murder, said one after another they would no longer under any circumstances support a candidate for President who was not pro-choice. They had done so in the past, of course, voting for Reagan twice, Bush at least once and sometimes twice, except for the ones who voted for Perot in 1992; almost none had voted in 1992 for Bill Clinton. Almost all would vote for him in 1996. The abortion issue this year, in another instance of how the power of the Religious Right had reached the point of diminishing returns, particularly in the shadow of Gingrich—whom women *despised*—took on a new and vivid pertinence that was much bigger than abortion itself, that had to do with the insult of old men with testicles the size of marbles and prostates the size of bowling balls presuming an insight into the matter of procreation that in fact no man could have, handing down self-righteous dicta to women who had carried life inside them and knew how it felt and what it meant in a way that no man could ever know. In all the ways that the abortion issue had in the past cut so strongly in favor of those who opposed abortion, which is to say those who had voted against abortion above and beyond everything and anything else, this year it was cutting back, women not so much voting for abortion or even for the concept of choice, but for themselves. It was at this moment in the zeitgeist that a perfectly serious solution occurred to me: a national referendum on abortion in which the only Americans allowed to vote were women. But in the meantime they would vote against Bob Dole, who now paid the price for how, in Clinton-like fashion, he had so overhauled and fine-tuned his position on abortion in order to win the Republican nomination in the first place.

Beset as America was by the reality of having to be America, however grandiose the larger contemplations of meaning seemed in comparison to that reality, none of this could contradict how prosaic America had become. The sorrow was that it had become prosaic by necessity: survival of the most prosaic; and you could almost see beyond your windshield America becoming detached from itself, every generation from every other, every race from every other, every town from every other, down to the conjoined American twins of history and memory separating so bloodlessly that, in a weary gesture of such spiritual inertia, it was as though they had never been joined at all. In particular the America that Bill Clinton spoke to, his own generation that was born in nuclear light, felt rebuked on all sides: by disapproving parents, which is to say its past, for whom Bob Dole spoke; by contemptuous children, which is to say its future, for whom no one seemed to speak that hadn't already blown his brains out in a dark Seattle cellar. America might indeed have felt things were being taken care of, but it also felt the gust and hush of what it feared was its own twilight: a huge, preternatural sense that the best of everything was over after all, that having been drained first of all idealism and courage and delirium, it was now drained of the rage that had been the only thing keeping it alive. So in a way this election was not only important, but as the Great Anti-Election at the end of the Twentieth Century, it was perhaps the most important, for the way that, irrefutably and in a roar of silence, the American people were saying in the autumn of 1996 that this election *did not matter to their lives at all*. It had no bearing on them whatsoever, or on whichever America of the mind they or you or anyone else lived in. America had become completely detached from its own voice, not only the words but the mere sound.

As the days dwindled down, it was possible that America just waited to get this election and this Millennium out of the way so as to start something new. It was possible that America had become swallowed up by its own paradox—that having meant to propel itself beyond the dictates of history, having meant from the first to detach history from memory in order to be forever free of the past, as a true country of the imagination, now an America in which schoolchildren did not know which decade the Vietnam War was in or which century the Civil War was in realized that the currency of memory unsupported by the bullion of history was worthless. Now it was possible an America of 250 million different Americas that did not know if they were black or white, slave or slaveowner, righteous or evil, just meant to be finished with Bill Clinton and Bob Dole once and for all and start over, much like Lincoln who, realizing the first America was beyond salvation, secretly created a second America out of the Emancipation Proclamation and his speeches at Gettysburg and his second inauguration. It was possible that the unspoken collective will of some secret country had resolved, after 250 million secret Antietams, Shilohs, Chancellorsvilles, Vicksburgs, Bull Runs, Chickamaugas, Cold Harbors and Gettysburgs, that the second America was beyond salvation and now a third was to be created, perhaps with the election in the year 2000 of the man America had really wanted in 1996, and who refused. It was even possible, though a distinct long-shot, that a Republican Party open enough to nominate him, as it had once nominated Lincoln, could be trusted with such a mission. A year later the country could look back at Colin Powell's refusal and see precisely the moment when The Election That Was Supposed To Be instead became The Election The Country Didn't Want; and so the meaning of America would have to wait until the country was ready to confront the moment of truth—in a Zone of Perceived Faith where faith isn't now or never—as to whether it still had the faith to make Joe Christmas President of the United States. And while one would not want to sink into messianic illusions about Powell, or suspend reservations about putting a career military man in the chair of commander-in-chief (though it didn't work out so badly with Washington or Eisenhower, who knew enough about the military to be unimpressed by it), there could be no overstating the sheer transformative symbolism of a black man's election, as much as the hardheaded might want to argue such symbolism was just liberal goo. If and when such a thing came to pass there could be no pretending that a third America, hopefully and presumably still bonded to the first two by the Declaration of Independence and the Constitution, was not at hand.

You drive down I-55 from Chicago and turn left at St. Louis, and drive another ten minutes outside St. Louis and, as dusk falls, find the grave of Cahokia. Cahokia is the great lost America: not utopia, not Atlantis, not a myth, not an alternative or parallel America, but as much America the Real in the Thirteenth Century as the America the Real of the Twentieth. The Americans of Cahokia, whom scientists now call Mississippians for where the Mississippi, Illinois and Missouri rivers met, built the greatest city of its time, a city greater than London or Paris, greater than the cities of the Mayans who were already on the wane, the greatest of all American cities until the New York City of the Nineteenth Century, stretching over seventy miles and populated by twenty thousand Americans who built at Cahokia's center a pyramid fifty feet high. Now this pyramid lies beneath the mounds of earth that roll southwest to the Ozarks. But if you are somewhere on the road just between a momentary stability and the craziness that's been waiting for you around the bend, you might almost see at dusk twenty thousand American ghosts rise from the grave of this America that was secret from the rest of the world, secret from history, the last America that presumed it might cut off history from memory once and for all, before it died. Its death remains unfixed by science. There are no earthly shows of trauma by cataclysm, either natural or manmade, no gashes of devastating war, there is no sign of rot from some sweeping plague. There are only the geological and archeological hints of social suicide, of an America that slipped away into a great catatonia of the soul, cavalierly ravishing the land and water around it until the land and water could offer nothing in return, an America indulging itself into a fatal national lethargy until, as the desperation of the situation suddenly became clear, it was too late, when those who had less were repressed by those who had more, when resentment just answered resentment and a meeker nihilism was answered by a nihilism more rapacious. And when you pull up to the curb of Cahokia and gaze across the grave of the secret country you may find yourself, not unlike a ghost, suddenly set free of history and memory after all, floating to some place that knows neither nation nor millennium—which is all we ever really wanted of America to begin with.

But driving homeward, wherever home happens to be at the moment, that safe space you have commandeered between stability and craziness, between the history that made you and the memory that names you, cracks apart. On those occasions when you remember how lost you are, the half-moment that it surprises you meets the half-moment you knew it was there all the time, which threatens to leave you scrambling toward whatever dark passion still makes you feel like an American. By now you've spent days or weeks or months draping your life on one prosaic function after another in an interminable series of prosaic functions that are accepted, performed, accounted for and cashed in exchange for the luxury of telling yourself that you're functioning, since the only alternative is the breakdown that your pride and ego and instinct for survival won't allow you to have but that your heart has been begging for. And then finally there's just one function, without significance or metaphor, that's more than you can hang your life on; and when your life sags, you peer over it and see the gaping black beyond and it catches your breath. Then you would like to offer, as an answer to that void, an approximation in yourself of something just as black, but unless you're Charles Manson or Jeffrey Dahmer or Jesse Helms such a feeling is too far beneath you to be touched, let alone articulated. On the car stereo is not Sinatra or Springsteen but another Jersey punk, except that whereas Sinatra and even Springsteen sang so as to never be called punks again, Patti Smith always sang so as to ennoble the title, presenting herself as the maternal nexus between Dylan who sang for young America's ideals and Cobain who sang for young America's despair. Patti sings over and over of death and though in your head you know she sings of resurrection too, as history slips behind you and memory rushes toward you, just outside your windshield the dying is all you can hear. You finally turn the tape player off, the radio on, and almost as a joke the radio immediately plays a Kurt Cobain song; and the pathetic and monstrous passion that left him still feeling alive before it felt too bad to be alive is beyond any ideology that could either drain his desire of rage or his violence of need.

This is an American pain translated into a passion that's beyond excuses, let alone redemption. It is a passion that has no faith, hard as you try for it; it is a passion that finally only serves the function of keeping you alive because you know that without it you would just blow your head off. It's possible that you've never seen yourself as faithless, that the recurring image of a gun in all your American songs is just a whimsical coincidence. It's possible that you would give just as much—everything—for your ideals as you do for your despair, that your wrathful and lovely country, blistered by loss as it is, was always intended as the testament of some affirmation you have never really believed you deserve, your own ideals muttered from the dreamy aquahaze of lithium and heroin:

> *I'm so happy because today*
> *I've found my friends,*
> *they're in my head.*
> *I'm so ugly but that's OK, so are you,*
> *we've broken our mirrors.*
> *Sunday morning is everyday for all I care,*
> *I'm not scared.*
> *Light my candles in a daze,*
> *because I've found God*

at which point the song comes crashing down on you, having been launched from under the surface of its own melody and ripping skyward faster than the speed and ascent of its own sound; the half-moment that it charges you with the bellow of its refusal to succumb to either delusion or pain or anything else meets the half-moment that it terrorizes you with its passion. When you were younger and America was vast before you, the test of your country's meaning was whether it had the power to frighten and change you, driving alone on I-55 at night and heading back one last time to Chicago. And the test of your country's meaning was whether, as time passed, the fear turned to a terrible exhilaration, in part because you learned to live with the fear and in part because you were left with no choice but to be liberated by it since there was no becoming liberated from it. Then one night in history the nature of fear changed, maybe it was the night the Wall came down and there was nothing on the other side to be afraid of anymore except for some horror too personal to tear down as easily as a wall; somewhere in the dark, somewhere in that void beyond the sag of your life from a line of failed functions, somebody buried your secret country in the mud, and the darkness that came roaring over the horizon was the shadow of the Secret Millennium and though it should have been everyone's shadow, it was somehow only yours. Before the edge of the shadow touches us, the meaning of America has become the way we're so willing to challenge and offend every value but the one we blindly hold as true. At the intersection of assault and nurturing, you will either turn the music up, or off. Forgetting the pain again that you never wanted to remember in the first place, returning to your life of functions, you may opt for off. But sooner or later there will be no more forgetting, the remembering will be irrevocable, and then off is just another function. Up is a direction.

63

I was driving one morning from Chicago to St. Paul for the Fitzgerald hundredth birthday party. I had been invited by my friend Frances, who gave me my first job out of college almost twenty-five years before as a writer and editor on a West Coast magazine; years before that she worked for the studios, and years before that, as a very young woman, she had been Scott Fitzgerald's last secretary, smuggling his empty liquor bottles out of his house for him under cover of night so people wouldn't know he was drinking, and tossing them off the side of the road in Laurel Canyon. When Fitzgerald died young Frances was the one who took care of the arrangements while Sheila Graham was off having her breakdown somewhere. Now she was a guest of honor at the Fitzgerald centennial, and it would give me the opportunity not only to see her but to take in the festivities.

It was a long day's drive from Chicago to St. Paul, in a pouring rain, and I hadn't been on the road an hour before something happened. I'm still not sure if I hit an oil slick on the road or simply lost traction in the rain, or if something went very wrong with the car itself. It had been a rather star-crossed car, bought by my father a week before the doctors told him he was dying; in the six years since I inherited it, it had been hit, vandalized, broken into and stolen from under my nose. All I remember clearly, not because I lost consciousness but because everything happened so fast, was the car pulling a little to the left as I drove; I wasn't doing anything untoward, I wasn't changing lanes or taking a curve, just driving straight—and as I corrected the course from the pull to the left, suddenly the car spun completely out of control. At fifty miles an hour it spun out to the right across three lanes of expressway traffic, off the highway and down into a ravine and then back up onto a knoll, where it slammed to a stop in a row of hedges. That I somehow hit no other car and was hit by none was miraculous perhaps to the point of religious conversion. That the spin-out happened to coincide with the one part of the expressway not lined by a low concrete wall meant that I didn't smash into the wall or bounce off of it back into oncoming traffic, or hit the wall at such an angle as to flip the car over, coming down on its roof and flattening me like a pancake. Almost immediately a trucker stopped in the rain to see that I was all right and phoned in a report to a state trooper. Two other cars stopped as well; the front end of one was crumpled, and I was stunned so senseless by the crash that I actually said to myself, "Look, there's a woman who's had an accident too." It wasn't until days later it occurred to me she had just smashed into the car in front of her, who had suddenly hit his brakes to keep from hitting me.

The trooper came and took my report. A tow truck came to get the car. Ridiculously, my first thought had been to get back in the car, drive back up onto the highway and just head on to St. Paul, another six hours away. The car, in fact, was a total loss, every part of its body coming apart and the suspension twisted beyond repair. I rode with the tow truck into the little Illinois town of Shaumberg, where I left the car and called a cab to take me back to Chicago. For some reason the cab company sent a limousine, driven by a man who gave every indication of having gotten off a boat from Eastern Europe that very morning. I gave him the address of some friends in Chicago who lived near Wrigley Field, and since I only knew the city a little, it wasn't until its skyline was passing by my limo window that I realized the cab driver from Romania or Bosnia or wherever he was from didn't have the faintest idea where he was going. By now the adrenaline was wearing off and I was in some pain. "Do you know where you're going?" I said to the Bosnian.

"Wrigley Field, yes?" he answered.

"Wrigley Field yes," I said, "but we're not going toward Wrigley Field right now. Right now Wrigley Field is behind us."

"Oh no," he assured me, "this way Wrigley Field." That way was not Wrigley Field. I ordered him to turn around and head in the other direction. It quickly became clear that he hadn't the slightest idea where Wrigley Field or anything else was in Chicago; since the fare was a flat rate that had been agreed upon up front, he wasn't making any money prolonging the trip. For an hour we drove up and down this street and that, getting quite a little tour of the city. I finally got him back on the Kennedy Expressway and back to the right part of town, Wrigley Field peering over the neighborhood rooftops three blocks away. He still didn't believe it was Wrigley Field.

My friends in Chicago drove me to the emergency room of the closest hospital, where after several hours I was prescribed some glorified aspirin and sent home. The next morning I woke to a terrific spasm that ran from my neck to my lower back. It came so suddenly and furiously that my heart felt as if it was going to jump out of my chest. Over the next forty-eight hours the spasms increased until I became completely incapacitated; the slightest movement, from coughing to rolling my eyeballs to breathing irregularly, to things that involved no movement at all such as an anxious, treacherous thought wandering unexpectedly across my brain, felt as if someone was hacking up my back with an axe. My body was now in complete revolt against me. In the ambulance on the way to the hospital I screamed at every bump in the road, and I was still screaming when they wheeled me in for X rays and then up to my room. Hospital attendants peered in to see what all the racket was. "This is going to hurt, I won't fool you," one nurse said upon plunging an intravenous tube into the top of my hand, but it was so innocuous compared to what I had been going through that I would have laughed, if laughing wasn't such an act of recklessness.

I was in the hospital four days while the doctors checked for internal injuries and flooded me around the clock with Demerol and muscle relaxants to break the chain reaction of spasms. My roommate was Dennis. Dennis was a homeless junkie who was being regularly administered Methadone while treated for swollen feet and a grotesquely extended stomach covered with strange cysts and erupting tumors. He was on a diet seriously restricting his intake of fluids, which he constantly tried to circumvent, insisting to the nurses that the doctor had been by just moments before and approved another milk or ice cream, though of course no doctor had said any such thing or had been by at all. Dennis considered himself quite a charmer and master manipulator, verbally abusing the nurses one moment and sweet-talking them the next. "I'm in pain!" he yelled at them, "don't you understand? What's the matter with you? I gave up my fruit juice at lunch so I could have another ice cream, don't you remember? Why would I want to have fruit juice when I can have ice cream? What's the matter with you?" And then: "I'm sorry, darling, I didn't mean to yell. I just want to get better." He would fall asleep mid-sentence and wake mid-rant, raving at everyone, and he was always trying to wheedle my milk and ice cream out of me. When the nurses weren't around he would slip into a wheelchair and take off down the corridor, only to be found later in the hospital kitchen trying to scam some ice cream. Of course, he really didn't want to get better at all; the fact was that Dennis hadn't had it this good in a long time. He had everything he could want, except the smack, naturally—free room and board, free TV, and lots of women to yell at and order around and generally make miserable.

I never got a chance to say goodbye to my old pal Dennis because the morning I was scheduled to leave the hospital, when I was taken downstairs for one last physical therapy session, a nurse walked into my room to find him hovering over my bed with sixty dollars in one hand and my open wallet in the other. My credit cards were scattered out across the sheets. Dennis explained to the nurse that he had seen the sixty dollars lying on my bed and was thoughtfully doing me the favor of putting the money back in my wallet just so I would be sure not to lose it. The nurse called the armed security guard, who came down to physical therapy to present the situation to me; when I first saw him I couldn't help thinking I had once again been caught some place I didn't belong, like the Republican Convention or the press gallery of the United States Senate. After establishing that none of the money or credit cards was missing, the nurse and security guard advised that I should press charges, but of course I didn't. For one, I would have had to return to Chicago for a trial at some point in the future, and two, Dennis was not only one of life's losers, barely worth his own trouble let alone mine, but I couldn't help feeling that, there in our hospital beds side by side, we were sort of the yin and yang of the American nomad at his most absurd. "Yeah," Viv wondered later, "but did you ask him who he was going to vote for?"

64

Three days after getting out of the hospital my friends in Chicago put me on an airplane and shipped me home in a prescribed daze of Demerol, Valium, Flexiril, codeine and Motrin, and it was only upon coming out of that daze that I found myself sitting at my desk in my house overlooking the canyon in L.A. and gazing at a strange memento in my hand. It was a mysterious emerald card with a riddle, and in the days that followed I wandered the house studying the card, trying to solve its meaning and wondering from what secret American tarot the card had come. It wasn't until the haze of drugs lifted that I realized, not so much with a start as a growing comprehension, the answer to the riddle that was written across the card in large black letters: I HAVE VOTED. HAVE YOU?

It was a ballot stub. And now it occurred to me that, hard as the winds of history had tried to blow away all the evidence of it, there had been an election recently, maybe even very recently. There had almost certainly been an election even as there was not a single sign any such national ritual had taken place. Nothing gave any indication of being the slightest bit different: the man who had been President of the United States for the last four years, and whom the history of the last four years suggested could not possibly survive such an election, was still President; the Congress of the United States, which the history of the last two years suggested could not possibly survive such an election, was still the Congress; there had been no terror, no American Thermidor, no total collapse of the American Weimar into the American Reich. And yet, despite the conspiracy of history to wipe out all memory of the event, this ballot stub in my hand proved there had indeed been an election, a culmination of many months and many hundreds of millions of dollars, albeit an election of the most curious sort, one that meant to undo completely the previous two elections by ratifying each in contradiction of the other, history undoing memory and memory undoing history. In fact, for the first presidential election not simply of contemporary political history, not simply of our lifetimes, nor even of our parents' lifetimes, but for the first election since Robert Dole was one year old and Calvin Coolidge was President, more registered voters had not voted than voted, which is to say that America had voted *against the election itself*. Memory might argue that this was either a sanguine signal of national bliss or a forceful protest against a system that had broken down in failure. But history was as likely to answer it was a final weariness with democracy after all, an indifferent slip into American sleep.

The only truth of the election that was beyond contention, except for the way it was contested by so many commentators who had a vested interest in resisting the truth, not to mention a political establishment too thick even to be accused of running from the truth, was the final collapse of all ideological meaning. America obviously did not believe anymore in ideology, which was not to say that America didn't believe certain conservative things or certain liberal things, or even that America didn't believe more conservative things than it did liberal things. It was to say that orthodoxy had become as politically irrelevant to America as it was intellectually bankrupt, and one could only answer that it was not a moment too soon, and take some slim hope that of all the significant political figures on the American scene, Bill Clinton was the one with the most developed instinct for this collapse and with the most imagination to realize that some other political idea lay beyond this collapse, even if he did not have the imagination to conceive what that idea might be. It was always one of Bill Clinton's greatest virtues, his complete lack of principles, other than what one might hope was a commitment, perhaps even as passionate and deathless as ideology, to the Bill of Rights, the second sentence of the Declaration of Independence, and the better angels of our nature, to which Clinton at least spoke from time to time in his otherwise vacuous and often dishonest reelection campaign. Years later it might be argued that the political resurrection of Bill Clinton began not with his demagogic television ads on Medicare, not with an improved economy for which he might take some undetermined measure of credit with his deficit-cutting 1993 budget, not with his victory over the hamfisted Gingrich Congress in the 1995 budget battle, not with his displacement by the Speaker of the House as the most dubious figure in American politics, but with Oklahoma City: in a fashion not unlike Ronald Reagan's single greatest moment—his inspired soothing of the nation following the *Challenger* disaster of 1986—Clinton had soothed a nation badly shocked by the smoking rubble of its own fracturing; even Americans enraged at their government felt the need to calm down. And if Reagan was better at addressing the nation's anxiety from the Oval Office, Clinton was better at holding the nation's anxious hand. If Reagan was the Great Communicator, Clinton was the Great Consoler.

That might yet prove to be no small thing, in a country where one of the other things that hadn't changed at all, election or no election, ballot stub in my hand or no ballot stub, was that you and I are still the Enemy, even if we don't want to believe it. In fact, now that I gave it some thought, now that I could focus a little on the matter, I could almost swear that through my Valium fog I heard, that last weekend before the election, the all-too-familiar whine of Ross Perot, in a huge two-hour TV buyout, and George Bush, at a campaign rally for Dole, dropping the usual last-minute dark hints about "honor" and "duty" and draft dodgers, the true gist of which was pretty unmistakable and all of it only having the effect of delivering my vote back to the Draft-Dodger-in-Chief, after I had resolved to write in someone, perhaps Colin Powell. I was still the Enemy they always said I was, and if anything at all about that had changed in the course of this past campaign and this past year, it was that I was now quite happy to be the Enemy, because I had had enough of the likes of a financial shark like Ross Perot and a patrician political courtesan like George Bush lecturing the rest of us about honor and duty, and not so subtly questioning everyone's Americanism in the process. While I would happily entertain a discussion of Vietnam with any American male between the ages of forty and fifty-five, or anyone else who was actually over there, as far as I was concerned nobody else had anything to say about it worth hearing. None of this, of course, changed the fact that I still admired Bob Dole, even as I mourned the tarnished end of his long political journey, and hoped history and memory would do us and him the favor of forgetting it ever happened.

65

And as though an election had never taken place, life returned so quickly to "normal" I could barely decompress for it, not to mention reorient myself to how much conceptions of American normality had changed. From the country's highways came a rash of news reports that crazed drivers were crashing into one another and chasing each other down in traffic and shooting each other. On Veterans Day weekend the United States Army exploded with charges of male officers and drill sergeants raping, assaulting and threatening to kill female enlistees. It was confirmed that Michael Jackson was fathering a baby, a startling example of how in a universe defined by Einsteinian paradox, a fact can somehow be correct without being *true*. A probe was launched to Mars that would determine, once and for all, whether life ever existed there, while at the same moment three pieces of Martian rock were being auctioned in New York by a mysterious seller who called himself "Mr. Meteorite." And like a stray ballot stub, history offered one last strange glimpse of the otherwise invisible election in TV images of a Robert Dornan insane with defeat, Republican candidate for President of the United States only months before, now not only refusing to concede the loss of his congressional race but appearing ready to raze all of Orange County in the process. At home I read magazines and watched old movies on TV, and every week I drove into town with Viv for physical therapy.

A few days after the election I tried calling John Buckley and James Carville. I wanted to ask Buckley if he thought the presidential race could ever have been won by Dole, though I fully expected he would answer no, and he might have been right; and I wanted to ask if any other Republican might have run a better race, to which I also expected he would answer no, though I wasn't so sure. But Buckley's number had already been disconnected. As for Carville, well, naturally I wanted to ask Carville what happened to that most interesting election of our political lifetimes that he had forecast back in September of 1995. Maybe that was why he didn't call back.

As the autumn of 1996 passed it was sporadically hot and dry in the canyon, and I was sitting at my desk working one afternoon when I looked up to see the huge mushroom cloud of smoke billowing over the nearest hill. At that point the fire was about two miles away as the crow flies, in a wind blowing seventy miles an hour; so I thought I better call Viv, who was in the city that day working, since I no longer had a car, after all, and no means of escape if the fire came my way. Viv returned home and we packed some boxes of papers and manuscripts and books and whichever of Viv's sculptures seemed manageable. Her grand steel-mandala butterfly windows we left hanging on the house's walls. By the next day the fire was completely out of control, and the sky was filled with smoke that turned the full moon a bloody glob in the night, and Viv and I went into town with our things loaded in the car.

With me I took this book you're reading, though I knew by then what a selfish thing that was to do. I knew by then that the real reason for the fire had nothing to do with vicious Santa Ana winds; by then it was obvious that this was a book I was just never supposed to write: time and events, from biblical blizzards to jinxed hotel heaters to Jann Wenner to Bob Dole glaring at me in bathroom doorways to lipstick traces on Vegas mirrors to rain and the malevolent American highway, kept trying to tell me, and I was too self-absorbed to pay attention. I didn't doubt for a moment that if Viv and I were to just turn the car around and drive back to the edge of the fire and I were to toss the book into the flames, the whole infernal holocaust would vanish in a puff. So the only question was whether Los Angeles, nothing more than a mere megalopolis in the scheme of things, after all, where megalopolises come and go all the time, was worth the sacrifice, and I was still riding around the streets of the city contemplating this existential dilemma when, tens of thousands of acres and a week later, the fire was over.

Though it would be exciting to insist otherwise, the fact was that our house was never in real danger. The fire raged closest to us on the first day and then burned the other direction: we were on the good side of the wind's caprices. When we returned from the city on the second evening, our house was still there, perfectly safe and unscathed, none the worse at all except for a silt of ash that had blown in through our windows. When we got inside, nothing about the house seemed in the least different, not at first glance, anyway.

66

It was several minutes before I saw it, though I think I must have known right away that something was amiss, and my heart sank. Viv, however, was entirely sanguine: the windows of her steel mandalas hanging on all our walls were vacant, not a single glittering wing of a single butterfly to be seen. From one room to the next, from upstairs to down, was an array of livid white windows emptied of all the color they had held, even though the glass in all the windows that had protected the intricately executed butterfly designs was intact, unbroken, uncracked. We didn't talk about it. We just sat on the couch together in the twilight; and though I couldn't help believing that they had all blown away in the hot gust from over the hill where the fires burned, I think down deep Viv knew the butterflies just metamorphosed one last time, and had flown to the sea.

ACKNOWLEDGMENTS

In writing this book, some portions of which have appeared elsewhere in different form, I am indebted for many reasons to many people, including Jonathan Alter, Ron Athey, Gary Bauer, Martine Bellen, Arion Berger, Marian Berger, Will Blythe, Sonja Bolle, John Buckley, Greg Burk, Kateri Butler, Tom Carson, James Carville, Frank Culbertson, Sue Cummings, David Davis, Mike Davis, Joe Dolce, John Ellis, Jodie Evans, Larry Fink, Lynell George, Mikal Gilmore, William Greider, Amy Gross, Tom Hayden, Bret Israel, Pamela Klein, Dale Kuehne, Bob LaBrasca, Brooks Landon, Lynda Leidiger, Jane Levine, Judith Lewis, Stacey Lewis, Larry McCaffery, Paul Malcolm, Greil Marcus, Laura Marmor, Harold Meyerson, Diane Mooney, Susan Murcko, Tobias Perse, Kevin Phillips, John Powers, Sylvia and Ralph Precious, Richard Reeves, Jack Rems, Lew Richfield, Frances Ring, Joe Rosenthal, Walter Shapiro, David Shipley, Randy Michael Signor, Katharine Smalley, RJ Smith, George Stephanopoulos, Clark Stevens, Ella Taylor, Jennifer Unter, Emily White, Francis Wilkinson, and the doctors and staff of the Illinois Masonic Medical Center. I especially want to thank Melanie Jackson, Allen Peacock, Michael Naumann, Kit Rachlis, Fred Cohn, Patricia Cohen, Ann Patty, Michael Ventura,

Lori Precious—who besides now having inspired the best character in two books offered such invaluable advice as, "This book isn't going to be *completely* cynical, is it?"—and Joanna and Milton Erickson, who always supported their son's decision to be a writer even at times when it must not have seemed like such a great idea.